POPULATION AND SOCIETY 1750–1940

THEMES IN BRITISH SOCIAL HISTORY

edited by Dr J. Stevenson

This series covers the most important aspects of British social history from the renaissance to the present day. Topics include education, poverty, health, religion, leisure, crime and popular protest, some of which are treated in more than one volume. The books are written for undergraduates, postgraduates and the general reader, and each volume combines a general approach to the subject with the primary research of the author.

* THE GENTRY: the Rise and Fall of a Ruling Class
    G. E. Mingay
* THE ENGLISH FAMILY 1450–1700 *Ralph A. Houlbrooke*
* A SOCIAL HISTORY OF MEDICINE *F. F. Cartwright*
* EDUCATION AND SOCIETY 1500–1800: the Social Foundations of Education in Early Modern Britain *Rosemary O'Day*
  RELIGION AND SOCIETY IN TUDOR AND STUART ENGLAND 1500–1700
  POVERTY AND ENGLISH SOCIETY 1500–1660
* CRIME IN EARLY MODERN ENGLAND 1550–1750 *J. A. Sharpe*
  THE LABOURING CLASSES IN EARLY INDUSTRIAL ENGLAND
* THE PRESS AND SOCIETY: from Caxton to Northcliffe
    G. A. Cranfield
* POPULAR DISTURBANCES IN ENGLAND 1700–1870 *John Stevenson*
* POPULATION AND SOCIETY 1750–1940: Contrasts in Population Growth *N. L. Tranter*
* RELIGION AND SOCIETY IN INDUSTRIAL ENGLAND: Church, Chapel and Social Change 1740–1914 *A. D. Gilbert*
* BEFORE THE WELFARE STATE: Social Administration in Early Industrial Britain *Ursula Henriques*
* THE ARMY AND SOCIETY 1815–1914 *Edward M. Spiers*
* LEISURE AND SOCIETY 1830–1950 *James Walvin*
* SEX, POLITICS AND SOCIETY: the Regulation of Sexuality since 1800 *Jeffrey Weeks*
  CRIME AND CRIMINAL POLICY IN ENGLAND 1878–1978
  CRIME AND SOCIETY 1750–1900
  BRITISH SOCIAL POLICY SINCE 1870

* already published

POPULATION AND SOCIETY
1750–1940
Contrasts in Population Growth

N. L. Tranter

LONGMAN
London and New York

LONGMAN GROUP LIMITED
Longman House, Burnt Mill, Harlow
Essex CM20 2JE, England
Associated companies throughout the world

*Published in the United States of America
by Longman Inc., New York*

© Longman Group Limited 1985

First published 1985

BRITISH LIBRARY CATALOGUING IN PUBLICATION DATA

Tranter, N. L.
  Population and society 1750–1940.—(Themes
  in British social history)
  1. Great Britain—Population—History
  I. Title   II. Series
  304.6′2′0941   HB3583
ISBN 0-582-49224-6

Set in 10/11pt Comp/set Times
Printed in Singapore by
The Print House (Pte) Ltd

CONTENTS

Acknowledgements   vii
Introduction   1

1. Sources, methods, objectives   3
    Listings of inhabitants   6
    Civil censuses   8
    Church registers   14
    Civil registers   18
    Techniques and objectives of parish and civil register analysis   20
    Migration   26

2. Population growth and its mechanisms   34
    Migration   37
    Natural increase   43
    Mortality   44
    Marriage and celibacy   49
    Illegitimate and legitimate fertility   55

3. The decline in mortality   64
    Autonomous influences   65
    Innovations in medicine   68
    Public health and personal hygiene   78
    Nutrition   82
    Conclusion   87

4. The rise and fall of fertility   92
    Illegitimate fertility   93
    Legitimate fertility   100
    The Character of employment   103
    The employment ratio   105
    Rising per capita real wages   106
    Conclusion   122

5. Migrants and their motives   126
    Overseas migration   128
    Internal migration   141

6. Population growth and the economy   153
    Population and the British Industrial Revolution   154
    Population and the British economy, 1850–1940   164
    Population and the Irish economy   171

7. Some social implications of population change   177
    Age and sex structure   178
    Household and family   181
    Other social implications   189

Bibliography   200
Index   225

ACKNOWLEDGEMENTS

As a work of synthesis, this book relies heavily on the work of the many scholars who in recent years have done so much to improve our understanding of the historical relationships between population, economic and social change. It could not have been written without their labours and I wish to record my gratitude to them. I trust that none is entirely dissatisfied with the way in which his work is presented in the subsequent pages.

I would also like to thank John Stevenson, editor of the series, for his many helpful comments and Miss Margaret Hendry for typing the manuscript so speedily and efficiently despite the numerous other calls on her time.

To Heather, Rachel and Sarah

viii

INTRODUCTION

Ten years ago I attempted a synthesis of available work on English population history which, given the prevailing deficiencies in our understanding of population trends, their mechanisms, causes and consequences, I described merely as an 'interim report' (Tranter 1973a). I suspect that I might have assumed that a decade later it would be possible to dispense with the adjective 'interim'. Such an assumption would have proved over-optimistic. Despite major advances in many areas of the subject, the gaps in our knowledge of the history of population change, its determinants and effects, remain substantial. In many respects, therefore, the conclusions reached in the present volume are no less tentative than those in its predecessor. In view of the laborious and complex nature of the techniques required for work on the evolution of population and social structure, the shortcomings of many of the available source-materials and the undoubted complexities of the relationship between the variables of demographic, economic and social change, this is perhaps not surprising. It will require much effort yet before the nature of the association between demographic and non-demographic behaviour in past ages becomes clearer and more secure. The conundrums of historical demography have only been partially resolved.

Broadly, three principal lessons emerge from a comparison of British and Irish demographic experience in the period between the mid-eighteenth and mid-twentieth centuries. First, in spite of their geographic proximity and the closeness of their political and cultural ties, how great were the variations in the levels, causes and consequences of population growth in the different countries of the British Isles. Second, how long it took for the process of economic and social change during the eighteenth and nineteenth centuries to break completely the demographic mould of the pre-industrial past. In some respects, of course, the demographic regime associated with the modern world had begun to emerge as early as the late eighteenth and early nineteenth centuries. In England, at least, in complete contrast to the experience of

1

earlier ages, from as early as the 1780s high rates of population increase were no longer equated with a sharp deterioration in standards of life. For the first time population and per capita real wages rose in unison (Wrigley 1983). Likewise, the modern trend towards urban living was already firmly established by the opening years of the nineteenth century. Otherwise, however, many, perhaps most, of the major changes which occurred in Britain's demographic system between the mid-eighteenth and mid-twentieth centuries – in levels of mortality, norms of marital fertility and habits of migration for example – began only in the later decades of the nineteenth century, yet another reminder of the gradualness of the developments associated with the Industrial Revolution. Third, how very dependent were population trends themselves on the character of the economic and social environment within which they took place. The causes and consequences of population change are intricately intertwined within the general fabric of human institutions, attitudes and behaviour and cannot be evaluated thoroughly without adequate reference to this fabric. It is this inter-relationship which makes the role of demography in the evolution of man's economy and society so difficult to assess and predict.

Chapter 1

SOURCES, METHODS, OBJECTIVES

More so than in most branches of the discipline of history, the study of historical demography depends heavily on the reliability of statistical data. Accurate information on variations in the size and rate of growth of populations, and in the demographic mechanisms responsible for them (marriage, fertility and mortality rates and alterations in the balance between in- and out-migration), is a vital requirement for any meaningful discussion of the relationship between the processes of demographic, economic and social change.

It is, therefore, particularly unfortunate that for much of the period before the middle of the nineteenth century both the quantity and quality of the statistical data available to historians have serious limitations. All too often, for the years prior to the introduction of improved methods of census-taking and the adoption of state responsibility for the registration of births, marriages and deaths, the historical demographer is forced to rely on sources which were not originally compiled for demographic purposes and which, as a result, are frequently incomplete and prone to distortion. In the shortcomings of the statistical data lies much of the explanation for the confusion which continues to exist about the nature of the relationship between population, economy and society in earlier times.

In this chapter we will take a close look at the character of the principal sources available for studying the history of population and social structure in Britain and Ireland since the middle of the eighteenth century:

1. The various kinds of listings of inhabitants compiled by private individuals and institutions for a variety of different purposes – ecclesiastical visitation records, taxation returns, detailed local censuses and the like, many of which become more abundant in the second half of the eighteenth century than ever before.
2. Civil censuses, begun in England/Wales and Scotland in 1801 and in Ireland in 1821.

3. The registers of baptisms, marriages and burials kept by parochial ministers of the established churches, originating in legislation passed in the sixteenth and seventeenth centuries and extant for large areas of England and Wales, though not of Scotland or Ireland, during the eighteenth and early nineteenth centuries.
4. The civil registers of births, marriages and deaths which were begun in England/Wales in 1837–8, in Scotland in 1855 and in Ireland in 1864 and which provide the first truly effective system of vital registration.
5. The records of passengers travelling between the United Kingdom and countries outside Europe, regularly available from 1815, for departures, and 1855, for arrivals, though not properly distinguishing the genuine from the temporary migrant until 1912.

Special attention will be paid to the deficiencies of the source-materials for population history before the mid-nineteenth century and to the various procedures devised, not always successfully, to overcome them.

Until the adoption of better methods of census-taking in 1841 and 1851, information on the size and rate of growth of populations, their age, sex and marital structures, household, family and kinship arrangements, is found only in private listings of inhabitants and, for the period 1801–31, in the first state censuses. Neither source yields the same profusion of accurate, detailed data contained in the procedurally novel census returns of 1841 onwards. The number of surviving listings is small and the listings themselves vary enormously in the range and quality of the material they include. Compared with the censuses of the later nineteenth century those of 1801–31 yield only scant and relatively imprecise data. For statistics on levels of nuptiality, fertility and mortality in the period before the beginning of civil registration we rely almost entirely on totals of marriages, baptisms and burials entered in the parish registers of the established churches. As we shall see, these registers are too scattered over time and place, too defective in their content or too unrepresentative of the communities to which they relate to be utilized without the application of elaborate procedures designed to combat such problems. Unfortunately, the procedures themselves are sometimes of doubtful and uncertain value and, even when applied with the requisite stringent care, can never provide results comparable either in quantity or quality with those obtainable from the civil registers of a later era. Sources of statistical data on patterns of migration within each of the countries of the United Kingdom during the eighteenth and first half of the nineteenth centuries are reasonably plentiful – birthplace entries in some of the better listings of inhabitants, statements on place of residence in ecclesiastical court records and marriage registers, nominative listings of various kinds which permit estimates of the rate of surname turnover. But, useful though they are, none give as complete or reliable a picture of human mobility as the birthplace data contained in the manuscript census returns from 1841/1851 onwards. Statistical data on the movement of people into and out of the United Kingdom and its constituent countries are much less plentiful. In fact, not until the adoption of effective census and civil registration procedures and the introduction of an extensive series of passenger statistics in the second half of the nineteenth century can variations in net and gross levels of overseas and inter-country migration be estimated with any reasonable degree of precision.

In view of the inadequacies of so much of the numerical data for the eighteenth and first half of the nineteenth centuries, it is all the more ironic to note that almost from the very moment when innovations in methods of census-taking and registration improve the quantity and reliability of his statistical material, in the interests of confidentiality, the historical demographer faces increasing difficulty gaining access to it.[1] Census enumerators' manuscript books, for instance, are not usually available to researchers after 1881 (in England) or 1891 (in Scotland). Restrictions on access to the data on births, marriages and deaths collected by civil registrars are even tighter. Until 1974, historians in England/Wales were allowed by personal arrangement to consult the original civil registers kept by local superintendent registrars, though not the copies of these registers held in the General Register Office. In 1974, however, registrars were instructed to withdraw this facility.[2] By way of partial compensation, the General Register Office began the process of removing the older civil registers to the Public Record Office, where they were to be microfilmed and eventually made available for general use. Unfortunately, access is to be restricted by the application of the same hundred-year rule as currently applies to the census enumerators' manuscripts. At the same time, the centralization of access to the registration data poses a very real threat to the future of work on purely local or regional population history.[3] Such restriction of access to the manuscript census and civil registration returns is extremely disturbing. Useful though they are for some purposes, the published census and civil register data are too generalized to satisfy the needs of anyone interested in the demography of particularly small communities or of specific sub-groups in different communities, and the information they contain cannot be retabulated to consider questions not asked by their authors. The published data rarely provide the depth of detail and range of cross-sectional material necessary for thorough demographic analysis. Since the relationship between the variables of population, economic and social change is highly intricate, even to begin unravelling the way it works requires an abundance of demographic information which only a painstaking analysis of the original, manuscript census and civil registration data can provide. Troubled enough by the scarcity and unreliability of his data for so much of the nineteenth and earlier centuries, the historical demographer has every reason to feel aggrieved about the restrictions imposed upon access to the more abundant and reliable material available for the later nineteenth and twentieth.

5

LISTINGS OF INHABITANTS

Relative to the size of the total population and length of period involved, the number of extant, privately-compiled listings of inhabitants available for the centuries before the introduction of the civil census is small even for England and, to a lesser extent, Scotland where they appear to be most common. For Wales and Ireland, either because fewer were carried out or because fewer have survived, they are especially scarce. The listings which are extant vary greatly both in the extent of their geographic coverage and in the range and reliability of the information they contain. Only Alexander Webster's 'Account of the Number of People in Scotland, 1755', which gives the total population of each parish, and the Irish hearth-money returns, with their totals of the number of hearths and houses taxed, cover nation-wide areas.[4] Others, like the English and Welsh ecclesiastical visitation returns which record parish-by-parish data on the number of houses or families and, for Ireland, the 1766 census of Protestants and Catholics, the estate maps of 1756–62 which return the number of occupied houses, the 1798–1800 lists of the houses in each corporate town or borough paying or exempt from the hearth tax, and the 1834 ecclesiastical survey carried out under the aegis of the Commission of Public Instruction are available on a regional basis. But the majority refer only to single communities or single parishes within a community. As a general rule the broader the area of their geographic coverage the less detailed and accurate the information such listings contain.

Webster's census of Scotland, long regarded as reliable, has recently been subjected to greater criticism. For those Highland parishes with SSPCK schools parochial ministers were asked to submit returns of either the number of inhabitants 'young or old' or the number of 'examinables'.[5] There is, however, no independent evidence available to test the accuracy of their returns and no way of knowing exactly how Webster converted numbers of 'examinables' into total population, except that he adopted a procedure of arithmetical conversion based on life tables. Worse still, we are completely ignorant about the procedures he used to arrive at his final population totals for those Highland parishes without SSPCK schools, for urban communities and all parishes in the heavily populated area of Lowland Scotland (Flinn 1977).

The weaknesses of the Irish hearth-money returns as sources for household totals have long been recognized. Those for the nineteenth century, when single-hearth householders (the great majority of the rural population) were no longer taxed, are of practically no demographic value. Those for earlier periods, reflecting the widely varying efficiency of the collectors, their confusions over how to treat households not eligible for taxation and the difficulties of enumeration in crowded urban centres and remote, scattered rural settlements, are only marginally more useful. According to Connell, the first modern user of the hearth-tax data, the number of households was understated by as much as 50% in all returns up to those of 1785, by 25% in those of 1788 and 20% in those of 1790 and 1791 (Connell 1950a). A more recent inquiry indicates a different level and trend of deficiency: while the hearth-money returns of the first half of the eighteenth century were between 14 and 34% deficient in the households they recorded and those of the 1790s only 10% inaccurate, the returns compiled between 1753 and 1788 suffer so severely from the carelessness and inconsistency of underpaid collectors, declining standards of central administrative supervision and the effects of an increase in the proportion of paupers in the population that their utility for demographic purposes is completely undermined (Daultrey, Dickson, O'Grada 1981). Whichever pattern of inadequacy turns out to be nearer the truth, any conclusions based on such fragile sources must be regarded more as an act of faith than a matter of detached, rational assessment.

Almost as unreliable are estimates of aggregate population derived from ecclesiastical visitations: all too often the parochial totals of houses or families these documents contain appear as neatly rounded numbers, a fact which does little to suggest that they were always the result of a careful enumeration by the parish clergyman or his nominee: too often their indiscriminate use of the terms 'house' and 'family' makes it difficult to convert their 'house' or 'family' totals into realistic estimates of aggregate population, a difficulty compounded by the fact that until recently there was considerable uncertainty about what the appropriate 'house' or 'family' multipliers should be (Pryce 1971).

Listings of national or regional geographic scope are in any case of limited appeal to the historical demographer since they usually include data convertible only into estimates of the absolute size of populations. For more direct and detailed demographic information, on the age, sex, marital, household and family structures of eighteenth century populations as well as their size, it is necessary to resort to listings that are more circumscribed in the extent of the communities they cover. The motives underlying the compilation of such listings were diverse. Some were devised to assist local government fulfil its obligations for public health or revenue collection. Some were compiled by town mapmakers or estate surveyors: others by parochial ministers as a basis for their replies to questionnaires received before episcopal visitations: one, for Ardleigh (Essex) in 1790, as a precaution against the possibility of a French invasion: another, for the parish of Ness (County Ross, Scotland) for the purpose of forming a Volunteer Corps: that for Drogheda (Ireland) in 1798 as a consequence of the declaration of martial law in the town. Many were the direct result of a growing interest in population questions per se during the later decades of the eighteenth century.

As might be expected from such a profusion of motives, the content

7

and reliability of even the more informative private listings varies enormously. The best of them, like that for Cardington (Bedfordshire) in 1782, compare favourably with the enumerators' books of the civil censuses from 1841 onwards, naming every individual in each carefully delineated household, consistently stating the relationship of each individual to the head of the household in which he lived and often incorporating additional information on age, marital status, place of birth, occupation, and so on. Most, however, are not so thorough and occasionally, as in the case of the census of the Trinity College (Dublin) estates in 1843, suffer from omissions which the apparent sophistication of the return makes it all too easy to overlook (Lee 1981). Nevertheless, compared with listings of a broader geographic coverage they are a treasure trove of demographic data. Of 126 local listings analysed by Law for eighteenth-century England/Wales, 25 include information on ages, 28 on sex ratios, 44 on the number of persons per family and 65 on the number per house, 14 on marital status and a few on occupations, birthplaces, boarders and lodgers, religious affiliation, even smallpox victims (Law 1969). The 1771 listing for Rothesay (Scotland) records all inhabitants family by family, sometimes specifying relationships within each family: the 1766 census of Perth (Scotland) the number of households, the sex of all inhabitants, the number of children under fifteen and of servants and lodgers in each quarter of the town: that for the Argyll estates in 1779 the men, women and children in every household, often with a statement of their family relationship (Flinn 1977). The 1795 census of Tullow (Ireland) gives the number of houses and inhabitants together with their occupations and religious persuasions (Dickson 1972) and that for the city of Armagh in 1770 the names of all household heads, their marital status, occupation, religious denomination and number of their children, servants and apprentices (Clarkson 1978).

In view of the extensive amount of information they contain it is unfortunate that so few detailed listings survive, especially since those which are extant are unduly biased in favour of small rather than large and rural rather than urban communities. In an age when most communities were small and most people were rural, not urban, dwellers the effects of this bias are not as serious as at first sight might appear. Nonetheless, there is a need for future research to unearth additional local listings in order to provide a better representation of the population over time and space than we have at present.

CIVIL CENSUSES

Nationwide, decennial censuses conducted by the civil authorities were introduced in England/Wales and Scotland in 1801 and in Ireland in

1813–15, though the first Irish census was aborted long before completion. Not until 1821 did effective Irish census-taking really begin (Froggatt 1965).

Responsibility for the 1821 and 1831 censuses of Ireland was vested in the county magistrates who appointed local enumerators, usually tax collectors, to enter the results of doorstep, viva-voce inquiries into special notebooks from which data were abstracted and processed by the central office. The enumeration of the first censuses of England and Wales (1801–31) was usually entrusted to poor law overseers or substantial householders and those of Scotland, where there was no official system of parish poor relief, to schoolmasters or 'other fit persons'. These, too, followed the viva-voce principle: enumerators visited each household sometime between 10 March and 30 April and entered on a prescribed form the replies given by householders to a limited number of set questions.

Few of the original enumerators' sheets for the early censuses survive. However, since with rare exceptions like the manuscript of the census of Thirsk (Yorkshire) in 1811 (Fieldhouse 1971) they contain no more information than is available in the published returns based upon them, this is no great loss. The 1821 and 1831 censuses of Ireland record the number of people, houses and occupations by county, barony, parish, town and village. In addition, the census of 1821, though not that of 1831, includes data on age and school. The early censuses of England/Wales and Scotland provide material on total population (by sex), age (in 1821 and 1831 – in the former by quinquennial age-groups up to the age of twenty and by decennial age-groups thereafter, in the latter only for adult males over twenty years of age), occupations (by the broad categories of: (i) agriculture; (ii) trade, manufactures or handicrafts; (iii) all others – in 1801 for individuals, in 1811, 1821 and 1831 only for heads of families except that in 1831 the occupations of all males over twenty are also given), the number of houses (inhabited, uninhabited, under construction) and the number of families.

As might be anticipated from the nature of doorstep, oral procedures the precise reliability of much of the data in the early civil censuses is questionable. The Irish censuses of 1821 and 1831 suffered particularly from clerical incompetence, public hostility towards the tax collectors who were charged with assembling the data, confusions over boundary areas, language problems, the effects of extensive seasonal labour migration, the poor quality of their enumerators and the ambiguous instructions given to them (Froggatt 1965; Vaughan and Fitzpatrick 1978). As a result the census of 1821 understated the true size of the population by as much as 6% while that of 1831 was only marginally more accurate in its coverage (Lee 1981). The 1801 and 1811 censuses of England/Wales probably understated the population by some 5 and 3% respectively.[6] John Rickman, the initiator of the first English censuses, had no illusions about the quality of the poor law overseers he used as enumerators, hence his decision to restrict the range of questions they were to ask of the householder, and he was probably wrong in assuming that Scottish schoolmasters were any better. Rickman was especially troubled by the shortcomings of the 1801 census – the failure of some parishes to submit returns, the particularly poor enumeration of the number of families, the considerable variations in the quality of the returns submitted and the difficulties involved in checking the accuracy of his enumerators' efforts. In some respects the censuses of 1811–31 were an improvement. No community escaped enumeration and, in 1831, the adoption of special tally-sheets for use by enumerators enhanced the accuracy of the data that were recorded. Even so, the assembled returns still lacked the lists of names and addresses so essential for an exact check on the reliability of their statistical summaries. There remained considerable confusion among enumerators about whether or not to include members of the armed forces and the militia. And the decision, in 1811, to enter the occupations of individuals rather than family heads probably increased the amount of error in statements of occupation just as low levels of literacy and the absence of an efficient system of birth registration seriously lessened the accuracy of the statements of age that were included in the 1821 and 1831 censuses. Above all, the early censuses of England/Wales and Scotland were the victims of two circumstances over which their agents had no control: the rapid growth of urbanization which posed problems of housing density, overcrowding and chaotic house numbering far beyond the capacities of even the most conscientious and energetic enumerators to solve completely: and the continued public prejudice against census-taking, a prejudice fuelled by fears of conscription, taxation or undue interference with individual freedom.[7]

In all four home countries the census of 1841 marked the beginning of a major improvement in methods of census collection. Firstly, in place of oral, tally-sheet procedures which usually took several weeks to complete, each householder received his own individual schedule to be completed for the designated night of the census. The schedules were then collected by the enumerators and copied into enumerators' books upon which the official census publications were ultimately based. Secondly, considerable efforts were made to improve the quality of enumerators themselves and to clarify the instructions by which they were expected to work.

In England and Wales the task of supervising the census was assumed by the Registrar-General of Births, Marriages and Deaths and its actual enumerators selected by the registrars of the various registration sub-districts. The local registrars were given the additional responsibility of checking the enumerators' returns for inconsistency and inaccuracy before transmission to the General Register Office in London where they were checked further before being analysed. With the introduction of civil registration, in 1855 and 1864 respectively, similar procedures were adopted in Scotland and Ireland. In the meantime the task of enumerating the Scottish censuses of 1841 and 1851 remained largely in the hands of local schoolmasters under the supervision of the sheriffs and provosts and the overall guidance of the Registrar-General of England and Wales. The Irish censuses of 1841–61 were conducted under the aegis of a specially appointed three-man census commission with the constabulary, assisted when required by other officials of central government, replacing the local tax collectors as enumerators.

The new technique of census-taking produced material of a sophistication previously available only in a handful of the most detailed, private local listings of inhabitants. Inter alia, the 1841 census of England/Wales and Scotland required each householder to record the name, age, sex, occupation and place of birth of every member of his household. The census of 1851, in an attempt to remove certain ambiguities and standardize procedures, asked for more precise data on place of birth and age, clarified the instructions concerning statements of occupation and required additional information on marital status and relationship to household head. Thereafter, the nature of the schedules changed very little, though additional questions were included from time to time – among them, whether imbecile, lunatic or idiot, Gaelic or Welsh speaker, employer, employee or self-employed; numbers of rooms and numbers of rooms with windows per household; education and religious affiliation; marital fertility; the whereabouts of all living children or stepchildren under the age of sixteen for each married or widowed adult; and place of usual residence as well as birth.

The 1841 census schedule for Ireland went far beyond that of the mainland in the detail it required, including questions on sex, age, relationship to household head, marital status and date of marriage, occupation, ability to read or write, birthplace, education, school attendance and housing. In the absence of a national system for registering vital events it also requested information on the number of births, marriages and deaths in each of the previous ten years and cause of death.[8] The 1851 schedule added questions about use of the Irish language and infirmities and introduced separate schedules dealing with the number of persons ill on a specified day, sickness among the inmates of various institutions and numbers of idiots and lunatics. From time to time thereafter further questions were added – on, for example, religious persuasion, unemployment and total live births per married woman. But the major change in the content of later Irish census schedules, a corollary of the introduction of civil registration in 1864, was the withdrawal of queries relating to births, deaths and dates of marriage. In view of the elaborate nature of their content it is unfortunate that, except for a handful of returns for County Cork and the parish of Killashandra (County Cavan) in 1841, none of Ireland's nineteenth and early twentieth century census schedules has survived. The enumerators' books of the censuses of 1861, 1871, 1881 and 1891 were never preserved

11

while those for 1821, 1831, 1841 and 1851, together with the material for the abortive 1813–15 census, were destroyed in the Dublin Record Office fire of 1922 (Royle 1982).

The new census procedures begun in 1841, helped by rising standards of education, lessening public suspicion of the motives of census-taking and a greater willingness to countenance state intervention in economic and social life, led to a marked improvement in the reliability of the data that were assembled. Even so, it is essential always 'to approach the enumerators' returns with critical faculties fully alerted ... particularly (in) studying small areas where the idiosyncracies of an enumerator might lead to quite a misleading set of returns' (Drake 1972b, p. 29). Basically, there are three potential sources of inaccuracy in post-1841 census material – the deliberate falsification of answers by household heads when completing the schedule, ambiguities in the questions asked of householders and in the procedural instructions given to enumerators, and deficiencies in the quality of the enumerators themselves.

Deliberate misrepresentation by household heads appears to have been rare. Comparisons of the consistency of information in different columns of the same census, for the same household in successive censuses and between census and civil registration data indicate that entries relating to sex, Christian and surname, marital status, relationship to household head and birthplace are as reliable as it is reasonable to expect. Where occasional inconsistencies do occur, they are relatively trivial and more usually the result of minor clerical failure than of deliberate falsification. Even statements of age, the most prone to error, are within acceptable margins of accuracy, albeit somewhat less reliable for females than males and for the elderly (elderly women especially) than for other age-groups (Tillott 1972; Thomson 1980).[9]

Ambiguities in the instructions relating to occupations, lodgers and visitors and in the definition of the term 'household' posed greater problems. Confusion over how to classify occupations, more serious in 1841 than in subsequent censuses, reflected the difficulty of finding a set of descriptive criteria simple enough to be easily understood yet sufficiently complex to incorporate the great variety of employment-types created by a diversifying economy. Least satisfactory are the occupational entries for women and children whose employment status was confused by the fact that so many of them worked part-time, often within the home. For the bulk of the adult male population however, though there was some diversity of practice among enumerators, serious errors were unusual. More troublesome was the lack of any clear and consistent definition of the terms 'lodger' and 'visitor'. So great was the confusion this caused that the modern researcher is usually forced to treat these classes of household resident as interchangeable. But it was the definition of the term 'household' which caused the greatest difficulties.

The instructions to the enumerators of the 1841 census did not make it clear whether separate schedules were to be left with the head of each household (co-resident domestic group) or of each house or tenement. The results were often chaotic. At Portpatrick (Wigtownshire), for example, it is frequently impossible to tell where one household ends and another begins: sometimes, residents described as relatives, servants or lodgers are treated as part of another's household: sometimes, households are equated solely with the nuclear family of parents and their offspring with relatives, servants or lodgers living in the same flat or house designated as a separate household. In 1851, in an attempt to resolve the uncertainty, enumerators were instructed to define a householder, or 'separate occupier', as any person who either owned or rented a whole house or any distinct floor or apartment within a house. This attempt at standardization was only partially successful. In particular, the treatment of lodgers remained very confused, some enumerators continuing to record them as members of another's household, others, as instructed, treating them as separate occupiers entitled to their own census schedule. Theoretically, the lack of consistency in defining the term 'household' poses problems for the analysis of household size and structure. Fortunately, recently devised standardized procedures for identifying separate households go a long way towards overcoming this difficulty (Anderson 1972).

If the case of East Lothian proves typical, the task of checking the enumerators' returns for consistency and reliability was carried out thoroughly and carefully by the local registrars and Census Office clerks (Collins and Anderson 1978). But how competent were the enumerators themselves? Contemporaries were generally unimpressed by their abilities, concluding that the work of enumeration required 'a better set of men than have hitherto been obtained'.[10] Historians have been more favourably disposed. Only a half-dozen or so of the ninety enumerators involved in the 1851 and 1861 censuses of selected areas of Yorkshire and Lincolnshire were obviously unsuited for their responsibilities (Tillott 1972). The majority of the East Lothian enumerators were artisans and skilled craftsmen, though they included a broad cross-section of the community ranging from university graduates and farmers to agricultural labourers and mole catchers: and all appear to have been chosen with some care (Collins and Anderson 1978). Without exception the enumerators responsible for the censuses of Portpatrick (Wigtownshire) over the period 1841–91 were literate, respectable and respected men, long resident in the parish and young enough still to be physically active. It is unlikely, therefore, that more than a small minority of census enumerators was unfit for their task.

Tillott has concluded that 'continued examination of the (census) returns suggests very strongly that they are reliable and that for almost all purposes the extent of error ... is slight' (Tillott 1972, p. 83). It is difficult to disagree with this judgement. Provided they are handled with care and analysed according to the standardized procedures devised by Armstrong, Anderson and others (Armstrong 1966; Anderson 1972; Tillott 1968), preferably in conjunction with sources such as rate-books, ordnance survey maps, tithe award plans and police charge-books,[11] the value of the civil census enumerators' returns for the historian of population and social structure is immense.

CHURCH REGISTERS

Apart from scattered data in urban Bills of Mortality – most of it in any case based on parish register material (Edwards 1969; Hollingsworth 1969; Glass 1973b), in the registers of various dissenting congregations (Eversley 1966, 1981; Steele 1970; Ambler 1972; Morgan 1973) and in the Irish censuses of 1841–61 – our knowledge of trends in numbers and rates of births, marriages and deaths for the period before the introduction of civil registration relies exclusively on the records of baptisms, marriages and burials compiled by the parochial clergymen of the established churches.

As a source for the study of historical demography the parish registers are seriously flawed. To begin with, the chronological and geographic incidence of their survival is extremely uneven, an obvious threat to the representativeness of the demographic conclusions based upon them. In theory, the registration of vital events in Ireland, among both Protestants and Catholics, dates back to the seventeenth century. In practice, few Irish registers have survived either because they have been lost or destroyed or, more probably, because for many areas none were ever actually compiled. For the Catholic majority of the population few registers exist for the period before the 1830s. Most of the Church of Ireland registers perished in the Dublin PRO fire of 1922. And such non-episcopalian Protestant registers as have survived relate mainly to the six counties of what is now Northern Ireland (Connolly 1979; Royle 1982). As late as the beginning of the nineteenth century only 99 of Scotland's 850 parishes had regular baptism and marriage registers and fewer still burial registers. Those which have survived are biased in favour of east-coast communities. Relatively few are available for the western lowlands, the northern islands, the Borders and the south-east, and hardly any for the Highlands and western islands (Flinn 1977). In England and Wales the situation is better. In Wales, for example, registers exist for about one-third of all parishes, though in many parishes of the diocese of St David's none survive for the period before the introduction of printed registers following Rose's Act of 1813 and in some other areas few date back beyond the middle of the eighteenth century (McDonald 1976).

The amount of detail given with each parish register entry varies considerably from place to place and, even within a single community, from time to time.[12] On occasions the entries are so brief that family reconstitution methods of analysis are impossible.[13] Generally, however, although the amount of entry detail is scantier for the eighteenth than the first half of the nineteenth century, it is usually sufficient to permit that accurate identification of individuals and families which is so essential for successful family reconstitution procedures (discussed below, p. 23). As a normal minimum, baptismal entries give date of baptism, Christian names of mother and child and full name of the father: those of marriage, the full names of bride and groom and, especially after Hardwicke's Act of 1753, their marital status, place of usual residence and, less frequently, age: those of burial, more variable in content, date of burial, full name of the deceased, relationship to a head of family (except in the case of family heads themselves and of unmarried adults no longer living with their parents) and marital status (except for married men and, usually, widowers).

The most serious disadvantage of parish registers as sources for population history is the problem of under-registration. Not even the very best ecclesiastical registers of baptisms, marriages and burials provide a complete record of all births, marriages and deaths occurring within the population to which they relate. Rapid population growth, the changing location of the population away from rural areas where church facilities were well established towards urban areas where they were not, the decline in religious zeal and the rise of Nonconformity all played their part in ensuring that 'the parish-books have been and are kept in a very uncertain and imperfect manner'.[14] Differences in local baptismal customs (which particularly affected the normal length of interval between dates of birth and baptism), in the personality and longevity of individual clergymen, in distances to the nearest church and the nature of local topography, the frequency of outbreaks of sickness and epidemics, the incidence of taxation and the costs of church services, and in the size, density and rate of growth of individual communities together produced a bewildering complexity in spatial and temporal patterns of under-registration.[15]

To varying degrees, under-registration was common to parish registers in all parts of the British Isles. The marriage registers of St Patrick's, Coleraine, between the 1770s and 1790s include only marriages in which the groom was a soldier or one or other of the partners was of an unusually high social status (Morgan 1973). Eighteenth-century Welsh parish registers contain numerous gaps, sometimes spanning many years (McDonald 1976). Such Scottish burial registers as exist often record only those which paid to use the parish mortcloth, not normal in the case of young children and usually provided free to paupers. According to James Stark, in 1851, from as early as 1794 not above a third of all births were captured by Scotland's parochial baptism registers. According to Bisset-Smith the number of baptisms registered in a group of West Lothian parishes during the 1840s was merely a quarter of what might have been expected from the size of the population (Flinn 1977). At Portpatrick (Wigtownshire) between 1820 and 1854 one in every three marriages, one in four of all male births and one in three of all female births escaped registration while the extent of birth under-registration varied considerably within the period – 32% in the early 1820s, 38% in the late 1820s and early 1830s, 36% ten years later and 50% in the late 1840s and early 1850s.

It is for England, however, that the greatest efforts have been made to unravel patterns of regional and secular variation in the quality of parochial registration. According to the traditional interpretation, for most of the eighteenth century the Anglican church registers recorded almost all marriages, 95% of all deaths and 90% of all births; between the 1790s and 1820 their coverage deteriorated sharply as the number of deaths and especially of births escaping registration rose alarmingly: and though rates of omission declined after 1820 the representativeness of the Anglican registers never again retained the levels current over much of the previous century (Krause 1965). Subsequent investigations have greatly modified this view.

During the late seventeenth century, following the troubles of the Commonwealth period, 'clandestine' marriages (unions celebrated by 'hedge priests' in private dwellings without benefit of church ceremony or contracted by an exchange of vows before witnesses without the presence of any kind of minister and not normally entered in the marriage registers of the established church) were so common in some areas that they amounted to almost half of all the marriages celebrated. By the early eighteenth century the Anglican church had regained much of its authority and the ratio of 'clandestine' to 'regular' marriages decreased dramatically (Wrigley 1973). Even so, throughout the first half of the century roughly one in ten marriages in England and Wales were 'irregular' unions of one kind or another evading 'capture' in the marriage registers of the established church (Brown 1976). The passing of Hardwicke's Act in 1753 (extended to Scotland in 1784), which recognized as legally valid only those marriages conducted by a clergyman in an Anglican church, reduced still further the frequency of 'clandestine' unions.[16] By 1821 the proportion of marriages omitted from the Anglican registers was as low as 2%. Not until 1836, when legal validity was restored to marriages celebrated in Nonconformist meeting houses, did the ratio once more begin to rise (Ambler 1972).

The conclusions of recent work on patterns of birth under-registration are less clear-cut. In stark contrast to the traditional interpretation, birth registration in the parish of Colyton (Devon) during the early nineteenth century appears to have been remarkably complete, at least 95% of all those giving Colyton as their place of birth in the 1851 census being traceable to an entry in the parochial baptism registers (Wrigley 1975). Similar comparisons of census birthplace data with parish register baptismal entries tell a very different story however. At Bottesford (Leicestershire) between 85% and 96% of all births were entered in the registers and the coverage deteriorated only slightly in the course of the period between the late eighteenth and mid-nineteenth centuries. In contrast, at neighbouring Shepshed, the quality of birth registration was much poorer and deteriorated rapidly between the late eighteenth century, when three-quarters of all births were registered, and the mid-nineteenth century, when only just above a third were recorded (Levine 1976a). In a sample of 45 mainly small, rural parishes in the period 1760–1834 one in every three births escaped registration, though there were substantial variations in the extent of omission from parish to parish: there is, on the other hand, no sign of any significant alteration in the extent of under-registration over time and nothing to support Krause's view that it was more serious between the 1790s and 1820 than either before or afterwards (Razzell 1972). Because they involve only those people who remained in a parish for relatively long periods, methods of assessing the extent of birth under-registration by means of a comparison of census birthplace statements with parish register baptism entries almost certainly understate the true level of under-registration and, by artificially smoothing out its volatility over time, obscure any tendency it may have had to increase in the course of the late eighteenth and early nineteenth centuries. To date, moreover, the task of cross-matching census and parish register data has not been undertaken for large urban communities where there is at least a prima facie case for supposing that the under-registration of births was more serious and increasing. Given these weaknesses in the recent methodology and the conflicting nature of the findings themselves, it is not yet possible to generalize about patterns of regional and secular variation in the efficacy of the ecclesiastical baptismal registers.

Whether the problem of under-registration was more or less prevalent in burial than baptism registers also requires more attention than it has so far received. Probably, over the eighteenth and first half of the nineteenth centuries as a whole, the burial to death ratio was more nearly complete than that of baptisms to births, if only marginally so (Krause 1965; Razzell 1972). At least one of the principal causes of under-registration, Nonconformity, was more likely to affect baptism than burial entries. Of 48 children born to a group of Nonconformist families living in the Bedfordshire parish of Cardington in 1782 fifteen had died before the 1782 listing of inhabitants was compiled: only one of the fifteen was not entered in the Anglican burial register despite the fact that all were interred in the dissenters' own burial ground (Tranter 1966). Possibly, during the first two decades of the nineteenth century, under-registration was at least as common for deaths as births, partly because of an increase in the number of Nonconformist burial grounds and partly because, until Rose's Act of 1812, Anglican ministers too often left the task of registering burials to negligent parish clerks or frequently delayed too long in entering the clerk's own lists in the registers (Razzell 1972). But this requires confirmation. For the moment, we know even less about regional and temporal variations in the under-registration of deaths than in that of births.

Obviously, a good deal more research is needed before we have a satisfactory understanding of the extent of under-registration in the Anglican church records of vital events. But however much this research modifies our present, somewhat confused appreciation of the extent of the problem it will surely merely confirm that in many, perhaps most, areas of the country, especially during the later eighteenth and first half of the nineteenth centuries, the shortcomings of ecclesiastical birth, death and, to a lesser extent, marriage registration are sufficiently severe to raise serious questions about the utility of church registers as sources for the study of trends in population growth and its vital rates.

CIVIL REGISTERS

The civil registration of births, marriages and deaths began in England and Wales in 1837–8, in Scotland in 1855 and in Ireland in 1864. That it came sooner to England/Wales than Scotland was due to a combination of circumstances: the larger size of the pressure-group in England favouring reform of the existing system, in part a result of the greater legal disabilities suffered by English than Scottish religious dissenters at the hands of the marriage laws: the relative weakness of the English established church in the face of this pressure: and the particularly vociferous opposition mounted by Scotland's burghs at the thought of what the new procedures would cost (Flinn 1977). In Ireland, the adoption of civil registration was delayed by the fact that data on vital events were already collected by the census authorities. The motives for its eventual adoption, however, were much the same everywhere and related in one way or another to the growing problems which stemmed from deficiencies in the existing system of ecclesiastical registration: its failure to supply adequate proof of identity and family relationship, so vital in matters of inheritance and claims to property: its inability to provide the reliable and detailed evidence on vital rates required by members of the medical profession interested in the causes of illness and death, by actuaries for their work on annuities, life assurance and Friendly Society benefits, and by the growing number of commentators anxious for a more precise statistical observation of social problems.

Above all, the introduction of an effective system of civil registration was increasingly seen as essential for the effective government of a rapidly changing society, all the more so since it had already been adopted by many other European countries (Glass 1973b; Cullen 1974).[17]

In order to avoid overtaxing the knowledge and powers of both informants and local registrars, from the outset the range of information required by the English and Welsh civil certificates was deliberately restricted. Marriage certificates requested details on age, marital status, rank or profession of the groom, bride and their fathers, and place of residence. Birth certificates sought information on the sex of the child, full name of the father and mother (including the latter's maiden name), father's rank or profession and place of residence of the informant. Death certificates asked for data on the sex, age, rank or profession of the deceased and cause of death. In Scotland, at least during the first year of the new system, the information required was much more extensive. The marriage certificate of 1855 asked for date and place of marriage, 'present' and 'usual' place of residence, age, occupation, place and date of birth of bride and groom and their relationship to each other (if any), name and occupation of their parents, number of the marriage (if a remarriage) and children by each former marriage. The 1855 birth certificate required, for the father, age, occupation, place of birth, date and place of marriage, children living and deceased; for the mother, age, birthplace and parity of the present birth. The death certificate for 1855 included questions on where born and how long resident in the district, occupation, age, names and occupations of parents, cause of death and duration of the fatal illness, to whom married and all children in order of birth, their ages or, in the case of those already deceased, their date and age at death.

Not surprisingly, the gathering of such a profusion of material imposed too great a strain on informants and registrars alike. Beginning in 1856 the questions relating to father's age, birthplace, place and date of marriage (reintroduced in 1861) and mother's age and birthplace were omitted from the birth schedules: those on the deceased's birthplace and length of residence in the district were removed from the death certificate (though a question concerning the marital status of the deceased was added): and those on 'present' and 'usual' place of residence, marital status, number of the marriage (if a remarriage), number of children by previous marriages and the birthplaces and dates of birth of bride and groom were taken out of the marriage certificates (from 1861 the relationship of bride and groom was also excluded). Thereafter, the information required by the Scottish civil certificates closely resembled that on those for England/Wales and Ireland. And until the Population (Statistics) Act in 1938, which extended the range of data required by the birth certificates, it remained largely unchanged.

As a register of the total number of marriages and deaths the civil

19

returns were almost completely accurate from the beginning.[18] For births, at least during the early years of the new system, the coverage was not quite so thorough. According to William Farr the registration of births in England and Wales during the 1840s was 93% accurate. Glass suggests that the proportion of births escaping registration fell from 7.9% (for males) and 8.6% (for females) in the period 1841–45 to 6.3% and 6.4% respectively between 1846 and 1850, 2.8% and 3.1% in 1861 and 1.2% and 1.6% in 1871 (Glass 1951): and Teitelbaum that it declined from 6.1% in the 1840s (both sexes), to 2.8% in the 1850s and 1.9% in the 1860s (Teitelbaum 1974). By 1880, apart from a temporary setback during the first decade of the twentieth century, the registration of live births in England and Wales was practically perfect. In Scotland, except for some, probably slight, under-registration of marriages and a 6% under-registration of births during the first year of the new system, the coverage of vital events was almost completely reliable from the outset, certainly from the end of the 1850s (Glass 1973b; Flinn 1977). [19]

Little attempt has been made to test the reliability of the various data included on the civil certificates. Statements relating to cause of death should certainly not be taken too seriously in view of the variety and uncertainty of contemporary medical diagnosis and terminology particularly before 1874 when anyone, whether a qualified medical practitioner or not, was permitted to inform the registrar of cause of death. This apart, however, if the results of such tests as have been carried out for the Scottish parish of Portpatrick are typical, most of the personal information given on the certificates seems reasonably reliable.[20]

TECHNIQUES AND OBJECTIVES OF PARISH AND CIVIL REGISTER ANALYSIS

For the period before the introduction of civil censuses parish register data have been widely used not only to illustrate geographic and temporal variations in rates of natural increase (that is, in the excess of births over deaths) but also to construct estimates of the total size of the population. Until recently, estimates of aggregate population based on parish register material followed one or other of two procedures. In the first, population totals are derived from a simple division of the number of baptisms, marriages or burials by the assumed level of baptism, marriage or burial rates per thousand population. In the second, use is made of the technique of 'counting-backwards', in which the size of a population at point 't' is estimated by subtracting the excess of births over deaths during the period '$t-t_1$' from the known size of the population at point 't_1'. Where parish register data have been used in these ways to construct estimates of the size of the population of England and Wales as a whole, historians have relied on the national aggregates of baptisms and burials given by John Rickman with the early census returns for every tenth year (1700, 1710, etc.) down to 1780 and annually thereafter.

There are several glaring weaknesses in these procedures. Firstly, assumptions about levels of birth, marriage and death rates at different times in the eighteenth and earlier centuries have all too often been made without any attempt to test their accuracy. Secondly, the technique of 'counting backwards', as usually applied, too readily assumes that the numbers of people migrating into a population roughly equate with the numbers who migrated out of it, a reasonable assumption for England and Wales as a whole but palpably absurd for its component areas. Thirdly, all estimates of the size of the population of England and Wales and its constituent parts based on Rickman's compilation of parish register data suffer from the serious deficiencies to which these data are subject (Schofield 1971). Marred by arithmetical errors (Wrigley 1976) and inconsistencies in the allocation of parishes to particular areas which make it difficult to treat the returns as a continuous record for given regions (Edwards 1976b), the number of vital events recorded by Rickman also falls short, sometimes far short, of the number actually entered in the parish registers (Wrigley 1976; Edwards 1976a). Rickman's data, therefore, cannot be regarded as a basis for constructing reliable estimates of rates of population growth in eighteenth-century England and Wales (Crafts 1974). In any case, as discussed above, the parish registers themselves give an incomplete account of the aggregate numbers of births, marriages and deaths actually celebrated. If the extent of under-registration over time and place and between baptism and burial series (on which estimates of natural increase and, usually, of population totals are based) had been uniform the problem would be less serious. Unfortunately, this was not the case and no-one has yet produced a set of correction ratios capable of resolving satisfactorily the dilemma posed by the complexity of under-registration patterns. To rely, as so many have done, on constant rates of omission is clearly unwise.

Recently, for England, the standard methods of estimating population size and growth from parish register data have been superseded by the Wrigley and Schofield technique of aggregative back-projection, which provides estimates of the population of the country at five-yearly intervals from 1541 onwards. Starting in 1871, when the size and age structure of the population are known, the aggregate population in each age-group in 1866 is calculated by estimating the number of people who died between 1866 and 1871 (through matching the total number of deaths in the quinquennium with an assumed age structure of mortality) and adjusting this number to take account of the balance between in- and out-migration (derived from an estimate of lifetime net migration for each age-group in 1871 adjusted to distinguish the proportion of this movement which occurred in the five years between 1866 and 1871). Having calculated the size and age structure of the English population in 1866, the same procedures are followed to estimate the size and age composition in 1861, and so on back to the middle of the sixteenth century (Wrigley and Schofield 1981). The validity of the technique depends, of course, on the accuracy of the authors' estimates of births (required to derive net levels of migration) and deaths as well as on the validity of their assumptions concerning the age structure of mortality in earlier centuries. As they readily admit, there must always be some doubt about the accuracy of data-inputs which have required such heroic efforts and assumptions to provide (Flinn 1982). Nevertheless, the estimates of English population growth which their labours have yielded are startling improvements on previous estimates and unlikely to be much modified in the future.

The main function of church and civil registration data, however, has always been to provide information on the behaviour of the demographic mechanisms which underlay the variations in rates of natural increase. A number of different methods of measuring levels of nuptiality, fertility and mortality have been utilized, the choice being determined by whether aggregative or family reconstitution techniques of analysis are adopted. In studies of the aggregative type the behaviour of marriage, birth and death rates is usually presented in the form of a crude rate (the number of vital events per thousand total population), a relatively unsatisfactory measure which takes no account of differences in age, sex or marital structure. Wherever possible, all too rarely before the nineteenth century, it is preferable to express birth rates in the form of a general or marital fertility rate (the number of births per thousand women or per thousand married women aged 15–44) and to subdivide death rates by sex and age-groups. Where the size of the population is unknown, aggregative measures of fertility usually rely on a simple division of the number of births by the number of marriages in a particular period and mortality is often expressed merely as a ratio of male to female, or infant and child to adult, deaths, procedures which also suffer from their inability to distinguish the effects of differences in migratory habits, age, sex and marital structures. The aggregative approach to the registration data can likewise be made to provide useful insights into seasonal fluctuations in the number of vital events (Spencer, Hunn and Deprez 1976), ages at marriage (Elliott 1973; Outhwaite 1973), the sex ratio of baptisms and the proportion of illegitimate to legitimate births (Schofield 1970b).

The technique of family reconstitution, which involves reconstructing each family's nuptiality, fertility and mortality history from parish and civil register entries of marriage, birth and death, presents its findings rather differently. From it can be derived ages at death (and, thus, age-specific death rates, by sex), the number of children per 'completed' family (defined as one which remains unbroken until the wife is at least 45 years old), the number of children born to women of different age-groups (age-specific fertility rates), the length of intervals between marriage and the birth of the first child and between the births of subsequent children, ages at marriage, duration of married life, the frequency of remarriage and the length of time between the end of one marriage and the beginning of another. In addition, family reconstitution data can be used to derive estimates of total population, age structure and levels of crude birth, marriage and death rates (Sharlin 1978).

In some respects aggregate procedures are preferable to those of family reconstitution. They are less laborious, more easily applicable to large populations and involve relatively little waste of information. They give a better indication of short-term fluctuations in the behaviour of vital rates and allow the speedy identification of those areas and periods to which the more intensive methods of family reconstitution might profitably be applied. Sometimes indeed – when the accurate identification of individuals so essential for successful family reconstitution analysis is prevented by the restricted range of names in use or insufficient detail in parish register entries, or when high rates of population mobility make it difficult to accumulate a sufficiently large and representative sample for study by family reconstitution procedures – aggregative techniques are the only ones possible (Eversley 1966).

Such advantages, however, are more than offset by disadvantages from which the technique of family reconstitution largely escapes. Apart from the fact that they penetrate less *effectively into the demography of a parish* than those of family reconstitution (Wrigley 1966a), aggregative techniques suffer more seriously from the twin problems of under-registration and ambiguous interpretation. Baptism, marriage and burial totals are of little use as guides to the behaviour of vital rates if they exclude, as they often do, many of the births, marriages and deaths which occur in a population. Even if the omission ratios recently derived for England as a whole prove acceptable (Wrigley and Schofield 1981), more research is needed to assess the extent of regional variation which obviously occurred around the national average. And even where registration does provide an accurate count of the total number of vital events, the inability of aggregative techniques always to relate their data on birth, marriage and death rates to the age, sex and marital structures of the population concerned or, in the case of fertility measures based on a simple ratio of the number of marriages to births, to the pattern of in- and out-migration severely lessens their usefulness as indices of the true behaviour of fertility, nuptiality and mortality. On both counts, family reconstitution has the great merit of yielding data applicable only to a population of known risk and free from the distortions arising from differentials in age, sex and marital composition.

Not that family reconstitution procedures are free of problems. To begin with, although the amount of detail given with parish register entries is normally sufficient to allow the accurate identification of individuals and families, there are occasions when this is not the case and when family reconstitution, therefore, is impractical (Henry 1968; Hollingsworth 1968). Secondly, in view of their laborious nature and their need to use only data of rigorously attested accuracy, family reconstitution studies have frequently been based on statistical samples that are far too small to be considered significant.

But perhaps the most trenchant criticism of family reconstitution concerns its representativeness, specifically its bias towards particular types of community and, within individual communities, towards particular types of resident. To date, the choice of parishes for analysis by family reconstitution procedures has been determined more by the adequacy of their registers than the representativeness of their economic and social characteristics (Santini 1972). Accordingly, almost all existing studies relate to small, rural communities. Larger, especially urban, populations, with more deficient registers and greater problems in ensuring accurate individual and family identification as a result of high rates of migration and a proliferation of people with the same name, have been neglected. Until the technique of family reconstitution is applied, successfully, to a wider variety of communities the representativeness of its findings is obviously debatable. Even in a single community the proportion of families which can be reconstituted is extremely small, from a minimum of 10% to a maximum of 30%–40% if the search for individuals and families is extended into the registers of neighbouring parishes (Hollingsworth 1969; Santini 1972). One reason for this is under-registration and its various causes. Another is the extent of migration. Four out of every ten couples marrying at Portpatrick (Wigtownshire) between 1820 and 1891 left the parish immediately after the marriage ceremony and never returned: a further one in ten left, never to return, immediately following the birth of their first child. Of 180 couples marrying in the parish between 1820 and 1860 and known to have remained longer a quarter stayed for less than five years, a little over a third for less than ten years and only just over a third for 25 years or more, the full length of a woman's child-bearing period.

The problem is to decide whether the minority of reconstitutable families – presumably those most attached to the established church, relatively immobile and more representative of the conservative than the radical and the richer than the poorer members of village society – are so uncharacteristic of the demography of a community that family reconstitution procedures are rendered valueless. Probably, though not yet certainly, the answer appears to be that they are *not* radically different in their demographic behaviour. It is unlikely, for example, that migrant couples would display markedly different demographic profiles from couples who remained to be 'caught' in the reconstituted population. Most migrants moved very short distances, usually within a radius of ten miles, and there is no reason to assume that those who moved across parish boundaries (thereby disappearing from the registers of the parish of departure) would have very different patterns of marriage, fertility and mortality from those who stayed put or moved only within the parish. In any case, the reconstitutable minority will itself include many families in which either the husband or the wife came from outside the parish and thus, to some extent, will incorporate some of the effects on the demography of a community which migration may have had (Schofield 1972a).

It is, however, the frequency of *temporary* migration (defined as the movement of couples who began their family-building in parish A, continued it in parish B and returned to parish A to complete it) rather than of *permanent* disappearance from the registers, whether due to emigration or other cause, which poses the greatest potential drawback to family reconstitution procedures (Schofield 1972a; Hollingsworth 1972). The frequency of temporary migration has never been fully assessed but it was undoubtedly extensive. In the dozen or so years before March 1891 John S., a 33-year-old ploughman with a wife and four children, had lived sequentially three years at Straiton, six months at Portpatrick, one year at Leswalt, three months at Kirkcolm, one year at Inch, two years at Portpatrick, six months at Stoneykirk, two years six months at Leswalt and one year eight months at Portpatrick. Similarly, John S., a shoemaker, married Grace W. at Portpatrick on 9 September 1830 where a son, Robert, was born on 3 October. For almost twenty years thereafter there is no reference to the couple in either the church registers or the censuses of 1832–4 and 1841 and they can be assumed to have left the parish. Some time before 1851 John and Grace returned to Portpatrick, the censuses of that year recording the birth in the parish of a daughter, Grace (not entered in the deficient baptism registers), and listing five other children aged between six and eighteen, all born at Leswalt. The absence of any reference to the family in either the church and civil registers of the 1850s and 1860s or in the census of 1861 suggests that it left the parish shortly after 1851. By 1871, however, Grace, now a sixty-year-old widow, had returned to Portpatrick with one of her daughters, where she died on 27 January 1887 aged 81. Where family reconstitutions are attempted on the basis of registration data alone, as so often they have been, migratory patterns of this kind can give rise to seriously distorted results.

In testing for continuity of residence and otherwise validating and extending the data derived from family reconstitutions based on church and civil registration material, it is obviously imperative to make full use of other available sources – wills, overseers' assessments and accounts, militia rolls, estate records, enclosure maps and, above all, private nominative listings of inhabitants and civil census enumerators' books (Brown 1971). And, even then, the strictest conventions must be adopted in deciding which of the data can be safely incorporated into the analysis and which must be omitted. Only if these conventions are consistently applied will family reconstitution, coupled with aggregative methods of analysing register data and the use of private and civil censuses, afford a satisfactory means of unravelling the demographic mysteries of the past.

MIGRATION

On the whole, historical demographers are better served by sources relating to the geographic mobility of people within each of the various countries of the United Kingdom than by those dealing with migration into and out of the United Kingdom or its constituent countries.

In the study of internal migration the sources used and the way in which they are used depend on the particular aspect of spatial movement under consideration – whether the net balance of migration between areas, the gross volume of movement into and out of different communities, regional and secular variations in rates of population turnover, distances travelled by migrants or migratory patterns by age, sex or socio-occupational group.

Analyses of the net balance of population movement between areas, devised by subtracting the level of natural increase from the actual increase in the size of the population over a specified period of time, require reliable data on total population and numbers of births and deaths. With the introduction of regular decennial censuses and the civil registration of vital events in the nineteenth century such data are readily available. For earlier times however, when census and registration data are less adequate, net migration is more difficult to measure. It is extremely rare for any single community, least of all a whole area, to have both the reliable listings of inhabitants and the registers of births and deaths required for a satisfactory analysis. In any case, the study of net migration, while it allows us to distinguish areas which attracted people from areas which lost them, tells us nothing about the *volume* of migrant flows. Recently, sophisticated techniques have been developed for estimating the volume of gross migration between counties (Friedlander and Roshier 1966; Baines 1972). But because these require information on age structure and age-specific mortality rates as well as on rates of growth of population and natural increase they, too, are generally impractical for the period before civil census and register material become available.

Estimates of the *frequency* of internal migration are easier to devise. The most common procedure for estimating rates of population turnover, albeit the one open to the greatest criticism, involves an assessment of the survival-rate of surnames in successive nominative listings – taxation returns, members' rolls of gilds and corporations, parish registers, ratebooks and the like (Buckatsczh 1951). Of course, the results of such methods are extremely crude. Although there are exceptions (Holmes 1973; Dennis 1977), they usually make no allowance for the influence of mortality on surname survival-rates. Too often, the nominative lists upon which they are based are incomplete or refer only to specific, perhaps unrepresentative, sections of the community. And, in areas like Wales, the utility of such studies is marred, if not destroyed completely, by the restricted range of surnames in common use.

More detailed and reliable analyses of migrational frequency, and also of distances travelled and differences in migratory habits by age, sex or social class, require sources which provide more than a mere list of names. Fortunately, these are reasonably plentiful. Private listings of inhabitants, church marriage registers and nineteenth-century census enumerators' and civil register returns are geographically the most extensive and most commonly used sources of data on place of birth or usual residence. Thus, the Cardington (Bedfordshire) listing of 1782 has been used to relate patterns of migration to age, lifecycle, occupational and marital status (Schofield 1970a). Anglican marriage registers have proved an invaluable source for tracing the origin of marriage partners (Maltby 1971). Census enumerators' statements on the place of birth of parents and their children are good indicators of patterns of *family* mobility (Gwynne and Sill 1977). Civil birth certificate data on place of residence have been used to illustrate the extent of inter-parochial mobility by occupational status (Gant 1977).

Among the many other important sources of information on migration are marriage certificates with their details on place of residence (Elliott 1973), police charge books which, besides details on the occupation, offence, earnings, number of children, height and facial characteristics of the accused, also give his place of residence and birth (Williams 1973), and eighteenth- and nineteenth-century Scottish chartulary books which record the title deeds to land purchased for housebuilding and include the name, occupation and place of origin of the household head (Lockhart 1978). On the basis of such materials, we already have a fair picture of the character of human mobility within each of the countries of the British Isles in past times.

Sources for the study of migration into and out of the United Kingdom and its constituent countries are more problematic. It is easy enough to provide estimates of the net balance of in- and out-migration, though only from that point in the nineteenth century when census and civil registration data allow a comparison between rates of natural

27

increase and population growth.[21] Again, from the middle of the nineteenth century onwards, there is little difficulty in compiling estimates of the number of foreign-born residents in each of the countries of the United Kingdom – from census entries on place of birth, given with all censuses from 1841 (from 1851 by precise country of origin) and, less satisfactorily, from records of alien immigrants kept by the Home Office or, during the interwar period, from the number of work permits issued to employers of aliens by the Ministry of Labour. Much of the remaining material on movement between Britain, Ireland and the outside world, however, is more flawed.

Among the most important, if under-used, sources on emigration are the data on immigrants compiled by the governments of Canada and the USA, the two most popular destinations for emigrants from the UK. Records of immigrants arriving at Quebec are available from 1828 onwards. In the USA the annual collection of data on immigrants was instituted by a Congressional Act of 1819 which required the masters of incoming vessels to supply customs officers with lists of all passengers embarking at a foreign port. The lists, covering the period 1820–1902 and extant for all Atlantic and Gulf coast ports, invariably include data on name, age, sex, occupation, country of origin, the date and circumstance of deaths on the voyage and, occasionally, family relationship and place of last residence.

But, although a source of considerable potential, the American ship-lists are not entirely devoid of problems. Some of the information they contain, notably on occupations, is far from completely reliable. More seriously still, they understate the level of immigration from the United Kingdom to the USA partly because the lists for those entering the USA through San Francisco have not survived, partly because the earlier lists were often deficient and registration procedures at American ports not always thorough and partly because they take no account of migrants who travelled to the USA via Canadian or Mexican ports (Erickson 1972; Brayshay 1979). Similar detailed sources are available for those emigrants from the United Kingdom to the British colonies whose passages were assisted by colonial government funds, though these too have been relatively little utilized (Duncan 1963–4).

For the second half of the eighteenth century lists of passengers leaving the United Kingdom for overseas destinations are extant only for the short period between December 1773 and April 1776 when customs officers were instructed to provide weekly returns of people 'who shall take their passage on board any Ship or Vessel to go out of this Kingdom, with a description of their Age, Quality, Occupation, Employment, and former Residence; and an Account of to what port or place they propose to go, and for what purpose they leave this country.' While large numbers of these lists survive we do not know how many have been lost or how many departing vessels escaped registration, and emigrant totals based upon them probably substantially understate the true level (Flinn 1977). The compilation of passenger lists was suspended during the American War of Independence and not resumed until 1803. In fact, a regular, annual series of statistics on the number of passengers leaving British and Irish ports for destinations outside Europe did not begin until 1815, compiled by the Customs Commissioners and the Treasury (to 1840), the Colonial Land and Emigration Commissioners (from 1841 to 1872) and the Board of Trade (from 1873 onwards). Only after 1825 do these statistics distinguish between emigrants from Scottish, Irish, English and Welsh ports. But until 1853, when ships' masters were required to state the nationalities of their passengers, their usefulness as a guide to the number of emigrants by nationality is diminished by the fact that many Irish and some Scots left from English ports.[22]

The weaknesses of the United Kingdom passenger lists as a guide to the volume of emigration are well-known. Before 1863 they refer only to steerage passengers (fortunately the large majority) and exclude both cabin passengers and those who worked their passage as crew members (Flinn 1977). Not until 1890 were ships' masters asked to provide lists of passengers travelling to European countries (except to Mediterranean ports) and only from 1905 were they required to do so by law (Ferenczi and Willcox 1929). Moreover, particularly before the widespread introduction of steamships on ocean crossings, many vessels evaded clearance through the customs and therefore failed to submit details of their passenger manifests to the authorities. Finally, not all ocean-going travellers were genuine emigrants. By the later decades of the nineteenth century a growing number of people travelling overseas had no intention of affecting a permanent change of residence, and it is only from 1912 that the passenger returns distinguish genuine emigrants from temporary departures by requiring statements on country of last residence and intended, permanent future residence (Thomas 1954).[23] Despite these shortcomings, however, as well as the useful data they contain on ages, occupations and country of destination (from 1876), the nineteenth- and early twentieth-century passenger statistics can be regarded as providing a satisfactory approximation to fluctuations in the volume of emigration from the United Kingdom, albeit only to extra-European destinations.

For Ireland, during the period 1851–1920, there is an additional major source of data on emigration. In May 1851 the Irish government ordered that records be kept of all persons embarking at Irish ports with the intention of permanently leaving the country. The data were to include migrants to Britain as well as to the British colonies and other overseas countries and information was required on the sex, age, conjugal status, county of origin (often not recorded, especially in the 1850s and 1860s) and proposed destination (from 1876) of each migrant. These statistics were published in the early census reports, from 1856–75 in the series of Irish agricultural statistics and, after 1876, in the annual reports on emigration produced by the Registrar-General's Office (O'Grada 1975; Vaughan and Fitzpatrick 1978). For all their apparent comprehensiveness, however, they understate the true level of emigration by anything between 12% and 25% (O'Grada 1975).

Sources of data on the volume and composition of migration into the individual countries of the United Kingdom are even rarer and still more problematic. Only from 1855 were masters of vessels arriving from countries outside the continent of Europe invited to supply lists of their passengers and only from 1870 were they required to do so by law. Not until 1876 do their returns distinguish between UK citizens and aliens. As a result, it is only from 1855 that estimates can be made of the net balance of passenger movements between the United Kingdom and extra-European countries, and of the net flow of UK citizens alone only from 1876 (Thomas 1954).

Except for the data provided by the Irish Registrar-General for the period 1876–1920 – on the numbers leaving Ireland for different countries of destination within and beyond the United Kingdom – there is no direct statistical information on year by year fluctuations in the volume of migrant flows between the countries of the British Isles. Much of this movement, of course, did not involve a permanent change of residence but was merely a seasonal flux of labour in search of employment. Seasonal migration was especially prevalent from Ireland and the Highlands of Scotland.[24] Only for the Irish is it possible to provide even the crudest estimates of the size of these seasonal labour flows: for the 1830s, from the answers given to queries contained in parochial reports to the Royal Commission on the Poorer Classes concerning the number of labourers habitually leaving their parish to find work elsewhere and the proportion of these going to Britain: for 1841, from statistics collected by the census authorities of the number of harvesters waiting in Irish ports for passage to Britain: for the first half of the nineteenth century, from scattered data assembled by the Irish Post Office and Railway Commissioners: and for the 1860s, from material included in the 1866 Commission on Irish Railways and in the reports of the Irish poor law inspectors of 1869–70 (Irvine 1960; Johnson 1967; O'Grada 1973). The estimates yielded by these documents vary considerably. Beginning in 1880 annual figures of seasonal migration from Ireland were compiled both by the constabulary and the railway and steamship companies. The constabulary returns – in part because the constabulary was so unpopular and in part because the returns were assembled in the month of June, before many potential seasonal migrants had yet to decide whether or not to go – are particularly suspect, probably recording only about 60% of the total seasonal flow (O'Grada 1973). For the other areas which contributed to seasonal migrant streams, notably the Scottish Highlands, there are no data which permit the measurement of volume.

NOTES AND REFERENCES

1. It is disturbing to note that recent discussions within the General Synod of the Church of England appear to threaten the access of bona-fide researchers to the parochial registers of baptisms, marriages and burials kept by the Anglican church, the principal source of information on the number of vital events before the introduction of civil registration. See, Parish registers: access and preservation, *Local Population Studies,* **4,** 1970; Fees for searches in church registers, *ibid.,* **10,** 1972; Fees for searches in parish registers, *ibid.,* **11,** 1973; Fees for searches in parish registers, *ibid.,* **12,** 1974; A new parochial registers and records measure, *ibid.,* **14,** 1975; The new parochial registers and records measure; a progress report, *ibid.,* **15,** 1975; Revising the parochial registers and records measure: an interim report, *ibid.,* **16,** 1976; The parochial registers and records measure, *ibid.,* **18,** 1977; The parochial registers and records measure: the last phase, *ibid.,* **19,** 1977; Parochial fees: the recent report by a sub-committee of the General Synod, *ibid.,* **21,** 1978.

2. In Scotland, researchers are still permitted unrestricted access to the nineteenth century civil register books held in the custody of the Registrar-General.

3. Access to General Register Office records, *Local Population Studies,* **3,** 1969; The office of population censuses and surveys, *ibid.,* **8,** 1972; Conversation at Somerset House, *ibid.,* **9,** 1972; Civil registers and the historian, *ibid.,* **11,** 1973; Access to local superintendent-registrars' records, *ibid.,* **13,** 1974; Civil registers and the local historian, *ibid.,* **14,** 1975; Access to civil registers, *ibid.,* **20,** 1978.

4. The Irish hearth-money tax began in 1662 and culminated in 1824. Surviving national nominal records for Ireland such as the Tithe Applotment Books of around 1830 and the Valuation Records of the 1830s contain only very sparse information (Royle 1982).

5. That is, of the number of persons old enough to be examined on the Catechism. The 'examinable' age varied greatly from area to area.

6. Taylor 1951; Krause 1958. Recent estimates for the censuses of England (less Monmouth) suggest rates of omission of 4.5% in 1801, 4.1% in 1811, 2.7% in 1821, 2.4% in 1831 and around 1.5% in 1841–71, mainly due to the under-registration of young children and of men serving in the army, navy and on merchant shipping (Wrigley and Schofield 1981, p. 595).

7. For a discussion of the weaknesses of the early censuses see Froggatt 1965; Vaughan and Fitzpatrick 1978; Glass and Taylor 1976; Benjamin 1954–5; Drake 1972b; Glass 1973a; Flinn 1977.

8. Data on cause of death were collected from the records of hospitals and other institutions.

9. My own tests of the reliability of the census enumerators' books for the parish of Portpatrick (Wigtownshire), 1841–91, confirm the conclusions of Tillott and Thomson.

10. Committee appointed by the Treasury to inquire into certain questions connected with the taking of the census, *Report,* BPP, 1890, LVIII, p. 21. In his evidence to the Committee Dr Ogle, superintendent of statistics at the General Register Office, described the enumerators as 'rather a poor

lot', many of the clerks at the Central Office as 'absolutely unfit for any work at all' and charged local registrars with 'very bad work' (Drake 1972b, p. 26).

11. See Williams 1973; Henstock 1973; Holmes 1973; Gwynne and Sill 1977.

12. For example, there was a marked improvement in the Church of Ireland registers for the parish of St Patrick's with the arrival of a new incumbent in 1807 (Morgan 1973).

13. Thus, the Welsh baptismal registers for the period before the middle of the eighteenth century sometimes record only the name of the child or the names of the child and his father (McDonald 1976).

14. Evidence of Edgar Taylor to the *Select Committee on Parochial Registration,* BPP, 1833, XIV, p. 590.

15. For a discussion of the factors influencing the extent of registration see Krause 1965; Eversley 1966; Loschky 1967; Pryce 1971; Schofield 1971; Mills 1973; Ambler 1974; Flinn 1977; Cook 1980; Doolittle 1980; Finlay 1980; McCallum 1980. On the tendency for birth-baptism intervals to lengthen in the course of the second half of the eighteenth and early nineteenth centuries see Berry and Schofield 1971; Mills 1973; Ambler 1974; Jones 1976; Jackson and Laxton 1977; Cook 1980; Doolittle 1980; McCallum 1980.

16. Marshall 1972; Wrigley 1973; Brown 1976. Only Jews and Quakers of all the Nonconformist sects were exempt from the provisions of the Act.

17. See also, The office of population censuses and surveys, *Local Population Studies,* **8,** 1972, pp. 4–9.

18. Except in the case of still births, the registration of which did not begin until 1927, in England/Wales, and 1939, in Scotland.

19. See also the comments of the Scottish Registrar-General in Registrar-General of Births, Deaths and Marriages in Scotland, *Fifth Annual Report,* 1859, Edinburgh, 1863, p. iii; *Fourteenth Annual Report,* 1868, Edinburgh, 1870, p. xv. Of 249 males and 236 females between 1855 and 1891 whose census entries indicate birth at Portpatrick 94% and 97% respectively were entered in the civil birth registers of the parish. In fact, the degree of inaccuracy in the birth registers is even smaller than this since a few probably erred in claiming Portpatrick as their place of birth. No estimates of the adequacy of Irish civil registration statistics are available, but there is no reason to suppose that they were any less satisfactory than those for England/Wales and Scotland.

20. In the absence of independent, alternative sources, much of the information on the certificates is difficult to test. But, for Portpatrick at least, statements of age at marriage, age at death and occupations given in the registers compare closely with those derived from sources like the census enumerators' books.

21. For England, on the basis of new data on population growth and rates of natural increase during the pre-civil census and registration era, crude estimates of net migration are available for as far back as the sixteenth century (Wrigley and Schofield 1981).

22. The estimates compiled by the Emigration Commissioners of the number of Irish-born leaving the United Kingdom for extra-European destinations during the period 1832–51 are little more than guesses based on the recorded movements of passengers from Irish ports and the

arbitrary assumption that two-thirds of all emigrants from Liverpool were Irish (O'Grada 1975).
23. The 1912 schedule also included more detailed queries on age and occupation. No similar provisions were made for travellers by air until 1947.
24. See Irvine 1960; Johnson 1967; O'Grada 1973; Collins 1976; Devine 1979.

Chapter 2

POPULATION GROWTH AND
ITS MECHANISMS

For countries as geographically proximate as England/Wales, Scotland and Ireland the differences in rates of population growth since the middle of the eighteenth century have been quite startling. Throughout the second half of the eighteenth century rates of population increase in Ireland were well above those in England/Wales and twice, possibly three times, as great as in Scotland. In the hundred years beginning around the close of the eighteenth century the rate of population growth in England/Wales and Scotland rose substantially (slightly more in the former than the latter and more quickly in the first half than the second half of the nineteenth century). By contrast, although rates of Irish population growth also accelerated during the late eighteenth and early nineteenth centuries, to levels exceeding those anywhere else in the United Kingdom, they began to decline rapidly in the decades immediately before the Great Famine (1845–51).[1] From the Famine until the mid-years of the inter-war period Ireland suffered a continuous decline in the absolute size of her population, a demographic phenomenon which made her unique among all her European neighbours. In the decades between the world wars rates of population growth in England/Wales and Scotland slumped alarmingly, Scotland's population actually declining in total during the 1920s. Here, too, the Irish experience was different. At some stage between the mid-1920s and mid-1930s the long period of demographic decline ended and between the censuses of 1926 and 1936/7 the country's population once more began to grow, albeit at a slower rate than elsewhere in the UK.

There were, of course, considerable variations in rates of population growth from region to region within each country. In Scotland, most of the increase in population since the middle of the eighteenth century has been concentrated in the relatively narrow geographic area of the Western and, to a lesser extent, Eastern Lowlands, roughly equating with the main centres of industrial and commercial development (Flinn 1977).[2] In England/Wales, where the geography of economic development was more diverse, the number of regions contributing to

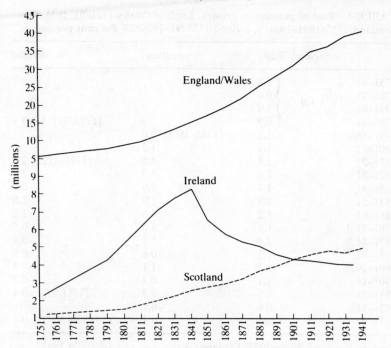

FIGURE 1   Total population: England/Wales 1751–1939; Ireland
1753–1936/7; Scotland 1755–1939 (in millions). *Sources*: Scotland, Flinn
1977; England/Wales, Lee and Schofield 1981 (1755–1801), Mitchell and
Deane 1962 (1811–1939); Ireland, Daultrey, Dickson and O'Grada 1981
(1753–91), Lee 1981 (1821–41), Vaughan and Fitzpatrick 1978
(1851–1936/7).

the growth of population was larger and regional differentials in rates of
population increase, therefore, less marked. During the second half of
the eighteenth and early nineteenth centuries population growth was
greatest in the industrial areas of the North West, Yorkshire/
Humberside and the Midlands and in the industrial and commercial
region of the South East centred on London. For much of the rest of the
nineteenth century the population of the North West, Yorkshire/
Humberside and the South East continued to grow relatively rapidly as
did that of the West Midlands before 1850. But, increasingly, from the
middle decades of the century the main foci of population growth,
reflecting the incipient problems of the traditional industries, shifted
away from the North West, Yorkshire/Humberside and the Midlands
towards the South East and the North. In contrast, the populations of
East Anglia and the South West stagnated in the second half of the
century and many rural areas, sometimes whole counties, suffered

TABLE 1 Rate of population growth, England/Wales 1751/61–1931/9, Scotland 1755/1801–1931/9, Ireland 1753/91–1926/37. Per cent per annum.

	England/Wales		*Scotland*	*Ireland*
1751–61		0.8		
1761–71	1.0	0.6		
1771–81		1.0		
1781–91		0.9		[1753–91] 1.4/1.9
1791–1801	1.1		[1755–1801] 0.6	
1801–11	1.1		1.2	
1811–21	1.8		1.5	[1791–1821] 2.1
1821–31	1.6		1.3	1.0
1831–41	1.4		1.0	0.6
1841–51	1.3		1.0	–2.0
1851–61	1.2		0.6	–1.2
1861–71	1.3		1.0	–0.7
1871–81	1.4		1.1	–0.4
1881–91	1.2		0.8	–0.9
1891–1901	1.2		1.1	–0.5
1901–11	1.1		0.7	–0.2
1911–21	0.5		0.3	[1911–26] –0.4
1921–31	0.6		–0.1	
1931–9	0.4		0.4	[1926–36/37] 0.1

Sources: Scotland, Flinn 1977; England/Wales, Lee and Schofield 1981 (1755–1801), Mitchell and Deane 1962 (1811–1939); Ireland, Daultrey, Dickson and O'Grada 1981 (1753–91), Lee 1981 (1821–41), Vaughan and Fitzpatrick 1978 (1851–1936/7).

absolute demographic decline. Between the wars, the loci of population growth shifted firmly towards the 'new' industrial areas of the Midlands and the South East. Significantly, regional variations in rates of population increase during the 1920s and 1930s were less pronounced than in the second half of the nineteenth century, the populations of rural areas in the South West, East Anglia and Wales growing at much the same rate as those of the older industrial regions in the North, North West and Yorkshire/Humberside. Particularly striking is the fact that whereas rates of population growth were generally lower between 1901 and 1951 than they had been between 1851 and 1901 in the rural areas of East Anglia and the South West they were actually higher (Lawton 1978).

Regional differentials in rates of population growth in Ireland contrasted with those on mainland Britain in two significant respects. First, because of the slower development of industry and commerce in Ireland they were a good deal less extreme. As a result, the geographic distribution of the Irish population altered relatively little between the mid-eighteenth and mid-twentieth centuries: extremes of demographic growth and decline to which the country as a whole was subject were not accompanied by equally extreme shifts in the spatial distribution of its inhabitants. Second, unlike the situation on the mainland, until at least the later decades of the nineteenth century rates of population increase were higher in poorer than wealthier areas. Before the Famine population grew more rapidly in the economically backward provinces of the west (Connaught) and south (Munster) than in the more prosperous and diversified economies of the north (Ulster) and east (Leinster). And although during the Famine decade itself it was the poorest parts of the country which suffered the greatest population losses once the Famine was over the traditional pattern re-emerged: between 1851 and 1881 it was the richer east not the poorer west which exhibited the most severe decline in population. Only from the 1880s, when the poorer western and southern regions declined in population more rapidly than those of the east and north, did a more usual relationship between regional economic and demographic trends come to prevail.[3]

MIGRATION

Variations in rates of population growth over time and from place to place are the combined result of changes in rates of natural increase and in the balance between in- and out-migration. Ever since the late eighteenth century migration has had a considerable impact on national trends in population growth. Indeed, the scale of the international movement of people is staggering. Between 1841 and 1931 almost three-quarters of a million Scots emigrated to other parts of the United Kingdom, chiefly to England. During the period 1825–1938 at least another two and a third million went to various destinations in the non-European world. Adding the more modest numbers who left Scotland during the second half of the eighteenth and early nineteenth centuries and who, throughout the period, emigrated to European countries the total gross outward flow from Scotland between the mid-eighteenth and mid-twentieth centuries probably exceeded three and a half million souls. The efflux reached its peak during the years between the middle of the nineteenth century and 1930. In the 1930s it subsided to the more moderate levels akin to those which had prevailed during the hundred years or so before 1850 (Flinn 1977).

The scale of emigration from Ireland was still more startling. Over the period 1780–1844 1.78 million people left the country, 40% for the British mainland, 60% for the United States, Canada, Australia and New Zealand. Between the Famine and the outbreak of the Second World War a massive 7.35 million left Ireland, just over a fifth for mainland Britain and more than three-quarters for North America and Australasia (Verrière 1979). Firmly established by the end of the eighteenth century, the Irish emigrant streams grew rapidly in the decade or so before the Famine before soaring to unprecedented levels during the Famine and the years immediately afterwards. Their volume declined between the mid-1850s and mid-1870s but remained greater than in any other period before or after the Famine decade (1845–54). From the mid-1870s to the outbreak of the First World War, except for a temporary upsurge in the early 1880s, the efflux stabilized at substantial but slightly lower levels. Only during the inter war period, with the exception of another short-lived rise in the second half of the 1920s, did the volume of Irish emigration slump to relatively insignificant proportions.

Although very few emigrants from England settled elsewhere in the British Isles, vast numbers went overseas. Excluding emigrants of Scottish origin and emigrants departing from Irish ports, almost twelve million people of UK nationality left England/Wales for countries outside Europe between 1855 and 1938.[4] The outflow was especially marked during the periods 1880–94, 1905–14 and throughout the 1920s and 1930s.

TABLE 2   Net outmigration as a percentage of natural increase, England/Wales 1841/50–1931/8, Scotland 1861/70–1931/9, Ireland 1871/80–1926/37.

	England/Wales	Scotland		Ireland	
1841–50	–19.1				
1851–60	5.5				
1861–70	1.2	27.7			
1871–80	4.5	19.8		144.8	
1881–90	16.6	41.0		275.9	
1891–1900	1.5	10.4		212.3	
1901–10	22.9	46.8		126.8	
1911–20	38.3	53.6			
1921–30	14.5	110.5		[1911–25]	146.1
1931–8	–29.3	[1931–9]	22.2	[1926–36/37]	92.7
1841–1938	10.2	[1861–1939]	54.5	[1871–1939]	164.7

Sources: Mitchell and Deane 1962; Flinn 1977; Verriere 1979.

To an extent, this huge outflow of people was offset by immigration. The perversities of the data make it impossible to quantify the volume of immigration. Fortunately, for the purpose of assessing the demographic implications of migration, the balance between in- and out-movement (net outmigration) is more significant and, from the middle of the nineteenth century, this can be measured with reasonable precision.

The influence of net outmigration on rates of population growth varied enormously over time and from country to country. In Ireland, as nowhere else in the western world, net outmigration overwhelmed variations in rates of natural increase in determining patterns of population growth. From the mid-nineteenth century onwards only in the closing years of the interwar period did the excess of births over deaths exceed the surplus of emigrants over immigrants and only in that period, therefore, did the population of Ireland grow. Otherwise, ever since the Famine, particularly during the 1880s and 1890s, levels of net outmigration far exceeded rates of natural increase. Between a half and two-thirds of all those born in Ireland during the period from the end of the Napoleonic wars to the mid-1860s had left the country by the time they were fifty years of age: among those born between the mid-1860s and mid-1880s almost a half: in the generations born since the last decade of the nineteenth century about a third (Verrière 1979). 'For both Irishmen and Irishwomen emigration became an expected episode in the life-cycle' (Fitzpatrick 1980, p. 126).

Scotland was a good second to Ireland in the influence of net outmigration on rates of population growth. In every decade between 1861 and 1939 the number of emigrants exceeded that of immigrants. During the 1920s, when the net outflow of people exceeded the level of natural increase, the aggregate population of the country actually declined. In the 1880s and first two decades of the twentieth century almost half of Scotland's natural increase was lost to emigration. At other times the effect of net outmigration on population growth was less severe. Even so, over the period as a whole, net outmigration absorbed the equivalent of more than half of the country's natural excess of births over deaths (Flinn 1977).

In England/Wales the consequences of net outmigration for rates of population increase were less dramatic. Nonetheless, except during the 1840s and the 1930s, in every decade since 1841 emigrants exceeded immigrants, here too the net outflow being especially pronounced during the 1880s and first two decades of the twentieth century. However, only between 1900 and 1920 did net emigration amount to a significant proportion of the natural excess of births over deaths and, even then, the ratio fell well below that for Scotland and Ireland. Throughout the period 1841–1939 net outmigration reduced the growth of population in England/Wales by a mere 10% compared with 54% in Scotland (1861–1939) and 164% in Ireland (1871–1939).

Before the introduction of census and civil registration the effect of net outmigration on national rates of population growth cannot be measured with the same accuracy. As in later years, the demographic impact of net emigration in the century before 1850 was greatest in Ireland and greater in Scotland than in England/Wales. But everywhere in the British Isles net emigration reduced rates of population increase much less before 1850 than afterwards. Even in Ireland net emigration in the period 1780–1845 probably reduced the growth of population by no more than a quarter, a significant figure but well below the level of post-Famine generations. In England, between 1751 and 1841, the loss by net outmigration amounted to less than one in every thousand inhabitants and reduced rates of population increase by a mere 8.5% (Wrigley and Schofield 1981).

Migration also played its part in determining regional differentials in rates of population growth within each of the countries of the United Kingdom. In Ireland the frequency of internal movement (other than of purely seasonal mobility) was relatively modest,[5] and both before and after the Famine regional variations in rates of population growth were most dependent on differentials in natural increase.[6] On mainland Britain, in contrast, regional differences in rates of population growth were due more to the influence of migration than to differing levels of natural increase. In England/Wales, and probably also in Scotland, only in the fifty years or so before 1831 were regional contrasts in demographic growth more the result of varying rates of natural increase than of migrant flows.[7] After 1831, in Scotland from at least as early as 1861, differences between in- and out-migration dominated regional variations in rates of population increase.[8]

Until well into the nineteenth century London and the Metropolitan area was the principal magnet for migrants, though large numbers were already streaming towards the nascent industrial regions of the North West, West Yorkshire, the West Midlands, and the coalfields of the North East and South Wales. These areas remained the chief attractions throughout the second and third quarters of the century. In the several decades before the First World War, however, rural emigrants began to turn their attention away from many of the older industrial centres of the North towards the South East and the Midlands. Generally, over the period 1851–1911 as a whole, the largest migrant flows were those from Central, West and South West England towards Glamorgan and Monmouthshire, from eastern, southern and south-western areas to London and the Home Counties and from a wide scatter of geographic origins towards Durham. By the inter-war years the greatest migrational gains were made by the South East and the Midlands while the greatest losses occurred in areas of depressed, staple industry or, less severely, in rural areas most remote from urban employment opportunities and services. Between 1911 and 1951 the most pronounced migrant streams involved people leaving London for neighbouring counties in the east, south and south-east: South Wales for North Wales, the Home Counties, the Midlands and Eastern England; and the North for counties in the east, south-east and south of the country (Friedlander and Roshier 1966; Lawton 1978). In Scotland, from the eighteenth to the twentieth centuries, migration patterns followed a roughly north to south geography as emigrants from the rural Highlands and Islands poured into the commercial and industrial areas of the eastern and, especially, western Lowlands.[9]

The most striking features of the character of internal migration in pre-industrial times were its frequency and its usually restricted geographic range. In seventeenth and eighteenth century England a majority of people, rural as well as urban-dwellers and women as much as men, changed their place of permanent residence at least once in the course of their lives, though few moved more than ten miles from their place of birth (Clark 1979). Perhaps half of the population of seventeenth century England died in a parish other than their place of birth (Spufford 1970). At Colyton (Devon) between 1765 and 1777 55% of all wives had been born outside the parish, almost two-thirds in parishes less than five miles away, nearly a fifth within a five to ten mile radius and none of the remaining fifth in a parish more than 25 miles distant (Wrigley 1977b). Three per cent of all families living at Cardington (Bedfordshire) in 1782 had entered or left the parish in the space of a single year and more than three-quarters of all male and nearly two-thirds of all female offspring of Cardington families aged thirty and above were living outside the parish when the census was taken (Schofield 1970a). The vast majority of household heads in 25 villages in North East Scotland between 1740 and 1850, mainly employed as tradesmen, fishermen and agricultural labourers, came from less than twenty miles away: where migration covered longer distances it usually involved only the more affluent groups of the community such as merchants and manufacturers (Lockhart 1978). In the parish of Greenlaw (Berwickshire), with a population of only 1,355, an astounding total of 810 moves into the parish and 533 moves out of it were recorded by the session clerk in the short period 1839–42 alone. Neighbouring parishes accounted for 30% of the inward and 36% of the outward moves, and other parishes in the Borders (chiefly in the counties of Roxburgh and Berwick) for 52% and 48% respectively: movement further afield was minimal (Flinn 1977).[10]

Internal migration remained extensive and typically short-distance through the nineteenth and twentieth centuries. In the Welsh village of Bow Street (Cardiganshire) 28% of the 1861 residents had moved in during the previous ten years and another 6% had changed their place of residence within the village. Twenty-one per cent of immigrants came from one or other of the three parishes into which the village itself intruded and 66% from immediately adjoining parishes. Of people who left the village between 1851 and 1861, 20% went to one of the three local parishes, 51% to adjoining parishes and just 29% further afield (Lewis 1966). Seventy per cent of the total population of Preston in 1851 had been born outside the town, four in ten immigrants less than ten miles and seven in ten less than thirty miles away. There was considerable movement within the town, too. In a sample of native-born Prestonians only 14% of males and 19% of females in 1861 were living at the same address as ten years previously (Anderson 1971).[11] The critical questions, of course, are whether there was any noticeable change in the frequency of migration or in the distance normally travelled by migrants during the nineteenth and twentieth centuries.

According to Deane and Cole levels of migration between counties were twice as high in the early decades of the nineteenth century than at the beginning of the eighteenth, an increase they regard as modest in view of the economic and demographic changes which had taken place in the course of the period (Deane and Cole 1967). Given that their data ignore all movement within county boundaries this conclusion is difficult to validate. But, on the whole, it is probably essentially correct. The proportion of people in England/Wales living outside their county of birth rose surprisingly little in the course of the nineteenth and first half of the twentieth centuries (Parish 1972–3). There is little to suggest that the frequency of internal migration has increased *dramatically* in recent times (Friedlander and Roshier 1966), and not until the closing years of the nineteenth century, perhaps not until well into the twentieth, was there any obvious widening in the geographic range of migratory movements (Friedlander and Roshier 1966; Lawton 1978). The life cycle mobility of married women at Colyton (Devon) altered hardly at all between 1765/77 and 1851. In 1851 41% of Colyton wives had been born within the parish (45% in 1765/77), 36% in parishes within a five-mile radius (34%), 11% within five to ten miles (10%) and 12% outside a ten-mile radius (11%). Of the 'foreign-born' wives at Colyton in 1851 62% had been born within five miles of the parish, 18% within five to ten miles and 20% beyond a ten-mile radius; exactly the same percentages for the same groups as in 1765/77 (Wrigley 1977b).

At Charlton-on-Otmoor (Oxfordshire) the proportion of marriages in which one partner came from outside the parish remained remarkably constant throughout the two hundred years between the mid-seventeenth and mid-nineteenth centuries – 38.5% (1651–1700), 32.6% (1701–50), 35.3% (1751–1800), 30.6% (1801–50): so, too, did the average distance travelled by 'foreign' brides and grooms – between six and eight miles. Not until after the middle of the nineteenth century was there a significant increase in the proportion of marriages involving a 'foreign' partner, 47.4% (1851–1900) and 63.2% (1901–50) (Kuchemann 1973). Among the labouring populations of 27 West Dorset parishes average marriage distances remained more or less unchanged between 1837 and 1886: over three-quarters of all marriages were of people from the same parish and in marriages where the bride and groom came from different parishes the distance between the partners was rarely more than two or three miles. By comparison, between the late 1880s and 1927/36 the percentage of unions involving partners from the same parish fell from a half to under a third, while the average distance between partners from different parishes widened.[12] It seems, therefore, that patterns of internal migration altered only moderately and gradually in the course of the nineteenth and twentieth centuries. And most of the changes which did take place in migratory habits appear to have occurred long after the process of industrialization, and the increase in rates of population growth which accompanied it, first began.

A good deal of the movement of people within each of the countries of the United Kingdom during the eighteenth and nineteenth centuries was temporary or seasonal rather than permanent in character, though in practice it is often difficult to distinguish one from the other. The extent of seasonal mobility cannot be measured very precisely but it was certainly widespread. In mainland Britain the stream of seasonal migrants temporarily deserting their homes in search of employment elsewhere grew rapidly between 1750 and 1850 but fell away thereafter until by 1914 it was little more than a trickle (Collins 1976; Devine 1979). In the case of Ireland, where it was greatest, most seasonal movement of labour occurred between Ireland and the British mainland rather than within Ireland itself. Temporary labour migrations from Ireland to harvest and building work in Britain, already common by the late eighteenth century, increased dramatically following the introduction of steamers in the 1820s and, except for a brief downturn during the years of the Famine, rose to a peak in the late 1860s and 1870s. They then began a long, gradual decline. At their height the numbers involved were enormous: 35,000–40,000 a year in the 1830s, at least 60,000 in the early 1840s, over 100,000 in the 1860s and 1870s. According to Hanley, whose figures may understate the actual level by up to 40%, the numbers then slumped, to 38,000 by 1880, 23,000 by 1890, 32,000 by 1900 and 13,000 by 1915.[13]

NATURAL INCREASE

Secular trends in rates of natural increase followed much the same pattern in England/Wales and Scotland – rising from the late eighteenth century to a peak in the first several decades of the nineteenth, declining in the 1830s and 1840s before recovering around the middle of the century and remaining roughly constant down to the outbreak of the First World War, and collapsing in the inter-war period to very low levels indeed during the 1930s. Judging from the levels of population growth and emigration, rates of natural increase in Ireland must have been abnormally high during the late eighteenth and early nineteenth centuries but probably fell sharply in the several decades before the Famine, a conclusion supported by the very marked surplus of baptisms over burials in the registers of the parish of Blaris (Lisburn) in the years around the beginning of the century and the notable decline in this surplus during the 1820s and 1830s (Morgan 1976). From the 1870s, possibly from as early as the third decade of the nineteenth century, to 1911 rates of natural increase in Ireland were distinctly lower than in

England/Wales and Scotland. In contrast to what happened on the mainland, however, they did not decline during the inter-war period, with the result that by the 1920s and 1930s the excess of births over deaths was very similar in all countries of the British Isles.

TABLE 3   Rates of natural increase as a percentage of total population at the beginning of each sub-period, England 1751/60–1831/41, England/Wales 1841/50–1931/9, Scotland 1841/50–1931/9, Ireland 1871/80–1926/37.

	England (excluding Monmouth)	England/ Wales	Scotland	Ireland
1751–60	7.5			
1761–70	6.1			
1771–80	9.9			
1781–91	10.4			
1791–1800	12.5			
1801–11	14.8			
1811–21	17.2			
1821–31	16.8			
1831–41	14.1			
1841–50		10.8	10.6	
1851–60		12.6	12.4	
1861–70		13.5	13.6	
1871–80		15.0	14.0	8.0
1881–90		14.0	13.6	5.2
1891–1900		12.4	12.4	4.7
1901–10		14.0	12.1	5.7
1911–20		8.1	9.1	
1921–30		6.3	7.2	[1911–25] 8.0
1931–9		2.4	4.4	[1926–36/7] 6.4

Sources: England, Wrigley and Schofield 1981; England/Wales, Mitchell and Deane 1962; Scotland, Flinn 1977; Ireland, Vaughan and Fitzpatrick 1978.

MORTALITY

Variations in rates of natural increase are determined by changes in the relative numbers of births and deaths. Until the introduction of civil registration these are difficult to estimate with any certainty. Only for England, thanks to the work of Wrigley and Schofield, do we have a reasonable understanding of the secular behaviour of fertility and mortality rates during the eighteenth and early nineteenth centuries. For Scotland and even more so for Ireland, because of the particular deficiencies of their parish register material, no such data are as yet available.

In those areas of England where industrial and urban growth led to a deterioration in environmental conditions mortality increased in the course of the late eighteenth and early nineteenth centuries. At Shepshed (Leicestershire), where the environmental deterioration produced by the development of a domestic framework knitting industry was aggravated by serious economic depression after 1825, infant and child death rates rose sharply: children born between 1825 and 1849 had a life expectancy seven years lower than those born during the period 1750–1824 and twelve years lower than those born in the seventeenth and early eighteenth centuries (Levine 1976b). At Carlisle crude death rates rose from 25 per thousand population in the 1780s to 27 per thousand in the 1840s and would have climbed still higher but for shifts in the age-structure of the resident population which helped to keep mortality down: death rates in the age-groups 0–4 and 15 and above rose by a fifth and a quarter respectively, most of the rise occurring after 1813 (Armstrong 1981a). Over the country as a whole, the growth of urban living with its attendant environmental squalors almost certainly worked to keep death rates higher than they would otherwise have been (Loschky 1972). Despite this, national average levels of mortality in England declined between the middle of the eighteenth and middle of the nineteenth centuries. English crude death rates fell from 25–26 per thousand in the 1750s to 22 per thousand a century later, most of the decline taking place in the decades following the Napoleonic Wars.

Mean life expectancy at birth, which had hovered around 36–37 years in the 1750s, remained at about 36 at the turn into the nineteenth century but had reached 40 by the 1850s (Wrigley and Schofield 1981). Evidence from other studies confirms the improvement which had occurred. Among women of the British aristocracy life expectancy rose from 36–37 years in the first half of the eighteenth century to 45 years between 1750 and 1774, 49 by the last quarter of the century and over 51 by the period 1800–24 (Hollingsworth 1964). Infant mortality rates among the aristocracy fell from 200 per thousand live births in the sixteenth and seventeenth centuries to 80 per thousand after 1775 (Wrigley 1968). The life expectancy at birth among males in the county families of Hampshire and Northamptonshire rose from 37 (for those born between 1681 and 1730) to 48 (1731–80) and 50 (1781–1830), mainly due to a saving of lives among infants, children and young adults (Razzell 1965). Infant death rates among Quakers in the rural South of England fell from 135 (males) and 114 (females) per thousand live births during the period 1700–49 to 125 and 117 respectively between 1750 and 1799 and 93 and 83 during the period 1800–50. Mortality in the age-group 1–4, per thousand children alive at the age of one, declined from 106 (males) and 89 (females) to 76 and 80 and 51 and 48 in the successive half-centuries (Eversley 1981). In rural North Shropshire death rates in infancy (0–1), which had fluctuated around 200 per thousand between the mid-sixteenth and mid-eighteenth centuries, were as low as 130 per thousand by the end of the eighteenth century and 110 per thousand by the early 1840s (Jones 1976, 1980). In the Fenland parishes of Leake and Wrangle (Lincolnshire) infant mortality rates improved noticeably from the closing years of the eighteenth century (West 1974). At Methley (West Riding), though child death rates (1–14) were higher in the second half of the eighteenth century than the first, those in infancy and adulthood were decidedly lower (Yasumoto 1981).[14]

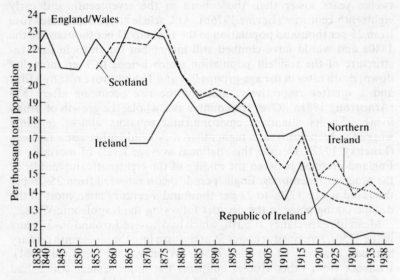

FIGURE 2   Deaths per thousand population: England/Wales 1838–1938; Scotland 1855–1938; Ireland 1865–1920; Northern Ireland and Republic of Ireland 1925–38. *Sources*: England/Wales and Scotland, Mitchell and Deane 1962; Ireland, Vaughan and Fitzpatrick 1978.

In Scotland, too, mortality appears to have fallen during the second half of the eighteenth and early nineteenth centuries – if the figures can be trusted – even more rapidly than in England. Tentatively, it has been suggested that Scottish crude death rates fell from 37–38 per thousand population, infant mortality from 236–238 to 163–164 per thousand live births while life expectancy at birth rose from 26–27 years to over 39 between the 1750s and the 1790s. In the Scottish case, however, the secular decline in death rates was interrupted by a temporary resurgence of mortality in the second quarter of the nineteenth century, a resurgence that was especially pronounced among urban populations (Flinn 1977).

TABLE 4   Infant mortality. Deaths 0–1 per thousand live births,
England/Wales 1840–1938, Scotland 1855–1938, Ireland 1865–1938.

	England/Wales	Scotland	Ireland	
1840	154			
1845	142			
1850	162			
1855	153	125		
1860	148	127		
1865	160	125	98	
1870	160	123	95	
1875	158	132	95	
1880	153	125	112	
1885	138	121	95	
1890	151	131	95	
1895	161	133	104	
1900	154	128	109	
1905	128	116	95	
1910	105	108	95	
1915	110	126	92	
1920	80	92	83	
			Northern Ireland	*Republic*
1925	75	91	86	68
1930	60	83	68	68
1935	57	77	86	68
1938	53	70	75	67

Sources: Mitchell and Deane, 1962; Mitchell, B. R. (1975) *European
historical statistics, 1750–1970*, London.

The absence of direct statistical data has given rise to widely divergent
opinions on the behaviour of Irish mortality rates during the eighteenth
and first half of the nineteenth centuries. Connell's belief that death
rates failed to decline was based solely on pessimistic and largely
uncorroborated assumptions about the growing severity of fever
epidemics, the lack of improvement in standards of sanitation, housing
and diet and the uselessness of such medical innovations as voluntary
hospitals, dispensaries and inoculation or vaccination against smallpox
(Connell 1950a). Drake and Razzell on the other hand, principally on
the grounds that the statistics on deaths collected by the census
enumerators of 1841 indicate lower levels of infant and child mortality
in Ireland than England/Wales during the late 1830s, have argued
equally forcefully that Irish death rates *did* decline in the course of the
late eighteenth and early nineteenth centuries (Drake 1963–4; Razzell
1967). As Tucker points out, however, it is likely that the census data
seriously understate the number of deaths which occurred in the 1830s

(Tucker 1970) – in the case of infant deaths perhaps by sufficient to raise mortality to levels 45% *higher* than those in England/Wales (Verrière 1979).

There are few detailed, local studies available upon which to test the strength of those competing claims. Those which have been carried out favour the view that in Ireland, too, death rates fell between the mid-eighteenth and early nineteenth centuries. Burial totals in the registers of Magherafelt (County Derry), St Patrick's (Coleraine) and Blaris (Lisburn) imply considerably higher mortality rates in the first half of the eighteenth century than the second and a further pronounced reduction in child mortality around the turn into the nineteenth century (Morgan 1973, 1974, 1976). Infant and child death rates among Irish Quakers fell more or less continuously throughout the period 1725–1850 and by the nineteenth century were generally lower than among Quaker families in the rural south of England.[15] Admittedly, this evidence is too scanty to be taken as complete confirmation of a general decline in Irish mortality in the century before the calamitous upsurge in death rates during and immediately following the Great Famine of 1845–51. But at least it reminds us to keep open the *possibility* that falling mortality was a demographic characteristic common to all constituent countries of the United Kingdom between the mid-eighteenth and first quarter of the nineteenth centuries.

With the introduction of civil registration we are on firmer ground. Following a period of relative stability in levels of mortality during the third quarter of the nineteenth century, from the mid-1870s onwards crude death rates in both England/Wales and Scotland declined almost continuously. In Ireland the decline was longer delayed, not beginning until the early years of the twentieth century, and more gradual when it came.[16] In the twentieth century Irish death rates were consistently higher than those in Scotland and England/Wales, where they were lowest of all.[17]

In Scotland the secular decline in death rates had begun in all age-groups up to the ages 35–44 (except infancy, 0–1) by the 1870s. In England/Wales child mortality (1–14) and mortality in the age-groups 15–24 also began to decline from the 1870s and in the ages 25–44 from the 1880s, for females, and 1890s, for males. Both in Scotland and England/Wales rates of mortality in infancy and at all ages above 45 did not begin their long-term decline until the start of the twentieth century (McKeown, Record and Turner 1975; Mitchison 1977). In Ireland, except for males aged 5–24 whose mortality fell from the 1870s or 1880s, the secular decline in age-specific death rates was delayed until the twentieth century and then proceeded relatively slowly: the twentieth-century drop in rates of infant mortality, for example, was much less noticeable in Ireland than on the British mainland. This had a significant effect on the comparative levels of Irish and British mortality. During the early 1870s, possibly in many earlier periods too,

Irish death rates by sex and age-group were consistently lower than in England/Wales and Scotland. Thereafter, the differential was less consistent and steadily less favourable to the Irish. By the beginning of the second decade of the twentieth century, although mortality among Irish males aged 0–9 and 45 and over remained lower than among their counterparts in England/Wales and Scotland, it was now higher for those aged between ten and 44: among Irish females aged 0–4 and 65–84 death rates were still lower than on the British mainland but were generally higher among those aged between five and 64 and above 85. What had happened is best illustrated by a comparison of infant death rates. During the late nineteenth and early twentieth centuries Irish infant mortality rates were lower than in Scotland and much lower than in England/Wales. From the first decade of the twentieth century, however, the gap closed rapidly. By 1938 levels of infant mortality were much the same in Ireland as in Scotland and higher than in England/Wales. As a result, the rise in life expectancy which occurred everywhere between the mid-nineteenth and mid-twentieth centuries was greater in England/Wales than in Scotland and least pronounced in Ireland (Glass 1963–4; Aalen 1963–4; Kennedy 1973).

MARRIAGE AND CELIBACY

In societies which lack an effective means of regulating levels of fertility within marriage variations in the timing and extent of marriage are the only way of restraining fertility to a level compatible with the maintenance of a balance between numbers of people and basic resources. *Potentially,* variations in nuptiality were a critical determinant of trends in rates of fertility and population growth in pre- and early industrial times. *In practice,* however, historians have always disagreed about the strength of their influence. To some, their impact was extremely limited (Drake 1963–4; Crafts and Ireland 1976b). To others, fluctuations in ages at marriage and proportions marrying were the principal determinants of demographic trends throughout the eighteenth and much of the nineteenth centuries (Connell 1950; Wrigley and Schofield 1981, 1983; Wrigley 1983).

During the period between the mid-eighteenth and mid-nineteenth centuries so few data exist on marital ages in Scotland that it is impossible even to guess at their trend.[18] Controversy over the behaviour of marital ages in Ireland in the century before the Famine has raged unabated since Connell first suggested that falling age at marriage, and thus rising fertility, were chiefly responsible for the acceleration in rates of population growth during the late eighteenth and early nineteenth centuries, and rising ages at marriage, and thus falling fertility, for their deceleration in the several decades immediately preceding the Famine (Connell 1950a).

Unfortunately, Connell's thesis rests on shaky foundations. In the absence of direct statistical data on marital ages for the period before 1830 it relied heavily on material compiled for the 1830s which supposedly demonstrated that ages at marriage were lower in Ireland than in England and that they rose in the course of the decade. The evidence to substantiate the first of these claims, however, rested solely on oral statements made to the Poor Inquiry Commission of 1836 about the usual age at marriage among the labouring populations, a section of the community known to have married earlier than other socio-occupational classes and from which, in any case, Connell tended to select data only from those parts of the country where marital ages were stated to be unusually low. The evidence for the second, based on retrospective statements of age at marriage collected by the 1841 census enumerators, may be no more than an artefact of the way the data were compiled or a natural consequence of changes which occurred in the age-structure of the Irish population during the 1830s (Drake 1963–4).

Yet, serious though these criticisms are, they do not necessarily invalidate Connell's conclusions (Lee 1968). Recent work on Londonderry and the parish registers of St Patrick's (Coleraine) suggests that age at marriage in late eighteenth and early nineteenth century Ireland may well have been slightly lower than elsewhere in Western Europe and tending to rise in the decades leading up to the Famine.[19] Obviously, additional work of a similar kind is required to test more thoroughly the truth of Connell's thesis. In the meantime, the possible contribution of falling ages at marriage to Irish population growth around the turn into the nineteenth century should not be overlooked.

For England there is now abundant evidence of a substantial decline in the mean age at marriage between the late seventeenth and early nineteenth centuries, a decline that was especially pronounced after 1750 and sufficient to account for over half the increase in gross reproduction rates which occurred during the period (Wrigley and Schofield 1981). Ages at first marriage among men and women in thirteen widely scattered reconstituted parish populations fell by between one and two years in the course of the second half of the eighteenth century and continued to fall during the early decades of the nineteenth (Wrigley and Schofield 1983). At Powick (Worcestershire) average ages at marriage fell from 31.8 to 22.4 years for bachelors and from 30.5 to 24.3 years for spinsters between 1663/1700 and 1751/75 (Johnson 1970): at Colyton (Devon) from 27.7 in 1720 to 25 by the mid-1830s for bachelors and from 29.6 in 1720 to 26 by the end of the century and 23 by the 1820s and 1830s for spinsters (Wrigley 1966b). In the town of Stratford-upon-Avon the mean age of brides at first marriage declined from 27.4 years (1745–54) to 26.8 (1790–4) and 23.8 (1795–9): at Napton-on-the-Hill from 27.3 (1715–49) to 26.3 (1750–79), 25.9 (1780–1800) and 23.5 (1820–9): and at Bidford-on-Avon from 27.7 (1750–69) to 24.5 (1780–99) (Martin 1977). To date, no reconstitution data have shown a contrary trend, though it would certainly be surprising if ages at marriage declined everywhere.[20] For England, and possibly for Ireland, falling ages at marriage obviously played a substantial part in the rise in rates of fertility which appears to have occurred in the late eighteenth and early nineteenth centuries.

Between the mid-nineteenth and mid-twentieth centuries crude marriage rates were always higher in England and Wales than in Scotland and consistently lowest in Ireland.[21] Generally, if the data for England and Wales are representative, they were higher during the third quarters of the eighteenth and nineteenth centuries than at other periods of comparable duration between the mid-eighteenth and mid-twentieth centuries, and everywhere marriage rates tended to rise during the inter-

FIGURE 3   Marriages, per thousand population: England 1750–1870; England/Wales 1840–1938; Scotland 1860–1938; Ireland 1870–1935. *Sources*: England, Wrigley and Schofield 1981; England/Wales, Mitchell and Deane 1962; Ireland, Vaughan and Fitzpatrick 1978.

TABLE 5 Mean age at first marriage, England 1700/49–1911, Scotland 1861–1931, Ireland 1861–1937, England/Wales 1900/2–1936/40.

	Male				Female			
	England	Scotland	Ireland	England/Wales	England	Scotland	Ireland	England/Wales
1700–49	27.5				26.2			
1750–99	26.4				24.9			
1800–49	25.3				23.4			
1851	26.9				25.8			
1861	26.4	26.9	30.1		25.4	25.1	26.7	
1871	26.4	26.8	30.2		25.1	25.0	26.4	
1881	26.6	26.8	30.9		25.3	24.9	27.3	
1891	27.1	27.3	31.6		26.0	25.3	28.2	
1901	27.3	27.5	31.9	[1900–2] 27.3	26.3	25.6	28.7	[1900–2] 26.0
1911	27.7	28.0	32.5	[1910–12] 27.7	26.3	26.0	28.8	[1910–12] 26.3
1921		28.2	32.0				26.0	
1926							28.2	
1931		28.1		[1930–2] 27.6				[1930–2] 25.6
1936			31.6	[1938] 27.0			28.3	[1938] 24.6
1937			28.9	[1936–40] 27.3			26.4	[1936–40] 24.8

Sources: England, 1700/49–1800/49 for twelve reconstituted parishes only, Wrigley and Schofield 1981; Scotland, Flinn 1977; Ireland, 1926 and 1936 for the Republic only, 1937 for Northern Ireland only, Dixon 1978; England/Wales, Hajnal 1947; Coleman 1980.

war years. Otherwise, they followed no obvious secular trend.

Since the beginning of civil registration, in all countries of the British Isles, secular variations in mean ages at marriage among both men and women have been very moderate. Everywhere, for both sexes, the singulate mean marital age rose slightly in the course of the late nineteenth and early twentieth centuries and declined during the inter-war period, the start of a prolonged fall in ages at marriage (Hajnal 1953; Coleman 1980). Overall, however, the extent of these variations was too modest to have had a significant impact on levels of fertility, even in the late nineteenth century when rising ages at marriage coincided with the onset of a secular decline in rates of marital fertility. Fertility continued to fall throughout the inter-war years despite the tendency for age at marriage to decrease. From the middle of the nineteenth century to the outbreak of the Second World War ages at first marriage, particularly for men, have always been higher in Ireland than in either England/Wales or Scotland.

Temporal variations in the proportion of the English population remaining unmarried reinforced the effects of secular changes in age at marriage on trends in levels of fertility. Lifetime celibacy rates were highest when ages at marriage were relatively high and lowest when the latter were relatively low (Wrigley and Schofield 1981). The percentage of women who lived through the child-bearing ages without ever marrying halved in the course of the eighteenth century (Wrigley 1983). Together, in the absence of any obvious increase in the frequency of childbearing within marriage (see below), falling ages at marriage and declining levels of lifetime celibacy were wholly responsible for the rise in rates of English fertility which characterized the late eighteenth and early nineteenth centuries (Wrigley 1983; Wrigley and Schofield 1983).[22] The tendency for celibacy rates to increase in the twentieth century – among both men and women in Ireland and Scotland and women in England/Wales – certainly contributed to the decline in birth rates which took place during the period.[23] Indeed in Ireland, where ages at marriage remained relatively constant, variations in the extent of lifetime celibacy were the dominant influence on levels of nuptiality (Dixon 1978).

In Scotland and, to a lesser extent, England/Wales levels of celibacy since the middle of the nineteenth century have been higher among females than males. In Ireland by contrast, at least from the closing decades of the century, permanent celibacy has been noticeably greater among men, a feature closely related to the unusual character of the population's sex structure (see below, p. 180). In Ireland too, lifetime celibacy rates, except when compared with those of Scottish women in the second half of the nineteenth century, were consistently higher than elsewhere, especially among men. Ever since the middle of the nineteenth century English men and women have been less likely to remain unmarried than those of Scotland or Ireland.

TABLE 6 Lifetime celibacy, England 1751–1861, England/Wales 1851–1931, Scotland 1861–1931, Ireland 1841–1936.

	England Both sexes	England/Wales Male	England/Wales Female	Scotland Male	Scotland Female	Ireland Male	Ireland Female
1751	107						
1761	73						
1771	77						
1781	36						
1791	49						
1801	68						
1811	65						
1821	71						
1831	75						
1841	96						100
1851	110	115	122				120
1861	107	105	119	135	201	140	140
1871		97	121	132	200	160	150
1881		96	119	127	194	160	160
1891		100	124	134	187	200	170
1901		110	136	146	192	240	200
1911		121	158	160	208	290	240
1921		120	164	168	207	[1926] 310	
1931		108	164	162	215	[1936] 340	250

Sources: England, celibates per thousand people aged 40–44 (Wrigley and Schofield 1981); England/Wales and Scotland, celibates per thousand males and females aged 45–54 (Mitchell and Deane 1961); Ireland, celibates per thousand males and females aged 45–54 (Kennedy 1973).

ILLEGITIMATE AND LEGITIMATE FERTILITY

Comparisons of variations in the frequency of illegitimacy and bridal pregnancy from country to country or from area to area and time to time within the same country are not as easy to undertake as is sometimes supposed.[24] To begin with, one of the most common measures of the extent of bastardy, the illegitimacy ratio,[25] is flawed by its failure to take account of differences in the ratio of females to males in the fertile age-groups, in the sex and marital structures of communities or in the effect of changes in rates of *legitimate* fertility on the total number of births. Second, recorded levels of illegitimacy and bridal pregnancy are greatly affected by the reliability of registration procedures. Particularly during the period when the church was responsible for registering vital events the quality of registration varied considerably from area to area and time to time – a fact which existing studies of bastardy and bridal pregnancy all too often ignore. Third, regional comparisons of levels of illegitimacy and premarital pregnancy can be seriously distorted by the tendency for unmarried, pregnant women to leave their homes for areas where their condition was less shameful or less of a hindrance to marriage and employment. On balance, however, these considerations are unlikely to negate the general conclusions suggested by the available data and summarized below.

So far as one can tell, levels of illegitimacy and bridal pregnancy always appear to have been markedly lower in Ireland than in England/Wales and highest in Scotland. In spite of the trend towards celibacy, rates of premarital conception and illegitimacy in Ireland altered little throughout the period from the mid-eighteenth to mid-twentieth centuries (Connell 1968b). Just 2.5% of all births in nine predominantly Catholic parishes between 1755 and 1865 were born outside wedlock, with no sign of the rise in levels of bastardy which occurred in England from the later decades of the eighteenth century. In 1864, the first year of civil registration, the illegitimacy ratio for Ireland as a whole was a mere 3.8%. It fell to a low of 2.3% by the mid-1870s and remained under 3% throughout the rest of the nineteenth century. From 1922 to 1974 the proportion of illegitimate to total births in the Republic of Ireland fluctuated between 1.6% and 4%, well below the levels prevailing on the British mainland (Connolly 1979). Parishes like St Patrick's (Coleraine) – a seaport with a high percentage of transient and pregnant girls escaping the censure of their native community and attracted by the tolerance of the local rector, where illegitimacy rates were somewhat higher (Morgan 1973) – were probably exceptional. Compared with England, rates of bridal pregnancy in Ireland were also low. In six late eighteenth and early nineteenth century parishes, though there were considerable variations from parish to parish (correlating positively with inter-parochial differentials in levels of illegitimacy), the

55

proportion of brides conceiving their first child before marriage averaged only 9–10%, and in only three of the six parishes did rates of bridal pregnancy increase in the course of the period (Connolly 1979).

Too little work has been done for any meaningful conclusions to be drawn about levels and trends in Scottish bastardy and bridal pregnancy before the introduction of civil registration in 1855.[26] From the middle of the nineteenth century, however, rates of illegitimacy in Scotland always exceeded those in England. This, together with the fact that rates of illegitimacy were greater in rural than urban areas and, within rural populations, greatest in the North-East and Border counties, was a feature which observers then as now found extremely puzzling.[27] Scottish illegitimacy did share one trait with that of England, however. In both countries, mirroring trends in marital fertility, levels of bastardy declined steadily from the 1870s onwards (Flinn 1977; Mitchison 1977).

TABLE 7   Illegitimacy in Scotland, 1861–1931.

	Illegitimacy ratio	*Illegitimacy rate*
1861	9.4	21.6
1871	9.4	23.0
1881	8.4	20.2
1891	7.6	16.1
1901	6.3	12.6
1911	7.4	13.0
1921	7.2	12.4
1931	7.3	9.7

Source: Flinn 1977. The illegitimacy ratio is the number of illegitimate births per hundred total live births: the illegitimacy rate, the number of illegitimate births per thousand unmarried and widowed women aged 15–49.

High rates of illegitimacy in Scotland were coupled with high levels of bridal pregnancy. According to Dr Strachan, in a third of all marriages celebrated in thirteen widely scattered rural parishes during the period 1855–69 the first child was born within six months of the wedding. Bridal pregnancy like illegitimacy, Strachan maintained, was more prevalent in rural than urban areas and in the Lowlands than the Highlands (Flinn 1977). At Portpatrick, in the south western Lowlands, almost a third of all women marrying between 1855 and 1891 were pregnant at the time of their marriage (Tranter 1978).

In the case of England there is no doubt that an increase in rates of illegitimacy and bridal pregnancy occurred between the middle of the eighteenth and middle of the nineteenth centuries. Thomas Batchelor's observation that rising illegitimacy was 'an acknowledged characteristic of the times' has been amply supported by recent research.[28] Allowing for considerable regional variations – bastardy was highest in the West and North West and lower, in descending order, in the South, North East and the Midlands, while premarital conceptions were most common in the more northerly counties – rates of bastardy and bridal pregnancy rose almost everywhere in England during the late eighteenth and early nineteenth centuries. From less than 2% between the early seventeenth and early eighteenth centuries, illegitimacy ratios began to climb after 1730 to reach 6% and over during the first half of the nineteenth century before falling to between 4% and 5% during the later decades of the nineteenth and first half of the twentieth centuries (Laslett and Oosterveen 1973). Whereas before 1700 around one-fifth of all brides were pregnant on marriage, after 1700 the proportion rose to two-fifths (Hair 1966, 1970).[29]

On the whole, long-term trends in illegitimacy, bridal pregnancy and legitimate marital fertility moved roughly in unison. When rates of marital fertility were high and rising, in the later eighteenth and early nineteenth centuries, rates of illegitimacy and premarital pregnancy were also relatively high and increasing; when marital fertility began its prolonged, secular decline in the late nineteenth century so, too, did levels of non-marital fertility. Age at marriage, on the other hand, varied *inversely* with levels of illegitimacy and premarital conception, a fact which rules out the possibility that periods of peak premarital sexual activity were the result of sexual frustrations caused by delayed marriage.

The paucity of direct statistical data on levels of Irish marital fertility in the period before the Famine makes it difficult to test the claim that rising fertility was the demographic mechanism principally responsible for the rapid growth of Ireland's population during the late eighteenth and early nineteenth centuries (Connell 1950a). Age-specific marital

TABLE 8 Legitimate births per thousand married women aged 15–44, England/Wales 1870/2–1935/7, Ireland 1836/40–1935/7.

	Ireland	England/Wales
1836–40	313	
1866–70	341	
1870–72	307	295
1880–82	284	275
1890–92	287	250
1900–2	292	230
1906–10	307	
1910–12	305	191
1925–27	271	140
1931–36	259	
1935–37	256	111

Sources: Kennedy 1973; Verrière 1979.

fertility rates among Irish Quakers were consistently higher than among Quaker families in the rural south of England and rose steadily in the course of the eighteenth century to a peak between 1775 and 1825, from which point they began to decline (Eversley 1981). Conceivably a similar trend prevailed among the Irish population at large. Irish fertility ratios in the 1830s certainly appear to have been higher than those in England/Wales though, because it is based on possibly untenable assumptions about relative levels of infant and child mortality, this conclusion must be treated with caution (Tucker 1970). Since the Famine marital fertility rates in Ireland have always been well above those in England/Wales and Scotland, the differential actually widening from the late nineteenth century onwards. Whereas in Ireland the fertility of married women declined by just 16% between 1870/2 and 1935/7 in England/Wales it fell by 62%. And whereas in England/Wales and Scotland marital fertility rates began to decline from the 1870s and 1880s in Ireland they did not begin to do so much before the inter-war period. By the mid-twentieth century levels of Irish marital fertility were among the highest in the western world. To the modest extent that Ireland shared in the general decline of crude birth rates which began in the last quarter of the nineteenth century it was the result of decreasing nuptiality, not, as in England/Wales and Scotland, of a sharp fall in the frequency of childbirth within marriage. Despite high rates of marital fertility, extreme levels of lifetime celibacy since the middle of the nineteenth century have resulted in a crude birth rate lower in Ireland than almost anywhere else in Europe.

For Scotland, too, there is little direct statistical evidence on the behaviour of fertility rates before 1861. Mitchison's suggestion that there is 'some evidence for an increase in family size and possibly of marital fertility during the eighteenth century' (Flinn 1977, p. 289) is, therefore, surely premature. Scottish fertility rates began a long-term decline in the 1870s and 1880s, the pace of the decline accelerating in the course of the twentieth century. Though marginally greater in urban than rural areas, the fall in fertility occurred at much the same pace in all parts of the country. Overall levels of fertility in Scotland have fallen more gradually than in England/Wales since the late nineteenth century, particularly in the younger adult age-groups (Flinn 1977).[30]

Recent research has fully endorsed the validity of Professor Krause's long-standing contention that English fertility rates rose in the course of the second half of the eighteenth and early nineteenth centuries (Krause 1958–9). Gross reproduction rates, after following a gently rising trend in the seventy years before 1756, increased sharply in the late eighteenth century, to a peak in the quinquennium around 1816, declined between 1816 and 1846 and then rose moderately down to the mid-1860s (Wrigley and Schofield 1981; Wrigley 1983).[31] Practically the whole of this increase in fertility is explained by declining ages at marriage and levels of celibacy. To judge from an admittedly small sample of

TABLE 9 Births per thousand population, England 1751–1871, England/Wales 1841/5–1938, Scotland 1861–1931, Ireland 1836/40–1931/5.

England		England/Wales		Scotland		Ireland		
							(i)	*(ii)*
1751	34.2							
1761	34.8							
1771	35.2							
1781	35.5							
1791	38.4							
1801	33.9							
1811	40.0							
1821	40.9							
1831	35.2					1836–40	37.2	33.0
		1841–45	35.2					
1841	36.0	1846–50	34.8			1846–50	35.2	
		1851–55	35.5					
1851	36.4	1856–60	35.5			1856–60	31.0	
		1861–65	35.8					
1861	35.9	1866–70	35.7	1861	34.8	1866–70	31.0	25.8
		1871–75	35.7					
1871	35.7	1876–80	35.4	1871	34.7	1876–80	27.7	25.7
		1881–90	32.4	1881	33.6	1886–90	24.2	22.4
		1891–1900	29.9	1891	30.8	1896–1900	23.4	22.6
				1901	29.5			
		1901–11	27.0	1911	25.8	1906–10	23.5	23.1
		1921	22.4	1921	21.5	1921–25	22.2	21.1
		1931	15.8	1931	19.1	1931–35	20.1	19.6
		1938	15.1					

Sources: England, Wrigley and Schofield 1981; England/Wales, Teitelbaum 1974 (1841/5–1876/80), Glass, 1951 (1881/90–1901/11), Mitchell and Deane 1962 (1921–38); Scotland, Flinn, 1977; Ireland, Verrière 1979 – column (i) based on the number of children recorded in decennial censuses allowing for mortality and emigration: column (ii) based on census (1836–40) and civil register data of the number of live births.

reconstitution studies, the regularity of child-bearing within marriage (marital fertility) remained more or less unchanged between the seventeenth and early nineteenth centuries (Wrigley and Schofield 1981). Combined age-specific marital fertility rates in thirteen reconstituted parish populations were actually lower among couples conceiving their children during the period 1750–99 than in any of the three preceding half-century periods (Wrigley and Schofield 1983). At Shepshed (Leicestershire) gross reproduction rates climbed from 3.94 in the first half of the eighteenth century to 5.53 between 1750 and 1824 and 5.68 in the period 1825–51. Yet, here too, levels of marital fertility in the

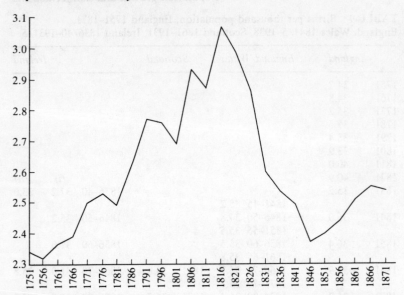

FIGURE 4   Gross reproduction rates, England 1751–1871. *Source*: Wrigley and Schofield 1981.

age-groups where most children were conceived (25–34) were no higher between 1750 and 1850 than they had been in the seventeenth or first half of the eighteenth centuries (Levine 1976b).[32] If, as seems likely, rising fertility rather than falling mortality must be accorded the 'lion's share' of the responsibility for the acceleration in rates of English population growth after 1750 the rise in fertility itself was principally due to the trend 'towards earlier and more universal marriage' (Wrigley and Schofield 1983, p. 132).

Beginning in the quinquennium around 1876, English fertility rates entered a long period of continuous decline partly, in the last quarter of the nineteenth century, due to a rise in age at marriage and a reduction in the proportion of females in the reproductive age groups (stemming from changes in the age structure of the female population) but chiefly, and after 1901 entirely, to declining levels of fertility within marriage. Mean completed family size fell from 6.2 for marriages celebrated in the 1860s to 5.3 among those of 1881, 4.1 for those of the 1890s, 3.3 during the first decade of the twentieth century, 2.8 in 1911, 2.4 in 1921, 2.1 in 1931 and 2.0 in 1941 (Simons 1978).[33] The extent of this decline differed remarkably little from area to area so much so that regional differentials in marital fertility rates at the close of the inter-war period were practically identical to those of 1876 (Simons 1978; Brass and Kabir 1978).

Of course, among some socio-occupational groups – the peerage for example (Hollingsworth 1964) – the onset of the secular decline in fertility pre-dated the mid-1870s. Even before 1876 there were considerable socio-occupational differentials in fertility levels. The average size of completed families in a group of eighteenth century Lancashire parishes, for instance, was noticeably larger among gentry, farmer, craft and trading classes than among labourers (Loschky and Krier 1969). Between 1840 and 1864 retailers' wives at Ashford (Kent) had fewer children in their first five years of marriage than labourers' wives and whereas the fertility of the latter rose in the course of the period that of the former fell (Pearce 1973).

From the mid-1870s to the outbreak of the First World War the pace of fertility decline, in the main, correlated positively with socio-occupational class, fertility falling most rapidly among employers, professional groups and skilled workers, less quickly among unskilled manual workers and least of all among the wives of agricultural labourers and coalminers (Haines 1977). During the inter-war period, by contrast, fertility fell most rapidly in those social groups which at the beginning of the period had the highest fertility rates and the pace of fertility decline displayed a broadly negative association with socio-occupational class (Innes 1938; Matras 1965). Nevertheless, despite the narrowing of social class fertility differentials during the 1920s and 1930s, significant socio-occupational differences continued to prevail at the end of the inter-war period: fertility was lowest in social classes I (professional and administrative personnel), II (employers) and III (clerks) and highest in classes V (unskilled industrial workers), VII (miners) and VIII (agricultural labourers), with the fertility of textile workers, shop assistants and personal service employees (VI, XI and XII) and of semi-skilled manual workers, farmers and 'other ranks' in the police and armed forces (IV, IX and XIII) lying between the two extremes (Hopkin and Hajnal 1947).

NOTES AND REFERENCES

1. It is possible that in some parts of the country, on the estates of Trinity College, Dublin, for example (Carney 1975), the absolute size of the population had already begun to fall. But for a critique of the reliability of the Trinity College evidence see Lee 1981.
2. The Western Lowlands include the counties of Renfrew, Lanark and Ayr: the Eastern Lowlands the counties of Perth, Kinross, Angus, Fife, Clackmannan, East, West and Mid Lothian, Stirling and Dumbarton.
3. Cousens 1963, 1963–4, 1964, 1966; Horner 1969.
4. Calculated from data in Walshaw 1941; Mitchell and Deane 1962; Flinn 1977; Verrière 1979.

5.   Johnson 1959; Cousens 1960, 1965; O'Grada 1973.

6.   Connell 1950a; Cousens 1963, 1963–4, 1964, 1966; Johnson 1970.

7.   Only the London area relied solely on net immigration for its population growth. By comparison, the major industrial areas of the North, North West and the Midlands depended chiefly on their own high rates of natural increase (Deane and Cole 1967).

8.   Cairncross 1949, 1953; Webb 1963; Deane and Cole 1967; Lawton 1968, 1978; Flinn 1977.

9.   There has also been considerable movement between Eastern and Western Lowland areas of the country (Flinn 1977).

10.   For similar conclusions see Maltby 1971; Baker 1973; Martin 1978; Long and Maltby 1980; Tranter 1974.

11.   See also data for Fleetwood (Foster 1975), Fleetwood and Lytham (Rogers 1976), Ramsgate (Holmes 1973), York (Armstrong 1974), Liverpool (Lawton 1979), Huddersfield (Dennis 1977), Caldicott and Portskewett in Gwent (Gant 1977), Portpatrick (Tranter 1974) and Scotland (Flinn 1977).

12.   Even so, in three-quarters of all marriages where the bride and groom came from different parishes the distance between the partners was less than twelve miles in 1927/36 (Perry 1969).

13.   Johnson 1959; Douglas 1963; Cousens 1965; O'Grada 1973.

14.   See also Razzell 1972; Schofield 1972b; Lee 1974; Wrigley and Schofield 1983.

15.   In the period 1700–49, 132 males and 102 females per thousand live births died before the age of one: by 1750–99, 121 and 95 respectively: by 1800–50, 59 and 39. Among males and females reaching their first birthday in the period 1700–49, 171 and 148 per thousand failed to reach their fifth birthday: by 1750–99, 143 and 130: by 1800–50, 48 and 71. Male and female death rates in the age-groups 5–9 and 10–14 showed less obvious signs of decline, but mortality at these ages was anyway relatively low (Eversley 1981).

16.   Lower death rates in Ireland than in England/Wales in the last quarter of the nineteenth century reflected greater levels of under-registration in the Irish civil registers.

17.   This was partly due to the fact that Ireland's population contained a relatively high proportion of elderly persons.

18.   In the parish of Laggan (Inverness) mean age of male and female marriage was lower among cohorts born after than before 1800 (Flinn 1977). But it would be unwise to suggest the possibility of a decline in age at marriage from the experience of one parish.

19.   At St Patrick's mean age at first marriage among men rose from 21.7 years in the 1820s to 24.0 in the 1830s and 26.4 between 1840 and 1846: for women from 21.0 to 22.0 and 25.1 respectively (Morgan 1973).

20.   On the other hand, work based on material in marriage bonds and allegations shows no general tendency for ages at first marriage to decline in the course of the late eighteenth and early nineteenth centuries. But, useful though this work is as an indication of differentials in marital ages among the better-off socio-occupational sections of society, it is an unreliable guide to secular trends in age at marriage, particularly for the community at large (Razzell 1965; Outhwaite 1973).

21. In the absence of data for Scotland and Ireland it is impossible to say whether the same pattern prevailed in the hundred years before 1850.

22. The evidence on lifetime celibacy rates in Scotland and Ireland between the mid-eighteenth and mid-nineteenth centuries is too scant and scattered to permit any generalization about levels and trends.

23. Somewhat oddly however, except in the case of Ireland where lifetime celibacy rates increased from at least as early as the mid-nineteenth century, the initial decline in fertility during the 1870s and 1880s took place against a background of relatively low levels of celibacy.

24. Bridal pregnancy is defined as a woman giving birth to her first child less than eight or eight and a half months after marriage.

25. The illegitimacy ratio measures the number of births outside wedlock per hundred total live births.

26. At Kilmarnock in the 1750s the illegitimacy ratio was as low as 2% and it was reported that 'antenuptial pregnancy was very uncommon' (Flinn 1977, p. 287). At Cathcart (Renfrewshire), however, illegitimacy ratios in the 1770s and 1780s were as high as 8% (Flinn 1977): at Portpatrick in the mid-1830s 7.6%, and more than a third of all first births celebrated in the parish between 1820 and 1854 were conceived before marriage (Tranter 1978).

27. In 1861 illegitimacy rates were a startling 33.6% in the North East and 27.9% in the Borders compared with 22.5% in the Western Lowlands, 20.6% in the Eastern Lowlands but only 9.5% in the Highlands and 8.9% in the Far North (Flinn 1977).

28. **Batchelor, T.** (1808), *General View of the Agriculture of the County of Bedford,* London, p. 610.

29. How far the trends in bridal pregnancy during the late eighteenth and early nineteenth centuries were determined by changes in registration procedures is hard to say. On the one hand, the tendency for the average length of interval between birth and baptism to increase during the period would tend to understate the rise in bridal pregnancy. On the other, the decline in the proportion of irregular to regular marriages following Hardwicke's Act of 1753 may work to overstate it if it is assumed that before the Act pregnant brides more often resorted to clandestine unions than to marriages based on a church ceremony.

30. In Scotland the number of live births per thousand women aged 15–49 (the general fertility rate) decreased from 132 in 1881 to 111 in 1901 and 71 in 1931: in England/Wales the general fertility rate fell from 148 in 1881 to 115 in 1901 and 64 in 1931 (among women aged 15–44) (Flinn 1977; Glass 1951; Mitchell and Deane 1962).

31. Gross reproduction rates are defined as the total number of female births per woman.

32. Exceptionally, at Colyton (Devon) age-specific fertility rates were significantly higher between 1770 and 1837 than in the period 1720–69 (Wrigley 1966b).

33. A completed family is defined as a marriage which remained unbroken until at least the wife's 45th birthday.

Chapter 3

THE DECLINE IN MORTALITY

Much the most significant element in the general decline in mortality which, at varying rates and not without temporary interruption, has occurred in all countries of the British Isles since the middle of the eighteenth century has been the reduction in deaths from infectious disease. Almost all of the decline in death rates during the eighteenth and nineteenth centuries stemmed from the reduced prevalence and fatality of infections. Even during the twentieth century, when a decrease in deaths from non-infective conditions played a larger part than ever before, falling mortality was predominantly due to the continued reduction in deaths from infectious disease.[1]

Altogether, three-quarters of the decline in English and Welsh death rates between 1848/1854 and 1971 was the result of reduced fatality from infections and only a quarter the result of falling mortality from non-infective causes. Forty per cent of the overall decline was explained by a diminution in deaths from air-borne infections: 21% by a decrease in deaths from water- or food-borne diseases: 12% by reduced mortality from other diseases originating in micro-organisms but not transmitted by air, water or food: and just 25% by a decline in mortality from ailments not associated with micro-organisms.[2] Roughly one third of the decline in mortality from air-borne infections, almost half of that from food- or water-borne diseases and over a third of that from other infections had already been achieved by the opening of the twentieth century. In contrast, only 10% of the saving of life from non-infective causes of death had occurred by 1901. Such of the decline in mortality from infectious diseases as had taken place before the middle of the nineteenth century involved mainly air-borne infections – respiratory tuberculosis and smallpox especially. The decline in mortality from food- and water-borne infections did not begin until the second half of the nineteenth century and from non-infective causes not before the twentieth (McKeown 1976).

The causes of the secular decline in mortality from infectious diseases, particularly that part of it which occurred before 1850 when unequivocal evidence of the kind of improvements in human and environmental conditions which lead to lower death rates is difficult to find, have long puzzled historians. Even for the late nineteenth and early years of the twentieth centuries, when improvements in general standards of life were more apparent, the relative importance of the various possible causes of falling mortality remains uncertain. Not until well into the twentieth century is it possible to identify more precisely the agencies responsible for declining death rates.

Broadly speaking, each of the complex array of agencies which have been suggested by one historian or another as having played a part in the reduction in mortality between the mid-eighteenth and mid-nineteenth centuries may be grouped into one or other of two categories: (i) autonomous agencies, that is, forces which were independent of improvements made by man to his own condition or environment; among them, a natural decrease in the incidence and severity of micro-organisms – possibly a consequence of changing climatic conditions, a reduction in the size of the animal, rodent or insect populations which carried micro-organisms, or a natural increase in resistance to disease among either the carrying vectors or human beings themselves – perhaps the product of a process of genetic selection emanating from long exposure to disease organisms; (ii) influences which arose from actions taken by man himself; innovations in medical practice – new drugs and therapies, larger numbers of qualified personnel and institutions offering effective medical treatment, or greater resort to quarantine procedures; rising standards of public health – better housing, improved methods of sewage disposal, purer water supply, increased environmental cleanliness, cleaner air and better quality foodstuffs; the agricultural enclosure movement which lessened the transmission of disease from animals to man; improvements in personal hygiene; or higher standards of human nutrition which raised man's resistance to micro-organisms.

AUTONOMOUS INFLUENCES

That the incidence and virulence of infectious disease can be, and sometimes has been, partly determined by forces over which man has no control is indisputable. It is conceivable, for example, that the disappearance of plague from western Europe at varying dates between the mid-seventeenth (in Britain) and early nineteenth centuries owed at least something to wholly fortuitous, autonomous influences – the replacement of the black or house rat by the brown or field rat, a natural weakening in the virulence of the plague bacillus, the emergence of a breed of rat with an inherited immunity to infection, or the gradual build-up of protective antibodies in human populations. Even Professor McKeown, the leading critic of autonomous interpretations of mortality decline, concedes that a reduction in the virulence of disease organisms and an increase in human resistance to disease arising from the process of genetic selection made some contribution to the decline in deaths from typhus during the late eighteenth and early nineteenth centuries, in deaths from scarlet fever during the nineteenth century and from scarlet fever, measles, nephritis and rheumatic fever in the twentieth (McKeown 1976).

In relation to the overall decline in mortality since the mid-eighteenth century, however, the role of autonomous agencies must be regarded as modest, even in the hundred years or so before 1850 when its contribution was probably greatest. To see the disappearance of plague as the consequence of a natural rise in human immunity overlooks a variety of considerations: among them, the irregularity of plague outbreaks, fluctuations in the virulence of the infection itself, the fact that recovery from plague does not convey a lifetime immunity from the disease and the fact that the last plague epidemics occurred not in areas which had previously been least susceptible but in those where plague had always been most prevalent. To interpret it as a response to changes in the ecology of rodent populations is equally implausible. Even if the brown rat replaced the black rat, and there is evidence that in reality they co-existed in many areas, the direction and timing of brown rat migrations from Central Asia into Europe do not fit neatly into the geographic pattern of the incidence of plague. In any case, plague can be carried as easily by human as by rat fleas. To see plague's disappearance as the result of a natural diminution in the virulence of the bacillus sits uncomfortably with the major outbreaks of the disease which continued to occur on the Indian continent into the twentieth century. Lastly, to explain it in terms of an increased resistance among rats founders on the difficulties of explaining why rats developed an immunity only from the later seventeenth century, why plague continued to ravage many parts of the world long after it had disappeared from western Europe and why it prevailed longest in cities with the worst historical record of visitation, where the rodent populations ought to have had the greatest opportunity to acquire a natural immunity. On balance, therefore, the causes of the disappearance of plague are more likely to lie in human agency – the substitution of brick for lath and plaster in house-building, the cutting of overland trade routes between the western and eastern worlds by the Ottoman advance into south-east Europe or, the most likely explanation of all, the adoption of more effective measures of public quarantine.[3]

Attempts to relate the declining influence of infectious parasites on human mortality to changes in climatic conditions have proved equally unsuccessful. There is nothing to support the view that the high and wildly fluctuating rates of mortality common to much of western

Europe between the later sixteenth and early eighteenth centuries were associated, directly or indirectly, with the general deterioration in climatic conditions which occurred during the period. The main killer epidemics – plague, smallpox, malaria and infantile diarrhoea – followed temporal rhythms quite independent of climatic variation (Appleby 1980a). Periodically, of course, as in Scotland during the 1690s and Ireland during the later 1840s, the influence of climate on livestock and crop supplies so depleted per capita food output and standards of nutrition that levels of infectious disease and mortality rose dramatically. But this occurred only where populations had failed to develop efficient methods of storing and distributing foodstuffs during periods of shortage or where they were dependent on a dangerously narrow range of food crops. By the mid-eighteenth century at the latest this did not apply to either England/Wales or Scotland. In England, throughout the eighteenth and nineteenth centuries, there was no obvious long-term association between variations in climate and the behaviour of death rates. Mortality was higher in the first half than the second half of the eighteenth century in spite of the fact that warmer winters and cooler summers, which would favour lower death rates, were more prevalent in the earlier period (Wrigley and Schofield 1981).

Clearly, either the effect of climate on mortality was negligible or its influence was consistently overridden by other forces. According to Wrigley and Schofield these forces originated chiefly in circumstances that were independent of any improvements affected by man to his own conditions of life. It should be stressed, however, that they provide no positive evidence in support of this conclusion. Indeed, it seems to follow solely from their conclusion that secular trends in real wages bore no relationship to those in mortality. But even if this was so, and their data on real wages are far from conclusive (see pp. 101–2), it does not *necessarily* mean that man's efforts to improve his environment were of only secondary, or negligible, importance to late eighteenth and early nineteenth century mortality decline. Real wage trends may have been of little relevance to the introduction of at least some of the innovations which, potentially, made a significant contribution to the saving of life. In any case, as McKeown points out, it is surely asking too much of coincidence to accept that there was a fortuitous reduction in the natural virulence of the large number of infectious diseases known, or suspected, to have become less fatal between the mid-eighteenth and mid-nineteenth centuries (McKeown 1976). It is equally hard to understand why it was only from the late eighteenth and early nineteenth centuries that man should have become naturally more resistant to diseases to which for so long previously he had been prey. Simply because it is difficult to offer conclusive proof of a connection between human activity and the decline in mortality which occurred during the period from the middle of the eighteenth to the middle of the nineteenth centuries is not by itself sufficient reason for turning towards autonomous agencies for our explanation. Generally, the mortality of very few diseases has declined by natural volition, even in the period before the mid-nineteenth century when the ability of man to influence his own life expectancy was more limited than it was later to become. Before, and certainly after, 1850 falling death rates were primarily the result of man's own successful efforts to improve his lot.

INNOVATIONS IN MEDICINE

So dramatic has been the development of medical services since the middle of the eighteenth century and so revolutionary the advances ultimately achieved in standards of medical treatment that it is easy to understand why many earlier historians accorded medical innovation much of the responsibility for the modern decline in mortality (Griffiths 1926; Buer 1926). More recent research, however, has tended to moderate their claims.

At the beginning of the eighteenth century the condition of the medical services was appalling. Access to 'qualified' medical help was generally restricted to the relatively well-off and, in certain cases, the very poorest. For the relative few who could afford to pay treatment could be obtained from 'qualified' physicians or surgeons and medicines from apothecaries. For the very poor, at least in parishes which had implemented the full provisions of the 1601 Poor Law Act, treatment was available from surgeons or apothecaries at parochial expense. Otherwise, with some resort to the cheaper services offered by a variety of medical quacks, the vast majority of the population treated their ailments themselves by means of folklore remedies or quasi-medical knowledge handed down from family and neighbours. The institutional facilities for the treatment of sickness were in even worse condition. In late seventeenth-century England there were just five hospitals and one dispensary providing help for the sick poor.[4] In late seventeenth-century Scotland the only free institutional provision of medical relief for the labouring population was that afforded by the Faculty of Physicians and Surgeons in Glasgow and the Royal College of Physicians at a dispensary opened in Edinburgh in 1682 (Pennington 1977). In Ireland there was not even this.

In the eighteenth and early nineteenth centuries there was an impressive increase in the facilities for medical assistance, a consequence, in part, of the burgeoning interest in questions of population growth and human physiology and, in part, of a heightened humanitarianism occasioned by the philosophy of the Enlightenment and a growing concern over poor standards of public health and high levels of mortality. One aspect of this development was a substantial growth in the number of people qualified to dispense medical treatment and in the number of institutions offering a formal medical education (Kett 1964). Another was the increasing willingness of parochial poor law overseers to use poor law funds for the treatment of sick paupers (Thomas 1980). But the most striking and significant feature of the development of medical facilities during the period was the establishment of numerous voluntary general and specialist hospitals and dispensaries, funded almost entirely by private charity and providing treatment and medicines free to considerable numbers of people who would otherwise have remained untreated.

In Ireland the first voluntary hospital opened in Dublin in 1718 and a further six were established in the city between 1733 and 1773. By 1804 there was at least one general infirmary in every county in the country, financed partly by the state but predominantly by charitable donations and subscriptions. The first specialist hospitals, for fever, opened in the late eighteenth century. On the eve of the Famine there were over a hundred. By 1845 Ireland had 632 dispensaries, all offering free medicine and medical assistance to the poor and financed largely through charitable bequests and subscriptions (Connell 1950a; de Bhal 1973).

In Scotland the first voluntary general hospitals opened in Edinburgh (1729), Aberdeen (1742), Dumfries (1776), Montrose (1782), Glasgow (1794) and Dundee (1799).[5] By the 1780s there were already dispensaries at Kelso, Montrose, Dundee and Paisley. A Glasgow dispensary appears to have been in existence between 1801 and 1815 and a Celtic dispensary, specifically for Highland-born residents in the city, between 1837 and 1847 (Flinn 1977; Pennington 1977).

Beginning with the Westminster Hospital in London (1720), a total of 33 voluntary hospitals had been founded in England by the close of the eighteenth century. In 1861 England/Wales had 23 voluntary teaching hospitals and 130 voluntary general hospitals providing free treatment for both in- and out-patients. Between 1800 and 1861 the number of beds available for in-patients in the voluntary hospitals rose from 4,000, when around 30,000 in-patients a year were treated, to 12,000. As early as the beginning of the nineteenth century dispensaries in the London area alone treated over 50,000 patients a year (Woodward 1974). Between 1851 and 1868 the physicians of the Stockton-on-Tees dispensary, founded in 1790, made 102,426 home visits to 10,347 different patients and in 1861 alone treated 1,724 patients, in a town with a total population of only 13,000 (Hastings 1973). In 1825 the Leeds Public Dispensary, founded a year earlier as an offshoot of the Leeds House of Recovery which had dealt with fever victims denied admission to the city's General Infirmary, assisted 1,814 out-patients and its staff made over four hundred home visits (Anning 1974). Throughout the United Kingdom as a whole a total of 154 charitable hospitals and dispensaries were opened between 1700 and 1825 (Singer and Underwood 1962).

After the middle of the nineteenth century the range of medical facilities expanded so rapidly that by the outbreak of the First World War most of the worst deficiencies in their geographic coverage had been resolved. In England/Wales the number of voluntary general hospitals had increased to 385 by 1891 and 530 by 1911, and the number of voluntary special hospitals – for fever, diseases of the eye, children and maternity – from 90 in 1861 to 161 by 1891, an increase well in excess of the growth of population. Primarily, of course, these served only the populations of urban communities and their immediate catchment areas. Beginning in the late 1850s, however, the problems arising from the lack of hospital facilities in more remote rural areas were gradually overcome by the creation of small cottage hospitals, the number of which had risen from sixteen in 1865 to 180 by 1880.

The work of the voluntary hospitals was supplemented and soon surpassed by the emergence of a state-run hospital system. Well before the establishment of the Metropolitan Asylums Board in 1867, and despite the traditional preference of the poor law authorities for granting outdoor rather than indoor relief to sick paupers, many poor law workhouses had come to include sick wards where paupers received treatment as in-patients. As early as 1861 there were more than four times as many beds in workhouse sick wards as in voluntary general and specialist hospitals. Following the establishment of the Metropolitan Asylums Board, the Poor Law authorities took further steps to expand the facilities for in-patient treatment in workhouses. The Board itself built a number of hospitals specifically designed for the treatment of victims of infectious disease, at first catering only for people in receipt of poor relief but subsequently admitting all infectious cases irrespective of income. It also actively encouraged poor law unions to band together to form 'sick asylum' districts with resources large enough to construct and maintain their own infirmaries.

By 1891 the public sector hospitals provided a total of 83,000 beds: by 1911, 154,000. As a result of the expansion of the state and private hospital system in the second half of the nineteenth century the ratio of hospital beds to total population in England/Wales increased from three per thousand population in 1861 to 3.9 in 1891 and 5.5 on the eve of the Great War (Abel-Smith 1964). By the opening of the inter-war period hospital coverage had more or less reached saturation point, the slower pace of hospital construction during the 1920s and 1930s merely reflecting the decrease in the rate of growth of demand for hospital treatment which came with the downturn in rates of population increase (Cowan 1970).

Although, initially, the Metropolitan Asylums Board had also intended to develop an extensive system of poor law dispensaries, to cater for those receiving outdoor relief and not requiring inpatient treatment, the intention was not pursued. In fact, from 1870 onwards, it became official policy to encourage indoor rather than outdoor treatment for sick paupers and to grant outdoor medical relief only when in-patient treatment was not available, much the same practice as had been adopted in Ireland after the Medical Relief Charities Act of 1851.

Accordingly, for ailments that did not require in-patient treatment, or were excluded from it, the poor continued to rely on voluntary agencies. Fortunately, these too expanded rapidly after the middle years of the nineteenth century. Many dispensaries evolved naturally from the out-patient departments of the voluntary hospitals. Some, of which there were 44 in the London area by 1890, were formed by poor law authorities in the wake of the Metropolitan Asylums Act. Many more, like the 927 provident dispensaries active in London in 1873, were run by friendly societies on the basis of members' subscriptions. Others were the product of the home medical mission movement begun in 1859 when the Edinburgh Association opened a small dispensary in the city for the purpose of training its students. In subsequent years, medical missions – each with several dispensaries and voluntary workers to carry out home visits, most with a convalescent home and a few with sleeping accommodation for patients waiting to enter hospital – were set up in Liverpool (1866), Aberdeen (1868), Glasgow (1868), Bristol (1871), Manchester (1871), Birmingham (1875), Oldham (1875), Dublin (1890) and, in London, at St Giles (1871), Marylebone (1876), Canning Town (1887), St Pancras (1888), Deptford (1889), Islington (1890), Lambeth (1891) and Forest Gate (1898). By the end of the nineteenth century most of the larger charitable societies like Barnardos and Fegans included at least one dispensary in their work (Heaseman 1964; Cope 1964).

Together, the dispensaries and out-patient departments of the voluntary hospitals treated considerable numbers of people. In 1890 the 44 London poor law dispensaries handled 54,149 attendances and made 53,272 home visits (Abel-Smith 1964). During the first six months of 1906 the Leeds Public Dispensary made 1,104 home visits and registered 11,773 out-patient attendances (Anning 1974). Between 1831 and 1890 the Stockton Dispensary treated an average of 1,200 patients a year (Hastings 1973). Although in the aggregate dealing with fewer patients than other dispensaries and out-patient departments, individually the medical missions too were extraordinarily active. The dispensary run by the Aberdeen medical mission treated seven hundred new cases every year: that at Bristol coped annually with 13,000 consultations and 5,000 home visits: that at Glasgow with an incredible 35,000 consultations a year.

There were good reasons for the particular popularity of the mission dispensaries. They offered treatment free to people whose incomes were too low or too irregular or whose mobility was too great to permit them to pay the subscriptions required by friendly society dispensaries or the medical clubs run by private doctors in the poorer areas. They were often the only resort for those who, for one reason or another, were denied treatment by poor law medical officers or who were simply too proud to suffer the taint of pauperism and especially valuable for people unable to acquire the subscriber's 'letter' required for admission to voluntary hospitals and many of the dispensaries in all but emergency cases. And, in their special emphasis on home visiting and the provision of 'medical extras' – food, medicines and surgical appliances – they displayed a greater concern for the needs of the patient's family than did most of the other institutions of medical care (Heaseman 1964).

The most significant institutional advances in medical treatment during the twentieth century related to the health of mothers and their children. Already by 1918, when the Maternity and Child Welfare Act came into operation, there were 1,278 maternity and child welfare clinics, nearly half of them dependent on private charity, providing invaluable advice on infant care, visiting mothers in their homes, distributing dried milk and other foods, organizing maternity savings' schemes and provident clothing clubs, selling cradles and so on (Dyhouse 1978). Their numbers increased considerably during the inter-war years.

The question is whether this undeniable expansion in personal and institutional facilities for medical treatment played any significant part in the decline in death rates which occurred between the mid-eighteenth and mid-twentieth centuries. To answer this question requires consideration of three additional questions. What proportion of the population had regular access to 'professional' medical facilities? Was the treatment provided by such services directed at the most common causes of death? And was the treatment they offered effective?

It is impossible to assess exactly the proportion of the population having regular access to medical services. Probably, by the inter-war period, coverage was more or less complete although even then, as shown by the reluctance of large numbers of working-class women to attend maternity and child welfare clinics, many people chose not to make use of the services that were available. In earlier times the situation was less satisfactory. Throughout the eighteenth and nineteenth centuries the location of medical services was heavily weighted in favour of urban populations: larger urban communities were better served than smaller urban centres and rural areas were particularly poorly endowed. Even where medical facilities were most developed their availability to large sections of the population was often severely restricted. As a matter of deliberate policy, for instance, the earliest voluntary hospitals excluded many people from treatment: sick paupers who were supposedly covered by the provisions of the poor law and whose demands for treatment were not to be permitted to overrun the facilities of the private sector: victims of infectious disease: patients whose illnesses were believed to be terminal or near-terminal, or those who required more than minor surgery: infants and young children: pregnant women: anyone who could afford to pay for the services of a private doctor or who was unable to obtain a subscriber's 'letter'. Only in cases of dire emergency were exceptions usually made (Cherry 1972, 1980b). The Leeds Public Dispensary initially excluded people who could pay for their own medicines, apprentices and servants whose employers were able to provide for them and, except in emergencies, only treated patients recommended by subscribers or trustees (Anning 1974). Beginning in the 1840s, the Stockton Dispensary refused to treat servants, recipients of poor relief or sickness benefits from provident clubs and friendly societies and anyone from households with earnings of more than 23 shillings a week (Hastings 1973).

Admittedly, faced by the growing demand for treatment, many of these restrictions were relaxed in the course of time. But, at least until the later decades of the nineteenth century, this does not mean that the proportion of the population benefitting from hospital and dispensary treatment necessarily increased. Demand for treatment was growing so rapidly that for a time it outran the ability of hospital and dispensary services to cope. The ratio of in-patients to population in the catchment areas served by the voluntary hospitals actually fell during the second and third quarters of the nineteenth century (Cherry 1980b). Only in the several decades prior to the outbreak of the First World War did the availability of medical services clearly begin to outpace the rate at which population and the demand for medical treatment increased.

Even on the eve of the First World War considerable deficiencies still remained. Before the National Health Service Act of 1911, even in areas where qualified medical practitioners were plentiful, the majority of the labouring population could not afford their fees and, for minor ailments anyway, continued to rely on folk remedies, herbal recipes or patent medicines (Schofield 1979). In spite of the absolute increase in the range of medical services after the middle of the eighteenth century it is by no means clear that they guaranteed the availability of regular treatment for the large majority of the population much before the later decades of the nineteenth century. Certainly, serious deficiencies in their coverage remained long after the secular decline in mortality first began.

From the very start the treatment provided by the medical services was, on balance, beneficial to the patients who came within their orbit. The view, popularized by McKeown and Brown (1955), that the early hospitals increased rather than decreased mortality is no longer tenable.[6] Of 26,596 patients treated at the Stockton Dispensary from 1851 to 1868 93.3% were discharged as 'cured', 2.1% as 'relieved', 0.8% for irregular or non-attendance, only 1.2% were transferred to the poor law union surgeon as 'hopeless' and a mere 2.6% died (Hastings 1973). Mortality rates among in-patients at the York County Hospital were as low as 1% in the early 1740s and 6% between 1825 and 1835. During the periods 1740–3 and 1784–1842 90% of the hospital's in-patients were discharged as 'cured and relieved' (Sigsworth 1966). In no single decade between the 1770s and 1870s did in-patient mortality at the Norfolk and Norwich Hospital exceed 5.7% while throughout the period 1780–1840 the proportion of patients described as 'cured and relieved' remained steady at around two-thirds (Cherry 1972). Over a wide sample of voluntary hospitals down to 1850 post-operative deaths never exceeded 10–15% and total in-patient mortality rarely averaged above 10%.

In the course of the second and third quarters of the nineteenth century, as the hospitals found it more and more difficult to cope with the twin problems of overcrowding and cross-infection caused by the rapid growth in demand for their services, rates of in-patient mortality rose and the percentages claimed as 'cured and relieved' fell. But the deterioration was not so dramatic as to suggest that they became little more than 'gateways to death' (Woodward 1974; Cherry 1980a and b). True, the statistical evidence upon which these optimistic conclusions are based exaggerates dispensary and voluntary hospital achievements. Relying as they did on subscriptions and charitable donations for their income, these institutions had good reason to display the results of their work in the best possible light. The term 'cured and relieved' is itself sufficiently vague to allow the inclusion of many patients whose condition was not permanently improved by treatment, and may well have been adopted for this reason. And the concern of voluntary hospitals and dispensaries to present a successful image to the public, initially at least, encouraged them to pursue policies which deliberately excluded the admission of cases likely to swell casualty rates. Nevertheless, their consistent attempts to exclude infectious diseases or to isolate them in separate fever wards and their obvious recognition of the need for spaciousness, ventilation and hygiene do imply that their statistical records are not dangerously misleading. It is surely unfair to deny that the treatment offered by hospitals, dispensaries and even medical missions, where religion sometimes took precedence over the practice of medicine (Heaseman 1964), did contribute something to the general decline of mortality, if only in those localities where they were widely established.

In the final analysis, *the extent to which* the new medical services contributed to the decline in death rates depends on whether they treated ailments prominent among the main causes of death and whether the treatment they provided was effective. Dispensaries and medical missions, by their nature, were less involved in treating potentially fatal illness and injury than the hospitals. Probably the majority of hospital patients, too, were treated for minor ailments not in themselves fatal – scalds, burns, cuts, dislocations and fractures, skin diseases such as scabies and scrofula, dental problems, dyspepsia, rheumatism and bronchial complaints. In their earlier years the voluntary hospitals actually excluded people suffering from many of the most common causes of death – among them certain kinds of infectious disease and tuberculosis. Moreover, until the introduction of anaesthetics in the 1840s and of antiseptic and aseptic procedures in the 1860s and 1890s respectively surgical techniques were too primitive and risky to permit other than relatively minor operations. In view of these limitations the contribution of the medical services to falling death rates was at best only modest, especially before the later decades of the nineteenth century.

On the other hand, a not insignificant *minority* of the patients treated by hospital and dispensary services did suffer from conditions which ranked high among the principal causes of death. Even the dispensaries attempted to tackle major killers like smallpox, bronchitis, influenza, pneumonia, cholera, scarlatina, measles, typhus and other fevers. In the course of the nineteenth century – partly because of the growing willingness of the voluntary general hospitals to admit infectious cases, partly as a result of advances in surgical technique and partly because of the development of poor law and specialist fever hospitals – the range of serious illnesses and injuries treated by medical institutions undoubtedly widened. Provided the treatment they offered was effective, the range of ailments tackled was certainly broad enough to have had at least a moderately beneficial effect on death rates (Hastings 1973; Cherry 1980a and b).

It is, however, about the effectiveness of this treatment that the greatest doubts have been expressed concerning the contribution of medical innovation to long-term mortality decline. Until the adoption after 1935 of chemotherapeutical drugs, sulphonamides and antibiotics there were few drugs capable of effectively combating fatal disease. Those which were effective – mercury (for syphilis) and cinchona (for malaria), introduced in the eighteenth century, antitoxin (for diphtheria) and salvarsan (for syphilis), in the twentieth – did not relate to diseases which figured prominently among the major causes of death. More typical of the drugs used to fight disease were those involved in the treatment of tuberculosis, none of which were effective until the introduction of streptomycin in 1947 (McKeown 1976). On the whole, the medicines supplied by qualified medical practitioners and medical institutions were little if any better than those available to the large numbers of men and women who relied on herbal remedies or patent medicines (Schofield 1979).

Advances in other aspects of medical therapy had a greater impact on levels of mortality. In the course of the nineteenth century the indiscriminate resort of earlier times to bleeding, purging and vomiting as normal methods of treatment gradually gave way to more selective, careful and less traumatic therapies (Hasting 1973). Surgical techniques became more conservative and safe. The introduction of anaesthesia in the 1840s reduced the number of post-operative deaths from shock and the fatalities which had always been associated with the need to carry out surgery quickly. At the same time, the adoption of antiseptics and aseptic methods, in the 1860s and 1890s, lessened the incidence of post-operative infection (Cherry 1980b). In the twentieth century reduced mortality from appendicitis, peritonitis, ear infections and various non-infective conditions owed much to specific improvements in surgical skills. Diarrhoeal diseases were successfully combated by intravenous therapy and puerperal fever by improved obstetric practices (McKeown 1975, 1976). From the beginning of the twentieth century, too, rising standards of medical practice, nursing and midwifery have contributed to a general improvement in levels of diagnostic skill and the quality of medical care, both of which have played a part in increasing the effectiveness of medicine in the battle against fatal disease.[7] But the innovations in medical therapy considered to have made the greatest contribution to the secular decline in death rates since the middle of the eighteenth century are those of inoculation and vaccination against smallpox, the increasing practice of isolating victims of infectious disease from contact with the rest of the community and the growing insistence on the need to maintain strict standards of hygiene and cleanliness in medical treatment.

Immunization against smallpox was not unknown before the middle of the eighteenth century, but it became common only during the second half of the century as a result of the development of safer, less severe techniques of inoculation pioneered by the Sutton family. By the end of the 1760s the Suttons alone claimed to have inoculated 40,000 people (Zwanenberg 1978). Even if this claim is exaggerated, there is abundant evidence that by the close of the eighteenth century the practice of inoculation, often financed for whole communities by parochial poor law overseers or private philanthropists, was widespread (Razzell 1965, 1967; Flinn 1977). By the early nineteenth century inoculation, together with Edward Jenner's new technique of vaccination, provided an effective therapy for combatting one of the greatest threats to life in earlier times. The question is how much credit to give it for the general decline in death rates in late eighteenth-century Britain and Ireland.

It was once argued that the reduction in mortality from smallpox due to the spread of inoculation was sufficient to account for the whole of the decline in mortality which occurred in England and Ireland during the late eighteenth century (Razzell 1965, 1967). This view is no longer acceptable even to its originator, partly because smallpox accounted for no more than a sixth and not, as was assumed, a third of all deaths in the pre-inoculation era and partly because mortality continued to fall through much of the first half of the nineteenth century when smallpox was no longer among the principal causes of death (Bradley and Razzell 1973; Razzell 1974b).

On the other hand, McKeown's attempts to deny inoculation and vaccination a major role in the decline of smallpox mortality itself also surely go too far (McKeown 1976, 1978). On grounds of expense, out of a reluctance to intervene in the workings of the natural order or because of a common, if erroneous, fear that inoculation and vaccination spread rather than contained the disease, there was unquestionably a good deal of popular opposition to the new techniques. And the recurrence of smallpox epidemics well into the nineteenth century indicates that too many people remained untreated for society to be free of the disease altogether. Even so, long before vaccination was made compulsory in 1852 and compulsion became legally enforceable in 1871, the extent of inoculation and vaccination was sufficient to reduce considerably the size of the population at risk from the disease and to curb the spread of the infection when it did appear. It is stretching cynicism too far to deny the significance of inoculation and vaccination when their adoption coincided with a decline in smallpox mortality from 16.5% of all deaths around the middle of the eighteenth century to just 1%–2% by the mid-nineteenth, especially since for the only alternative explanation – that it was the result of a natural decline in the virulence of the disease itself – there is no positive support.[8]

Without understanding, precisely, the mechanics of disease transmission, the importance of isolating cases of infection and of attempting to ensure decent standards of hygiene in medical treatment was accepted by many contemporary observers long before the beginning of the nineteenth century. The fact has not gone unrecognized by modern historians. Some relate the disappearance of plague to the adoption of stricter, more effective quarantine procedures (Flinn 1974, 1979, 1981; Post 1976, 1977). Some suggest that an important part of the reason for the success of the Suttonian method of inoculation was its insistence that those inoculated spend some time in isolation from the rest of the community (Zwanenberg 1978).

A large part of the expenditure incurred by parish poor law overseers in their battle against smallpox involved the costs of housing smallpox victims in buildings well away from their neighbours and of providing supplies of bedding, clothing and other essential goods which were destroyed immediately after use in order to minimize the risk of contamination. In their initial exclusion of infectious cases and their practice of isolating infectious patients in separate fever wards or buildings and in their frequent emphasis on the need for spaciousness and adequate ventilation, the regular washing of the walls of hospital wards with lime and the use of sulphur and nitre to fumigate wards, clothes and bedding, the voluntary hospitals, too, demonstrated considerable awareness of the importance of quarantine and cleanliness for effective treatment (Cherry 1972, 1980a and b). In practice, of course, as the increasing problems of cross-infection in mid-nineteenth century hospitals show, their endeavours were only partially successful. Yet it is possible that the efforts of the medical institutions to ensure the segregation of infectious disease and to improve the hygiene of their treatment played a more significant part in the contribution of medicine to declining death rates in the eighteenth and nineteenth centuries than has sometimes been allowed.

Ultimately, however, the role of medical innovation in falling mortality was only as effective as the drugs or therapies used for treatment. And in the main, with the exception of inoculation and vaccination against smallpox, for much of the period between the mid-eighteenth and mid-nineteenth centuries these were of relatively little value. Most of the decline in mortality from infectious disease, the principal element in the long-term reduction in death rates, came before the introduction of effective drugs and therapy.[9] Only for non-infective causes of death did innovations in medical technique play a more significant part. For most of our period, however, these were among the least important causes of death and, in any case, the bulk of the decline in mortality due to them did not occur until the twentieth century.

PUBLIC HEALTH AND PERSONAL HYGIENE

There is little to indicate that improvements in the standards of public health or personal hygiene contributed significantly to that part of the decline in mortality which occurred between the middle of the eighteenth and middle of the nineteenth centuries. True, many medical practitioners, foremost among them those who had served with the armed forces during the Napoleonic Wars (Mathias 1975), were beginning to emphasize the importance of personal cleanliness for the maintenance of health. But it is doubtful whether their advice was adopted by a sufficiently large proportion of the population to have had a major impact on civilian death rates.

A recent attempt to explain the early decline in mortality from the dirt-associated diseases of gastro-enteritis, typhoid, dysentery, relapsing and trench fever and typhus in terms of improvements in standards of personal hygiene (Razzell 1974) founders on a lack of adequate documentation. That there was an increase in the output of soap, cotton clothes and portable baths is undeniable. But it is by no means certain that it had any great effect on levels of human cleanliness. To what extent was the increased output of soap devoted to industrial rather than domestic uses? Were cotton clothes in fact washed more regularly than the woollens they replaced? Did the sale of portable baths or the use of soap for washing affect more than a small minority of the better-off sections of the community? Until these questions have been more extensively considered it is unwise to assume a substantial improvement in standards of human hygiene. And anyway, as McKeown reminds us, 'it is the condition of the water and food which determines the risk of infection rather than the cleanliness of the hands or utensils on which they are brought to the mouth' (McKeown 1976, p. 124).

A similar lack of supporting evidence also undermines attempts to explain the late eighteenth and early nineteenth century decline in mortality in terms of reduced levels of disease among animal populations and thus in the frequency with which animal diseases were transmitted to humans, in England a result of the enclosure of farm land, in Ireland of a switch from livestock to arable farming (Philpot 1975). Firstly, most of the land enclosed in England during the eighteenth century was open field, not the waste or common land on which animals had previously grazed indiscriminately. Secondly, the extent of waste or common land was too limited for its enclosure to have had any very marked effect on mortality rates. Thirdly, the mere erection of a hedge or fence around animal herds was not itself sufficient to contain the spread of animal disease, particularly in an age when disease could be transmitted so easily on the drove roads or at market (Turner 1976; Philpot 1975).

In reality, there was probably a general deterioration in environmental standards during the late eighteenth and first half of the nineteenth centuries. In England and Scotland the rapidity of urbanization gave rise to problems of overcrowding, poor housing, air pollution, impure water supply and grossly inadequate methods of sewage disposal unprecedented in their scale and far beyond the powers of the authorities to resolve.[10] Worse still, the risks to health arising from the squalor of urban surroundings were compounded by a problem of food adulteration which, in urban areas, had reached grotesque proportions by the middle of the nineteenth century.[11] Apart from the dangers caused by the poisonous ingredients that were added to many foods, adulterated foodstuffs were of little nutritional value and lowered human resistance to disease when it struck. For urban dwellers, at least, any improvement in health which occurred as a result of advances in standards of personal cleanliness was more than outweighed by the evils of the environment in which most of them had to live.

Conditions were little better in rural areas. There too, for instance, standards of housing declined in the face of increased rates of population growth.[12] By 1841 40% of all houses in rural Ireland were one-room cabins and another 37% contained between two and four rooms.[13] The high incidence of fever outbreaks in pre-Famine Ireland has been closely linked to poor housing and living conditions. In Ireland, as on mainland Britain, there is no indication of any environmental improvement during the period before the mid-nineteenth century.[14]

Such occasional, ad hoc improvements as were made in the procedures for administering public health during the worst periods of disease outbreak (Flinn 1974, 1981; Post 1976, 1977) were not sufficiently sustained or extensive to have done much to combat the widespread and continuous menace of environmental squalor. Indeed, in some areas public health conditions deteriorated so severely that rates of mortality actually rose. Thus, the failure of urban administrations to provide decent standards of housing, drainage, cleansing and water supply is blamed for the rise in Scottish death rates during the second quarter of the nineteenth century (Flinn 1977). Rising mortality at Carlisle between the end of the Napoleonic Wars and the 1840s has been attributed to overcrowding among the city's large community of domestic handloom weavers coupled with poor standards of water supply and methods of waste disposal (Armstrong 1981a). The growth of the framework knitting industry at Shepshed (Leicestershire) was accompanied by a similar deterioration in environmental conditions and an increase in infant and child death rates (Levine 1976b).[15] In England/Wales, as in Scotland, mortality rates around the middle of the nineteenth century would have been much lower had it not been for the march of urbanization and the appalling public health conditions it created (Loschky 1972). Life expectation rose during the late eighteenth and early nineteenth centuries despite a decline in average standards of public health not because of their improvement.

Not until the hundred years or so beginning around the mid-nineteenth century is there evidence of a steady improvement in the quality of public health and personal hygiene. By the 1850s concern over the scandals of food adulteration had reached such a pitch that subsequent improvements in the quality of food and drink products were inevitable. Initially, the improvement affected only the upper, middle and better-off working class sections of society, those with incomes high enough to be able to choose between pure and impure foods. For the bulk of the labouring population, relying on low-cost products most susceptible to adulteration, improvements in the quality of foodstuffs had to await the development of cooperative retail societies and multiple grocery stores and, in particular, the introduction of effective legislation designed to combat the worst problems of food and drink adulteration. Between the early 1870s, with the passing of the Adulteration of Food, Drink and Drugs Act in 1872 and the Sale of Food and Drugs Act in 1875, and the early twentieth century major advances were achieved in the quality of the nation's food and, to a lesser extent, drink supply.[16]

The effect of this improvement in the quality of food and drink products on standards of nutrition and rates of mortality since the late nineteenth century should not be underestimated. At the same time, however, its role must not be exaggerated. For example, Beaver's attempt to explain the early twentieth century decline in infant mortality in terms of the introduction of a safer, pathogen-free supply of cow's milk following the discovery of pasteurization or of the substitution in infant-feeding of dried, condensed or evaporated milk for cows' milk

(Beaver 1973) overlooks several vital considerations. Firstly, separated, sweetened and machine-skimmed varieties of condensed milk, which were widely sold despite the provisions of the Sale of Food and Drugs Act of 1899, were a much less satisfactory food for infants than 'desiccated' or unsweetened, full cream condensed milk. It was not, however, until the middle of the first decade of the twentieth century, several years after the decline in infant death rates had begun, that dried and unsweetened condensed milk began to sell in significant quantities. Secondly, the great majority of working-class mothers continued to breast-feed their babies, not least because it cost nothing; and it is not at all certain that the use of safe, artificial foods in infant feeding affected a sufficient proportion of children before 1914 to be accorded a major part in the initial decline in infant death rates. Finally, we need to know a good deal more about other aspects of late nineteenth- and early twentieth-century child care among the working classes before we can properly assess the relative contribution of artificial foods to lower mortality (Dyhouse 1978).

In the long-term the decline in mortality from infectious disease after the mid-nineteenth century, especially from diseases borne by water or food, owed much to a reduction in overcrowding, rising standards of housing and personal cleanliness, the provision of a purer water supply, cleaner air, better methods of refuse disposal and improved working conditions. Improvements in the environment of the home for instance, together with innovations in techniques of purifying and refrigerating foodstuffs such as milk, played an important role in lowering death rates among infants aged between six and twelve months during the 1930s (Winter 1979). Yet here, too, the contribution of hygiene and environmental improvement to falling mortality is more obvious after 1914 than before. There was little advance in standards of public and personal cleanliness before 1880 and only moderate improvements in standards of public health between 1880 and the outbreak of the First World War (McKeown 1976).[17] And although, even in the most deprived urban areas, basic standards of hygiene undoubtedly rose, it is hard to assess the effect of this on mortality rates. The absence of any marked correlation between spatio-temporal variations in mortality and general standards of sanitation in a city like Birmingham during the half century before 1914 suggests that one should not make too much of the contribution of sanitary improvement to the decline in death rates before the First World War (Woods 1978). And while the Birmingham data reveal a more striking association between housing conditions and mortality recent authorities are unanimous in concluding that the allied evils of overcrowding and poor housing had scarcely even begun to be tackled before 1914.[18] For the most part, the problems of housing, dirt and atmospheric pollution, which increasingly drove those who could afford it out of city centres into new, suburban communities, survived to be inherited and effectively resolved only by the post-war generations.

NUTRITION

In addition to the contribution made by improvements in the quality of foodstuffs themselves (in practice, of no significance before the later decades of the nineteenth century), rising standards of human nutrition may be achieved either by means of an increase in the overall per capita quantity of food consumed or by the development of more regular and egalitarian methods of distributing food supplies over time and between social classes. In turn, the former may result from either a general increase in the per capita output of existing food crops, the introduction of new foods or a rise in average real wages which enables lower income groups to maintain adequate levels of nutrition during periods of relative food shortage and rising prices: the latter, from better methods of storing and distributing food supplies which stabilize prices over time and reduce the likelihood of severe regional food shortages.

Numerous historians have seen rising standards of nutrition as the single most significant cause of the decline in mortality rates since the middle of the eighteenth century. To some, the reduction in Irish death rates during the second half of the eighteenth and early years of the nineteenth centuries was due, wholly or partially, to improvements in diet which stemmed from the introduction into the agricultural system of a new food crop, the potato.[19] To others, it was the result of a more general diversification and commercialization of Irish agriculture in which the potato was only one element: thus the decline in mortality between the 1750s and 1815 is explained by a decrease in the regularity of food shortages and the rise in death rates between the end of the Napoleonic Wars and the Great Famine by an increase in their frequency.[20] The spread of potato cultivation has also been seen as a significant factor in the reduction in Scottish death rates during the second half of the eighteenth century, if not as the initiator at least as a permissive agent which allowed a growing population to be fed satisfactorily (Flinn 1977).

In Scotland, however, the main causes of rising nutritional standards in the late eighteenth and early nineteenth centuries are seen to lie elsewhere. In part they stemmed from an increase in real wages which enabled people to eat better in normal times and to put by savings against times of deficient harvests and rising food prices; in part from improvements in methods of marketing food supplies which came with innovations in transport and the emergence of a more extensive system of commercial middlemen; but in the main from improvements in the administrative techniques for coping with the problems of food shortage during famine years. From the middle of the eighteenth century private landowners, poor law officials and central government agencies displayed a new sympathy towards the plight of the poor during periods of food crisis and, by means of more extensive relief measures and improved methods of distributing food supplies, took greater care to ensure that suffering was minimized (Flinn 1977).

For England, too, rising standards of nutrition have been given considerable credit for the decline in mortality both before and after 1850. According to Professor McKeown, increasing levels of agricultural productivity, and the improvement in dietary standards resulting from them, was the crucial element in the decline of death rates which occurred between the mid-eighteenth and mid-nineteenth centuries and continued to play an important role in their subsequent decrease. Higher levels of nutrition raised resistance to infectious disease among lower income groups and, by reducing the incidence of infection in the labouring population, promoted the life expectancy of those sections of the community which had always themselves been adequately fed but were at risk to the spread of disease from their poorer neighbours (McKeown 1975, 1976)[21] Similarly, declining rates of infant mortality during the late eighteenth and early nineteenth centuries have been equated with the greater availability of cows' milk for infant feeding, a consequence of the spread of mixed farming techniques in agriculture (Beaver 1973). Likewise, nutritional improvements – resulting from full employment, rising money wages, increased employment opportunities for women, the effective rationing of essential foodstuffs and the provision of separation allowances for the wives of men in the armed services, together with the substitution of condensed and dried milk for cows' milk, control over the liquor trade and improved sanitation and infant welfare facilities – have been seen as a significant factor in the persistent decline of infant death rates during the years of the First World War (Winter 1976).

To a considerable extent the significance of rising standards of nutrition to declining mortality after 1750 depends on the degree to which rates of mortality in earlier ages were determined by the state of the food supply. If the behaviour of death rates before 1750 can be shown to have exhibited a close association with levels of food output there is at least a prima facie case for supposing that dietary improvement was vital to the increase in life expectancy thereafter. If, on the other hand, mortality rates in earlier ages were determined by forces other than the state of food supplies the case for stressing the role of improving nutrition after 1750 is less logical.[22]

In Scotland and Ireland the quality of the harvest undoubtedly exercised a significant, though not necessarily dominant, influence on levels of mortality during the seventeenth and early eighteenth centuries. True, the Scottish mortality crises of the mid-1630s, later 1640s and early 1680s were not caused by food shortage. But those of 1623, the mid-1670s and the 1690s were, and it is probably no accident that unusually low rates of mortality between the mid-1650s and the end of the 1660s coincided with abnormally low corn prices. In the course of the eighteenth century, except regionally in the mortality crisis of

1739–41 and in the Highlands and Islands until well into the nineteenth century, the influence of harvests on death rates greatly diminished. From the eighteenth century onwards Scotland suffered no harvest failures as calamitous as those of 1623 or the 1690s and food shortages, when they did occur (in 1740, 1756, 1782 and 1799–1801), did not have the same devastating consequences for life expectancy as they had in previous centuries (Flinn 1977). In Ireland the appalling mortality which followed the poor harvests of 1740–1 suggests that there, too, the level of food output was, traditionally, a major determinant of mortality trends, as it was over much of Continental Europe until at least the second half of the eighteenth century (Flinn 1981).[23]

The experience of England appears to have differed. Secular trends in pre-industrial English death rates, perhaps from as far back as the early fourteenth century, show little association with variations in the food supply. The persistence of high rates of mortality in the periods 1350–1470, 1650–99 and 1720–50 coincided with generally low grain prices, abundant employment opportunities and high incomes and low mortality rates in the intervening periods, and again after 1750, with higher prices for food and stable, possibly falling, incomes (Chambers 1972). In London, epidemic disease ran rampant throughout the fifteenth century despite relatively high levels of nutrition while between 1550 and 1750 there appears to have been no regular association between periods of high bread prices on the one hand and outbreaks of plague, smallpox, consumption and tuberculosis on the other, and only a partial correlation between bread prices and the incidence of typhus, 'ague and fever' (Appleby 1975). For England as a whole, from at least as early as the middle of the sixteenth century, neither in the long nor short term was there any consistent relationship between death rates and variations in food prices. Even in years when the price of foodstuffs was extremely high mortality rates climbed only moderately (Wrigley and Schofield 1981). Whether because of the greater productivity and diversity of English agriculture or because of the relative ease with which food supplies could be transported from one part of the country to another (Appleby 1979, 1980a), long before the later eighteenth century temporal and regional fluctuations in English mortality had little connection with the availability of foodstuffs. In this respect, of course, England may have been unique and Ireland and Scotland more typical of the general experience. Even so, the English case should warn us not to make too much of the contribution of rising standards of human nutrition to the modern decline in death rates.

There are, moreover, other grounds for exercising caution over the nutritional interpretation of the rise in life expectancy since the mid-eighteenth century, particularly for that part of it accomplished before 1850. In the first place, the introduction of new food crops may not always have been beneficial. To suggest, for example, that an increase in the supply of cows' milk contributed significantly to the decline in infant death rates during the late eighteenth and early nineteenth centuries ignores both the fact that the overwhelming majority of children continued to be breast-fed and the fact that, until pasteurization, any increase in the use of cows' milk in infant feeding was as likely to raise as lower death rates. Again, not all the new food crops raised yields per acre. The introduction of maize to France tended to strengthen traditional systems of cropping and to retard the adoption of fundamental changes in agricultural methods which would have generated higher output.[24] This, however, did not apply to the potato, the principal crop innovation in Ireland and parts of Britain. Apart from its own direct contribution to higher standards of nutrition, the potato permitted the use of land which would not otherwise have produced crops and, when adopted in rotation with oats and wheat crops, played a major part in raising levels of productivity and the output of arable and livestock products generally (Mokyr 1981). The question is, was the adoption of new crops like the potato more a *response* to falling mortality and higher rates of population growth than their *cause*?

It would certainly be wrong to reject altogether the possibility that the potato had a beneficial effect on nutrition and mortality in those areas where it was widely adopted and where, in earlier ages, poor dietary standards had contributed to high death rates. On the other hand, rising rates of population growth during the late eighteenth and early nineteenth centuries were common to many areas, like much of England, which did not adopt the potato immediately and in which the state of the food supply less obviously determined earlier mortality trends. Even for Ireland 'there is no evidence that the potato was a necessary condition for population growth before the famine ... Population growth would probably have occurred even in the absence of potatoes although at a somewhat slower rate' (Mokyr 1981, pp. 27–8).[25] At most, therefore, the introduction of new food crops can be accorded only limited responsibility for the decline in death rates.

A further weakness in the nutritional interpretation of declining mortality is the absence of unequivocal proof of an increase in average standards of diet before the later decades of the nineteenth century. As late as 1914, low incomes and irregular employment, the skewed distribution of food in favour of adult males at the expense of women and children, the 'misuse' of income on drink and gambling and ignorance of the most effective methods of cooking and the type of foods providing the most nutritious diet kept standards of nutrition among women, children and large sections of the working classes deplorably low.[26] Nonetheless, in the wake of cheap food imports, developments in techniques of food processing, packaging and refrigeration, speedier and less costly methods of transport, advances in retailing services, rising real incomes and, in Ireland, the lessening pressure of population on resources brought about by demographic decline, dietary levels were clearly higher on the eve of the First World War than they had been half a century previously.[27] And, despite widespread economic depression, they continued to improve during the inter-war period.

In the century before 1850, however, the direction and intensity of trends in per capita food output and consumption are less certain. In England average real wages were twice as high in 1850 as 1750, a fact which ought to have been accompanied by a significant, if not necessarily proportionate, improvement in standards of diet.[28] This may not have been the case. Almost all the increase in real incomes in the century before 1850 came after 1820.[29] Until then real wage levels altered little one way or the other. Certainly, there was no improvement sufficient to have made a major impact on standards of diet.

Whatever the significance of real wage and dietary advances to falling mortality after 1820 it is hard to see a similar relationship in the fifty years or so before 1820. More disturbing still is the fact that, except during the period between the mid-sixteenth and mid-seventeenth centuries, from the sixteenth century to the nineteenth the correlation between short-term variations in levels of real wages and rates of mortality was extremely weak, much weaker than that between real wages and trends in either nuptiality or fertility. From at least the mid-thirteenth century long-term fluctuations in mortality were *positively* not *negatively* related to long-swing fluctuations in real wages: when real wages were high so also was mortality; when real wages fell mortality fell (Wrigley and Schofield 1981; Lee 1963).[30] The implication is that it was mortality, through its effect on the growth rate of population and the labour supply, which determined real wage levels rather than real wages which determined levels of mortality.

There is, in any case, no *necessary* association between variations in real income and dietary standards. Additional income may be used for items other than more, or better quality, food. At times of reduced purchasing power levels of nutrition may be protected by a reduction in non-food expenditures (Loschky 1976). Until we know more about patterns of expenditure in the past it is unwise to assume an automatic connection between real wages and variations in nutrition and mortality rates. There is, finally, no direct evidence to prove an increase in per capita food output in the hundred years or so before 1850. In absolute terms, of course, the aggregate supply of food rose substantially. But so did the number of people requiring a share in it. And, in the absence of any precise measurement of the extent to which total food output increased, what happened to trends in per capita supply is unclear.

Such little evidence as there is gives little cause for optimism. For Scotland references in the Old and New Statistical Accounts imply remarkably little change in diet between the 1790s and 1840s.[31] The appalling standards of diet among the Irish labouring population in the years immediately preceding the Great Famine can hardly be taken as evidence of an improvement over earlier times.[32] Dietary standards among agricultural labourers in Kent unquestionably declined during the period of the Revolutionary and Napoleonic Wars and improved thereafter only for those in regular employment.[33]

Neither of the recent leading historians of English diet has been able to demonstrate a significant improvement in human nutrition before the second half of the nineteenth century.[34] Of course, they may be wrong. The evidence on nutritional standards is notoriously fickle and difficult to interpret. Nevertheless, even if there was an increase in per capita food output and standards of nutrition in the course of the period 1750–1850 we need to know much more about the extent of the increase and the manner in which it was distributed throughout the community before we can conclude that it played a major, let alone *the* major, part in the early decline in death rates (Benson 1976).

CONCLUSION

The only safe conclusion that can be reached about the rise in life expectancy between the mid-eighteenth and mid-twentieth centuries is that its causes were diverse – a complex mixture of influences, each varying in strength from time to time and area to area. In view of the frailties of the supporting evidence, to suggest that any one of them predominated is premature and probably misleading. In part, particularly in the century before 1850, the improvement in life expectancy stemmed from an alteration in the relationship between micro-organisms and their hosts, a change for which man can be given no responsibility. But overall, perhaps even in the period prior to 1850, it owed most to man's increasing ability to reduce his contact with disease organisms or minimize their fatality when they struck. And, from the later decades of the nineteenth century certainly, the evidence of medical innovation, improvements in public health and personal hygiene and rising levels of nutrition is sufficient to suggest that, recently at least, man himself has been the primary cause of his own increasing longevity.

Precisely which aspects of these activities have been most responsible for the decline in death rates in recent decades, however, remains obscure. Some would give greatest emphasis to rising levels of income and nutrition (McKeown 1976). Others would point out that even without improvements in income and diet the life expectancy of Englishmen would have risen from fifty to seventy years between 1901/10 and the 1970s. Assuming that drugs and vaccines had little effect before the 1940s, the main explanation must lie with advances in health hygiene – better antiseptic and quarantine practices, purer food and water, improved methods of infant-feeding and higher standards of personal cleanliness (Preston 1975). For the period between the mid-eighteenth and mid-nineteenth centuries the degree of uncertainty is still greater. Not only is it unclear how much responsibility should be allotted to 'autonomous' forces it is equally difficult to assess the relative influence of each of the various, potential 'human' causes of rising life expectation. We simply do not know enough about trends in personal hygiene, standards of nutrition or the effectiveness of particular medical treatments to judge properly the significance of each against the other or their global influence compared with that of 'autonomous' agencies.

There remains, finally, the possibility that the current search for the origins of declining mortality fails to probe deeply enough. In so far as it has stemmed from improvements made by man to his personal and environmental circumstances we may need to look more closely at the motives prompting such improvements. *Why* is modern society more concerned with enhancing life expectancy than societies of earlier times – *why* its search for better hygiene, effective medical treatment, higher standards of nutrition and a fairer distribution of resources? Is it merely the result of a better understanding of how disease is transmitted? How far does it relate to the need for a healthier population in the economic, political or military interest? To what extent is it the result of rising humanitarianism or of economic, social and political changes which have altered the relationships of individuals, families and groups to the general community? It has recently been argued, for example, that improvements in the education of women are critical to the emergence of conditions which lead ultimately to lower death-rates in infancy and childhood. The more educated the woman, the greater her ability to provide satisfactory standards of food and child care without imposing undue strain on the family budget, the greater the ease with which she breaks with traditional methods of child care and the traditional resignation to illness, the more insistent she will be for effective medical treatment and the more likely to implement efficiently the advice received, the greater her influence on family decision-making processes and, thus, the more likely these decisions are to favour the interests of the child (Caldwell 1979). Could it be that part of the explanation for improvements in domestic hygiene and the facilities for maternal and child welfare during the twentieth century lies in the rise in standards of female education which occurred throughout the second half of the nineteenth?[35]

Or does the explanation lie elsewhere – in other economic, social or cultural forces which improved the status of women or reduced levels of marital fertility, thereby intensifying society's concern to ensure the survival of those who were born? As yet, we do not know. Until we have a deeper appreciation of the motives underlying the adoption of life-saving medical and public health innovations or the commitment to ensuring adequate supplies of food and other essential resources for even the very poorest our understanding of the causes of the secular decline in mortality between the mid-eighteenth and mid-twentieth centuries will remain seriously incomplete.

NOTES AND REFERENCES

1. McKeown and Record 1962–3; McKeown, Record and Turner 1975; Flinn 1977.
2. Air-borne infections include bronchitis, pneumonia, influenza, respiratory tuberculosis, scarlet and rheumatic fever, nephritis, whooping cough, measles, diphtheria, smallpox and infections of the ear, pharynx and larynx. The main food- or water-borne infections are diarrhoea, dysentery, cholera, typhoid, enteric fever and non-respiratory tuberculosis. Other ailments caused by micro-organisms include typhus, convulsions, teething, syphilis, appendicitis, peritonitis and puerperal fever. Among the principal causes of death not associated with micro-organisms are premature birth, alcoholism, rickets, non-infective respiratory diseases, various diseases of the digestive and nervous systems, infanticide and malnutrition.
3. For a discussion of the causes underlying the disappearance of plague see Appleby 1980b; Flinn 1979, 1981; Slack 1981.
4. The dispensary was opened in London in 1697 by the College of Physicians. It closed in 1725 (Woodward 1974).
5. In Glasgow, however, sick inmates at the Town's Hospital, founded in 1733 primarily as a workhouse, had long been treated free of charge by members of the Faculty of Physicians and Surgeons (Pennington 1977).
6. One possible exception to this was the 'lying-in' or maternity hospitals where the use of forceps in child delivery and a failure to improve standards of hygiene in the labour-room initially increased maternal and child mortality.
7. On the improvement in the professional competence of midwives following the Midwives Act of 1902, for example, see Forbes 1971.
8. On the contrary, according to one authority, the smallpox virus became more not less virulent in the course of the eighteenth century (Luckin 1977).
9. The various therapies used in the nineteenth century to treat victims of cholera, for example, are described as useless, unpleasant and often fatal (Howard-Jones 1972).
10. See, for instance, **Chapman, S.** (ed.) (1971), *The History of Working Class Housing,* Newton Abbott; **Butt, J.** (1971), 'Working class housing in Glasgow, 1851–1914', in *ibid;* **Trebble, J. H.** (1971), 'Liverpool working class housing, 1801–51', in *ibid;* **Gauldie, E.** (1974), *Cruel habitations: a history of working class housing, 1780–1918,* London; McKeown 1978; **Dingle A. E.** (1982), 'The monster nuisance of all': landowners, alkali manufacturers and air pollution, 1828–64, *Economic History Review,* xxxv, 4.
11. **Burnett, J.** (1968), *Plenty and Want,* London.
12. **Gauldie** (1974).
13. **O'Neill, T. P.** (1973), 'Poverty in Ireland, 1815–45', *Folk Life,* 11.
14. Connell 1950; **O'Neill, T. P.** (1974), 'Fever and public health in pre-famine Ireland', *Journal of the Royal Society of the Antiquaries of Ireland,* CIII.
15. Throughout western and central Europe areas of extensive handicraft industry had higher rates of infant mortality and lower levels of life

expectancy than areas where agriculture was the sole means of livelihood (Fischer 1973).

16. **Burnett** (1968).

17. See especially **Thane, P.** (1981), 'Social history, 1860–1914', in **Floud, R.** and **McCloskey, D.** (eds.), *The Economic History of Britain Since 1700,* vol. 2, Cambridge.

18. *Ibid.,* **Wohl, A. S.** (1971) 'The housing of the working classes in London, 1815–1914' in **Chapman, S.** (ed.), *The History of Working Class Housing,* Newton Abbott.

19. Drake 1963–4, 1969; Almquist 1979; O'Grada 1979; Daultrey, Dickson and O'Grada 1981.

20. Cullen 1972, 1981. The decline in infant and child mortality at Blaris (Lisburn) between the mid-eighteenth and early nineteenth centuries has also been explained by an increase in levels of nutrition (Morgan 1976).

21. It has been suggested that over half the total fall in mortality between the middle of the nineteenth century and 1914 was due to improvements in standards of living, among which the consumption of more and better foods was the most significant. **Baines, D.** (1981), 'The labour supply and the labour market 1860–1914', in **Floud, R.** and **McCloskey, D.** (eds.), *The Economic History of Britain Since 1700,* vol. 2, Cambridge.

22. A good illustration of the point is the German State of Bavaria where an increase in per capita food output in the first half of the nineteenth century was not accompanied by a fall in mortality because nutritional levels in the eighteenth century were not sufficiently low to have acted as the major determinant of high death rates. **Lee, W. R.** (1977), 'Primary sector output and mortality changes in early nineteenth century Bavaria', *Journal of European Economic History,* 6, 1.

23. In Ireland, as events in the second quarter of the nineteenth century show, any lessening in the influence of harvest conditions on mortality during the second half of the eighteenth and early nineteenth centuries was temporary.

24. **Hohenberg, P. M.** (1977), 'Maize in French agriculture', *Journal of European Economic History,* 6, 1.

25. See also the argument in Cullen 1968.

26. **Barker, T. C.** 'Nineteenth-century diet: some twentieth-century questions', in **Barker, T. C.** *et al.* (eds) (1966), *Our Changing Fare,* London; **Burnett** (1968); **Oddy, D. J.** (1970), 'Working class diets in late nineteenth-century Britain', *Economic History Review,* XXIII, 2; **Schofield, E. M.** (1971), 'Food and cooking of the working class about 1900', *Transactions of the Historic Society of Lancashire and Cheshire,* 123; **Thane** (1981).

27. **Blackman, J.** (1966), Changing marketing methods and food consumption, in **Barker, T. C.** *et al.* (eds), *Our Changing Fare,* London; **Burnett** (1968); **Johnstone, G. B.** (1976), 'The growth of the sugar trade and refining industry' in **Oddy, D. J.** and **Miller, D.** (eds), *The Making of the Modern British Diet,* London; **Mathias, P.** (1976), The British tea trade in the nineteenth century, in *ibid;* **Supple, B.** (1981), 'Income and demand 1860–1914' in **Floud, R.** and **McCloskey, D.** (eds), *The Economic History of Britain Since 1700,* vol. 2, Cambridge.

28. On real wage trends in England see **Lindert, P. H.** and **Williamson, J. G.**

(1983), 'English workers' living standards during the Industrial Revolution: a new look', *Economic History Review,* XXXVI, 1.

29. *Ibid.* See also **Flinn, M. W.** (1974), 'Trends in real wages, 1750–1850', *Economic History Review,* XXVII, 3.

30. It should be stressed, however, that the Phelps-Brown and Hopkins index of real wages upon which these conclusions are based may be a highly imperfect guide to trends in real purchasing power among the majority of the population. See below pp. 101–2.

31. **Campbell, R. H.** (1966), 'Diet in Scotland: an example of regional variation', in **Barker, T. C.** *et al.* (eds) (1966), *Our Changing Fare,* London.

32. **O'Neill** (1973, 1974).

33. **Richardson, T. L.** (1966), 'The agricultural labourer's standard of living in Kent, 1790–1840', in **Barker, T. C.** *et al.* (eds), *Our Changing Fare,* London.

34. Blackman in *ibid;* **Burnett** (1968).

35. For a discussion of female literacy rates see **Schofield, R.** (1973), 'Dimensions of illiteracy, 1750–1850', *Explorations in Economic History,* 10, 4; **Sanderson, M.** (1983), *Education, Economic Change and Society in England, 1780–1870,* London.

Chapter 4

THE RISE AND FALL OF FERTILITY

The causes of the rise in levels of legitimate and illegitimate fertility which occurred during the late eighteenth and early nineteenth centuries and of their subsequent, long-term decline from the last quarter of the nineteenth remain matters of considerable dispute. On only one aspect of the controversy is there any unanimity. Secular trends in fertility owed little to variations in human fecundity.[1] Rather, they were determined, overwhelmingly, by men and women exercising their choices about whether or not to marry, when to marry and how many children to have within and without marriage in response to the changing circumstances of the environment in which they lived. The suggestion that low rates of marital fertility at Colyton (Devon) between 1647 and 1719 were due to abnormally high levels of sterility and natural abortion among women who had contracted but survived the plague of 1645–6 takes no account of the fact that the numbers involved were too small to have had more than a marginal impact on aggregate fertility rates or of the fact that low rates of fertility persisted well into the eighteenth century.[2] To see rising levels of fecundity, the product of better health and diet, as a major contributor to the increase in fertility during the late eighteenth and early nineteenth centuries ignores the fact that advances in health and diet before 1850 were at best marginal. There is, in any case, no clear evidence of a connection between food intake and levels of human fecundity during periods of malnutrition.[3] To suggest, as did many contemporaries, that at least part of the long-term fall in rates of fertility which began in the late nineteenth century stemmed from declining levels of fecundity is obviously erroneous. Judging from the continued decrease in average ages at menarche,[4] human fecundity has risen, not fallen, in recent generations. It is, therefore, primarily in the area of human motivation, and the circumstances which determind it, that we must look for our explanations of secular and temporal variations in levels of fertility.[5]

ILLEGITIMATE FERTILITY

Theoretically, variations in rates of non-marital fertility may be due to one of a number of influences: the size of the population 'at risk' – itself determined by changes in the age at menarche, in ages at marriage and proportions marrying, in the sex ratio of the unmarried population and in the proportion of the total population in the age-groups at which illegitimacy was most common; the quality of registration procedures; the definition of what constituted a marriage; and variations in the likelihood of marriage taking place between conception and birth. In practice some of these agencies made little contribution to the most significant temporal and regional differentials in illegitimacy which have occurred in Britain and Ireland since the middle of the eighteenth century.

There is, for instance, no obvious correlation between rates of illegitimacy and variations in the size of the population 'at risk', whatever the mechanism responsible for such variations. Rising rates of illegitimacy in the late eighteenth and early nineteenth centuries cannot be explained by the effects of a decline in ages at first menstruation on the number of girls 'at risk' since the average age at menarche was already well below the age-groups at which illegitimacy was most common; and the decline in levels of bastardy during the late nineteenth and first half of the twentieth centuries took place in a context of falling, not rising, ages at menarche. Nor can regional and temporal differences in non-marital fertility be seen as a consequence of variations in ages at marriage or proportions marrying. High rates of illegitimacy were not caused by sexual frustration arising from delayed marriage. Whenever and wherever illegitimacy rates were relatively high, ages at marriage and proportions unmarried were relatively low. Low levels of bastardy invariably correlated with unusually high ages at marriage and rates of celibacy (Laslett and Oosterveen 1973). The increase in illegitimacy in late eighteenth- and early nineteenth-century England occurred against a background of falling, not rising, ages at marriage and increasing, not decreasing, marriage rates. In post-Famine Ireland levels of bastardy were low despite very high ages at marriage and proportions celibate. In nineteenth-century Scotland regional differentials in rates of illegitimacy bore no obvious relationship to ages at marriage and proportions marrying (Smout 1976, 1977; Flinn 1977). Indeed, since illegitimate offspring were more commonly born to working-class not middle-class girls, who tended to marry relatively late, and to girls in their late teens rather than their mid-twenties, the normal age at marriage, it is difficult to see how variations in nuptiality could have had much of an impact on illegitimacy rates.

Neither does there appear to be any sustained relationship between regional variations in bastardy and the ratio between the sexes. In nineteenth-century Scotland areas with higher than normal ratios of women to men did not necessarily equate with those of unusually high illegitimacy levels (Smout 1976, 1977; Flinn 1977). The rarity of bastardy in post-Famine Ireland, where the ratio of women to men was distinctly greater than on mainland Britain, itself negates the likelihood that high rates of illegitimacy had their origins in sex ratios that were unfavourable to women. Neither numbers in the age-groups most prone to bastardy nor the balance between the sexes and the extent of nuptiality in those age-groups seem to have had much of an effect on non-marital fertility. And while part of the explanation for low levels of Irish bastardy and for lower levels of urban than rural illegitimacy in nineteenth-century Scotland may involve relative deficiencies in methods of registering illegitimates, it is also inconceivable that variations in the efficiency of registration practices were responsible for the more significant regional and secular differentials in illegitimacy which have occurred since the middle of the eighteenth century. Rising rates of bastardy in the late eighteenth and early nineteenth centuries were associated with a deterioration, not an improvement, in the quality of birth registration, whereas in the second half of the nineteenth and early twentieth centuries, when rates of illegitimacy were low and falling, registration procedures were better than ever before.

Nor can regional and temporal trends in non-marital fertility be accounted for by differences in the definitions of marriage. For one thing, the explanation is of no relevance to the decline in illegitimacy which began in the later nineteenth century, by which time the definition of a legal marriage was standardized. For another, it is hard to see how it can account for the complex pattern of variation in illegitimacy rates from area to area, least of all from parish to parish.

A recent attempt to explain the rise in bastardy in late eighteenth-century England as merely an artefact of Hardwicke's Clandestine Marriage Act of 1753 is equally dubious. Before the implementation of the Act, it is argued, the children of 'irregular' unions were invariably registered as legitimate by parochial clergymen. After it, only unions celebrated in church were considered legally valid, and clergymen were instructed to regard the offspring of all other forms of marriage as illegitimate. Because the Act did not appreciably diminish the number of 'irregular' unions rates of bastardy necessarily rose (Meteyard 1980, 1981).

Whatever partial merit this thesis may have, its general validity is questionable on various counts. First, such was the mobility of men and women in the eighteenth century that it would have been difficult for parochial clergymen to attest the validity of many marriages even if they had wished to do so. Second, there is little doubt that the number of clandestine unions *did* decline considerably following Hardwicke's Act, to very low levels by the early nineteenth century. Third, it takes no account of the great variations in levels of illegitimacy which occurred in earlier centuries and which can only be explained in other ways. Fourth, if the change in the law relating to marriage was so important why was there no sudden, once-for-all, rise in levels of bastardy in the years immediately following its implementation and why did bastardy continue to rise during the later years of the eighteenth and early years of the nineteenth centuries (Stone 1981)? Lastly, it overlooks the fact that most illegitimate children were the result of casual sexual encounters by girls in their late teens and early twenties scarcely of an age to have formed a regular consensual union.

It follows, then, that variations in rates of non-marital fertility were essentially a product of genuine differences in sexual habits, differences which were largely independent of changes in sex ratios, nuptiality rates or the size of the group 'at risk' and which cannot be accounted for either by the varying adequacy of registration procedures or changing definitions of marriage.

According to one view, the increase in rates of illegitimacy which occurred in England and elsewhere during the late eighteenth and early nineteenth centuries was the result of nothing less than a revolution in standards of premarital sexual morality in the course of which the sexual chastity typical of earlier generations gave way to thorough-going sexual licence. Underlying this revolution was the process of industrialization and the increased opportunities this provided for women to find decently-rewarded employment outside the household and family. The greater independence and sense of self-determination among unmarried women to which these opportunities gave rise encouraged them to rebel against the constraints hitherto imposed by parents on the premarital sexual relationships of their children. Sex was no longer simply the means of procreation but a pleasure to be enjoyed. Inevitably, in the absence of effective methods of birth control, the consequence was rising levels of bridal pregnancy and illegitimacy. Only later in the nineteenth century, when effective birth control practices began to spread to the working classes, could premarital sex be enjoyed with less risk of conception. As the knowledge and means of contraception spread, non-marital fertility, like marital fertility, declined (Shorter, Knodel and Van de Walle 1971; Shorter 1973, 1977).

Apart from a lack of direct evidence to support the notion of a decline in standards of premarital sexual morality since the late eighteenth century, numerous critics have pointed to the inherent shakiness of many of the assumptions upon which the thesis is founded. To begin with, because of the value of their contribution to the economy of the family, pre-industrial women, even unmarried daughters living with their parents, were not as devoid of self-determination or influence within the household as Shorter and his supporters suppose. In any case, industrialization did not immediately revolutionize women's work. Even accepting that opportunities for female employment outside the home increased in the course of the Industrial Revolution, and at least one historian believes they did not,[6] the increase was moderate and, initially, brought little change in the type of employment women pursued. Long before the Industrial Revolution large numbers of young, single women worked away from their families, usually in the kinds of occupation which continued to dominate female labour throughout the nineteenth century – domestic service or the traditional craft and 'sweated' industries. Even at the end of the century the number employed in factory work was small.

Nor should it be too readily assumed that employment away from their families necessarily increased the sense of independence among young women. Women's earnings were usually too small to allow them to live independent lives. Their search for work outside the home was as much an attempt to strengthen than weaken family bonds by reducing the numbers immediately dependent on the resources of the household or increasing the amount of income available to it. Girls frequently sent part of their earnings back to their families and, invariably, maintained close contact with them. The good of the family – rather than self-interest – was the main motive underlying the search for work.

The Shorter thesis also sits uncomfortably with what is now known about patterns of bridal pregnancy and illegitimacy in pre-industrial England. Illegitimacy rates in late sixteenth- and early seventeenth-century England were not so far below those of the late eighteenth and early nineteenth centuries as to suggest that a major transformation in sexual conduct occurred with the onset of industrialization. In fact, in parts of Lancashire and Cheshire, levels of bastardy were noticeably higher in late Elizabethan times than in the early years of the nineteenth century (Laslett and Oosterveen 1973). And if, as Shorter maintains, the sexual revolution was a product of urban-industrialization, why did illegitimacy begin to rise from as early as the 1720s, why was the increase in bastardy common to so many Western European societies where industrial development and the growth of opportunities for female employment were less apparent than in England, why in England is there no evidence of a close regional correlation between levels of illegitimacy and the extent of urban-industrial development, and why, in nineteenth-century Scotland, were bastardy rates lower in urban-industrial than rural areas?

Recent research also tentatively suggests that high and rising rates of bastardy were due more to an increase in the number of illegitimates born to women already prone to bastard-bearing than to a general increase in the proportion of the female population bearing children outside wedlock (Laslett and Oosterveen 1973; Connolly 1979). Admittedly, the case for interpreting regional and temporal differentials in bastardy as a response to variations in the activities of a sub-culture of bastard-bearers rests on flimsy evidence. In some instances it clearly does not apply.[7] But if it does prove to be generally valid we must conclude that high and rising illegitimacy was not so much the result of sexual liberation among the unmarried female population at large as the consequence of an increase in the frequency of bastard-bearing among women who already displayed a considerable degree of freedom in their sexual behaviour. Perhaps the rise in illegitimacy during the eighteenth and early nineteenth centuries merely reflected the passing of a seventeenth-century Puritan discipline which had been hostile to bastard-bearers and had successfully curbed their activities (Laslett and Oosterveen 1973).

These criticisms do not imply that regional and temporal differences in attitudes towards pre-marital sexual behaviour had no influence on levels of illegitimacy. In specific cases they undoubtedly did. Of the various explanations for low levels of bridal pregnancy and bastardy in eighteenth- and nineteenth-century Ireland – the small size of the domestic servant population, the closeness of parent–child relationships, the absence of a bastardy law and, until 1838, of a poor law – the strength of popular disapproval of premarital sex, reinforced by the 'iron morality' of the Church and the great influence of its priests over their flock, was arguably the most significant (Connell 1968b; Connolly 1979). The lower levels of illegitimacy in urban rather than rural nineteenth-century Scotland similarly owed something to the sterner attitudes displayed in urban communities towards premarital sex, in this case a reflection of the presence of a middle-class population and of a 'labour aristocracy' of skilled artisans and clerks who were intolerant of sexual licence and whose own attitudes and behaviour may have percolated to other groups in the community (Smout 1976; Flinn 1977). We should not, however, too easily generalize the influence of such factors.

The assumption that the decline in rates of illegitimacy from the later decades of the nineteenth century was due primarily to the spread of new techniques of birth control rests on equally shaky foundations. After all, low levels of bastardy prevailed in Ireland despite widespread hostility to all forms of birth control other than delayed marriage or sexual abstinence. Again, it is likely that both the knowledge and practice of birth control was wider among urban than rural working-class girls. It is, therefore, surprising to note that the late nineteenth-century decline in Scottish illegitimacy rates began sooner and proceeded faster in rural than urban areas (Flinn 1977). Moreover, working-class women were already practising rudimentary methods of birth control – abortion, coitus interruptus, infanticide – long before the late nineteenth century (see pp. 109–12). New techniques developed by and for the middle classes towards the end of the century were at first little used by working-class society and cannot, therefore, be regarded as more than marginally relevant to the initial fall in bastardy levels. Of course, it may be that unmarried working-class girls of the late nineteenth century more often resorted to traditional birth control practices than their predecessors. But this is a very different proposition from that advanced by Shorter. And even if a greater resort to contraception did make a significant contribution to the decline in levels of bastardy it is still necessary to explain why this occurred. Shorter provides no such explanation.

The main alternative explanation for the secular rise and fall in rates of illegitimate fertility which has taken place in so many countries since the late eighteenth century also sees it as primarily a response to the forces of economic change. In contrast to the Shorter interpretation, however, it does not depend on a sexual liberation among women to account for the initial rise in bastardy or on the dissemination of new methods of birth control to explain its subsequent decline. Instead, its premise is that unmarried women engaged in sexual activity not to satisfy their desire for sexual pleasure or to demonstrate their independence from the family but simply in the expectation that it would lead to marriage: and the reasons why pregnancy less often led to marriage in the late eighteenth and early nineteenth centuries than ever before lay in the effects of economic growth on the circumstances of their lives. Economic development in rural as well as urban areas greatly increased the number of unskilled and propertyless men and women whose incomes were low and employment prospects uncertain and who lacked the protection traditionally afforded by family and kin. It also led to an increase in the extent of geographic mobility, particularly among the unskilled sections of the population. Driven by loneliness, poverty or the restrictions of domestic service into sexual liaisons in the hope that marriage would follow, young girls all too often found themselves deserted by poorly-paid, propertyless men, forced to be highly mobile in the search for work and lacking the supports of family and possessions to provide any alternative. The consequence was a rise in bastardy rates.

By the late nineteenth century circumstances were changing. The number of women in 'sexually vulnerable' employments like domestic service began to decline. So, too, did the flow of young female immigrants to the cities. The growth of factory employment and higher levels of working-class prosperity reduced the numbers of men and women forced to search for work far from the protection and security of their families. At the same time, increased working-class prosperity and the acquisition of goods and property which this facilitated endowed marriage with a new attractiveness (Tilly, Scott and Cohen 1976; Weeks 1981; Stone 1981). Perhaps, too, rising standards of education, improvements in transport and communications, a growing familiarity with the conditions of urban life and the slackening pace of urbanization itself helped to combat the loneliness and insecurity which had hitherto increased the likelihood of premarital pregnancy.

A similar interpretation has recently been advanced to account for the late nineteenth-century decline of illegitimacy in rural Scotland. There, also, reduced levels of bastardy are seen as the outcome of certain features of economic change, none of which required the adoption of new methods of birth control to work their effects: in the rural south-east, the demise of the bondager and bothy systems: in the rural north-east, the disappearance of 'chaumer' and 'kitchen' methods of housing farm labour: the general decline in domestic handicraft industries like millinery which made it more difficult for a woman to find the kind of work that allowed her to care for a child by herself; and the rise of working-class incomes which increased the desire for respectability and generated more hostility to illegitimacy (Flinn, 1977).[8]

Although further research is required to substantiate it, this interpretation of bastardy trends appears more convincing than Shorter's, not least because it provides a more acceptable explanation for the marked regional differentials which existed in rates of illegitimacy. Low levels of bastardy in Ireland, for example, can be readily seen as a combined result of the small proportion of domestic servants (the group most 'at risk') in the population (Connell 1968b), the limited extent of internal migration, the predominance of peasant farming (see pp. 145, 183), and the smaller, generally more settled nature of Irish communities. Higher levels of bastardy in the rural north-east and south than north and north-west of Scotland can be explained by the fact that, in the latter, courtship practices more often stopped short of sexual intercourse and, when pregnancy did occur, it was more likely to be followed by marriage.[9] Both factors were related to the strictness of parental supervision over the premarital sexual behaviour of their children and this, in turn, was conditioned by economic circumstances. In areas of keen parental control and low illegitimacy agriculture was dominated by small peasant farms which yielded a poor living and relied almost entirely on offspring for their labour supply. A daughter with an illegitimate child would impose a heavy financial burden on such a farm. In such areas the absence of a mobile wage labour force made it easier for parents to trace the man responsible for their daughter's pregnancy and to pressure his family into forcing him to marry her. By contrast, in those parts of rural Scotland where illegitimacy rates were higher agriculture was based on larger, more prosperous farms dependent on highly mobile wage labourers for their workforce. Agricultural workers, male and female, usually lived away from their parents and were therefore less subject to their influence. Their living arrangements in bothies, chaumers or farm kitchens, where they were left largely unsupervised, allowed them to mix freely with the opposite sex and positively encouraged sexual liaisons. Additionally, because of the dependence of capitalist farmers on hired labour and thus the relative ease of finding employment, unmarried mothers were less of a burden to their parents while the extreme mobility of male agricultural labourers in such areas made it difficult for parents to enforce marriage even if they wished to (Smout 1976, 1977; Carter 1977).

To date, little work has been done on the complex pattern of short-term and parish-by-parish variations in rates of bastardy. It is likely anyway that these will prove to be beyond the powers of generalized explanation. The nature and causes of longer-term, more broadly regional variations in levels of illegitimacy are more easily identifiable. On the whole, these appear to have depended on the economic forces of income differentials and differences in the level of employment opportunities and the character of productive systems. The influence of variations in sexual behaviour, in the availability of birth-control techniques and in the extent of a sub-culture of the bastard-prone was more limited, particularly since these factors are themselves to some extent determined by the pressure of economic conditions.

LEGITIMATE FERTILITY

In the pre-industrial world variations in ages at marriage and proportions marrying played a critical part in determining levels of legitimate fertility (Ohlin 1960–1; Lesthaege 1971; Chojnacka 1976). Even allowing for an increase in the frequency of child-bearing within marriage (marital fertility), much, probably most, of the rise in legitimate fertility in England and Ireland during the late eighteenth and early nineteenth centuries was due to rising rates of nuptiality. In the case of Ireland the behaviour of nuptiality remained the critical determinant of trends in rates of legitimate fertility throughout the nineteenth and early twentieth centuries. Only in the interwar period did changes in the frequency of childbirth within marriage begin to play a significant role in deciding the evolution of Irish fertility rates. In England/Wales and Scotland, however, though falling nuptiality made some contribution to the initial phases of the long-term decline in fertility which began in the late nineteenth century, the modern transition to lower fertility norms was mainly due to declining levels of marital fertility. It follows that any explanation for regional and secular variations in rates of legitimate fertility since the middle of the eighteenth century must take account of factors which affected both levels of nuptiality and the regularity of childbirth within marriage.

Reviewing the literature on the rise in English and Irish legitimate fertility rates during the late eighteenth and early nineteenth centuries suggests two possible explanations. The first sees it as a delayed and largely accidental response to an earlier period of rising nuptiality and fertility: the second as the outcome of various non-demographic changes which occurred only in the late eighteenth and early nineteenth century itself.

Professor Eversley, many years ago, was the first to argue that in part the late eighteenth-century fertility increase was merely the natural consequence of a 'bulge-generation' created during the third quarter of the century by the low mortality and high marriage and fertility rates which followed the passing of the demographic crisis of the years 1720–50 (Eversley 1957). Recently, a more sophisticated version of this 'delayed-response' thesis has been developed by Wrigley and Schofield. Their argument runs as follows. Children born and brought up in the relative affluence of the second quarter of the eighteenth century, when opportunities for employment were abundant and real wages high, were inclined to marry unusually early when they reached marriageable age in the third quarter of the century, despite the fact that economic conditions then were less conducive to early marriage than they had been for their parents. In the absence of effective means of controlling births within marriage, this rise in nuptiality inevitably swelled birth rates during the last quarter of the eighteenth century. Thus, the rise in rates of English fertility in the early years of the Industrial Revolution simply reflected what had happened to real wages half a century before. In the same manner, the reduction or stabilization of real wages during the 1770s and 1780s resulted in declining fertility between 1815 and the mid-1830s, while higher real wages in the early years of the nineteenth century were followed by rising levels of nuptiality after the mid-1830s and of fertility after 1851 (Wrigley and Schofield 1981; Wrigley 1983).

The validity of the Wrigley and Schofield thesis rests on the adequacy of three assumptions: first, that the Phelps Brown and Hopkins index of real wage trends upon which, with certain modifications, they depend is reliable: second, that children's attitudes to marriage are formed by the level of their parents' income rather than by other circumstances of the environment within which they are raised: third, that individuals base their nuptiality decisions more on the events of their 'remembered past' than on their immediate prospects for marriage.

All three assumptions are debatable. As the authors themselves admit, the influence of childhood experiences on the timing and extent of marriage, and the relative significance of parental incomes in determining such experiences, is entirely inferential. They provide no support for their contentions that the 'remembered past' was more important in shaping nuptiality rates than the immediate present and that the real incomes of parents were of greater importance than other factors in shaping the character of childhood experiences. The latest in a long line of critics of the Phelps Brown and Hopkins index as a guide to real wage trends roundly condemns it as of little relevance to incomes among the great majority of the labouring population.[10] It requires nerves of steel to assume that the wage *rates* of building craftsmen and labourers in the London and Lancashire areas satisfactorily represent average global trends in *actual earnings* when they take no account of the complexity of regional and occupational experience, of variations in the extent of unemployment and underemployment, in the significance of earnings in kind or the contribution of female and child earnings to family income. Price trends are better reflected than earnings in the Phelps Brown and Hopkins data. But even these are marred by a failure

101

to include costs of accommodation and to allow for the addition to the food supply of new crops like the potato. In short, the Phelps Brown and Hopkins price and wage indices are 'a terribly frail foundation for the very substantial superstructure erected on them' (Flinn 1982, p. 456). The Wrigley and Schofield thesis, therefore, remains unproven. In view of this, it is surely premature to dismiss the possibility that the rise in fertility which occurred in the late eighteenth and early nineteenth centuries owed at least something to conditions that prevailed contemporaneously with it.

What these conditions were is far from clear. One suggestion, that the increase in fertility was a result of the adoption of more liberal methods of poor relief in the years between the 1780s and the passing of the Poor Law Amendment Act of 1834 (Krause 1958–9), has too often been tested and found wanting to be acceptable. Apart from the fact that the more generous forms of outdoor relief associated with the Speenhamland system were restricted geographically, the overall level of allowances was far too small to encourage unduly early marriage and reckless breeding (Blaug 1963). County by county variations in fertility ratios in 1821 display no obvious correlation with variations in the level of per capita expenditure on poor relief during the years 1817–21 (Tucker 1975).

The evidence for two Kent parishes – Lenham, which gave allowances in aid of wages, and Barham, which did not – likewise shows no relationship between poor relief and the behaviour of nuptiality and fertility (Huzel 1969). Admittedly, by itself the Lenham/Barham analysis is inconclusive. The economies of the two parishes were not alike. Levels of employment and prosperity at Barham were higher than at Lenham and this may explain why the provision of poor relief by the latter failed to produce greater levels of nuptiality and fertility. The real question, to which Huzel's study does not address itself, is whether marriage and birth rates at Lenham would have been much lower in the absence of poor relief.

Results from a group of 22 parishes spanning fifteen counties and 49 parishes in the county of Kent are more difficult to deny, however. Here marriage and birth rates actually *rose* in the period following the abolition of allowances in aid of wages; allowance-paying parishes tended to have lower rates of nuptiality and fertility than those which gave no wage-supplements; parishes paying child allowances from the first child had lower, not higher, marriage and birth rates than most other parishes. It is more plausible, therefore, to see the adoption of 'generous' systems of poor relief as a response to rapid population growth, and the economic problems to which it so often gave rise, rather than its cause (Huzel 1980). The possible increase of fertility in Ireland, where liberal poor law allowances were lacking, reinforces this view.

Potentially more acceptable explanations of the late eighteenth- and early nineteenth-century fertility increase involve the effects of economic growth. Arguably this worked to stimulate birth rates in one of several ways:

(i) through the effect it had on the character of employment;
(ii) by increasing the employment ratio, that is, the proportion of the total population in work;
(iii) holding the employment ratio constant, by causing an increase in per capita real wages.

THE CHARACTER OF EMPLOYMENT

According to one variant of this interpretation the trend towards earlier marriage and higher fertility was related to the decay of apprenticeship systems in manufacturing and, in agricultural areas, to a decline in the frequency with which farmworkers 'lived in' with their employers (Habakkuk 1953; Krause 1958). A second variant argues that it resulted from changes in the distribution of the labour force towards occupations with traditionally high rates of nuptiality: from agriculture to manufacturing; from crafts and trades to coal-mining, factory textiles, metallurgy and engineering, pottery, brick and glass manufacture; from the low wage south to the high wage north; from rural to urban residence with its greater opportunities for employment and youthful age structures more favourable to early marriage (Habakkuk 1958). In Ireland, for example, rising levels of nuptiality and fertility have been explained partly by the switch from livestock to arable farming which came with population growth and rising English demand for grain and partly by the spread of the domestic, handicraft textile industry. Arable farms needed little capital to acquire or stock and provided more employment than those devoted to livestock. The adoption of the potato, together with the willingness of landlords to allow subdivision in order to swell the size of their rent rolls, made even the smallest arable holdings economically viable.[11] Handicraft industries, too, required little capital, and where they were common, in the north and west of Ireland, supplied the extra income necessary for early marriage and high levels of marital fertility (Almquist 1979; Collins 1982).

Closely associated with the decline in apprenticeship and 'living in' and changes in the occupational distribution of the population were the effects of an increasing proletarianization of the workforce. In those areas where it occurred, the transformation of peasants and artisans into propertyless wage- earners weakened the traditional social controls over marriage and fertility which had come from the ownership of property or possession of particular skills. Late marriage and controlled fertility were less essential for people having no skills to learn or property to protect and among whom rates of infant and child mortality were relatively high and the need for higher fertility norms therefore greater (Fischer 1973; Levine 1976b; Yasumoto 1981).

There is at least some evidence to support the view that changes in the nature of employment had not insignificant effects on levels of fertility. In eighteenth- and early nineteenth-century England regional variations in marriage and fertility rates correlated closely and positively with variations in the pace of industrial development (Deane and Cole 1967).[12] In England/Wales in 1861 regional differences in marriage patterns were also closely related to residential and employment conditions. Although the impact of urbanization on nuptiality was by no means consistent, men and women undoubtedly improved their prospects of marriage by moving from rural to urban areas and from agricultural to non-agricultural employments. More significant still was the relationship between levels of nuptiality and the extent of 'traditional' or 'non-traditional' occupations. In agricultural communities ages at marriage and proportions celibate were distinctly higher where small, subsistence farming and 'live in' farm servants predominated over larger-scale farming based on non-residential wage labour. In industrial communities ages at marriage and the proportions remaining unmarried fell as the size of manufacturing enterprises and the prevalence of wage labour increased (Anderson 1976). The scale of the transfer of labour out of agricultural into industrial occupations between the 1780s and the 1820s was certainly sufficient to have left its mark on national average rates of marriage and birth, while the reduced pace of this transfer may well have contributed to the decline of fertility which followed the end of the Napoleonic Wars.[13] One of the most striking correlations to emerge from the analysis of regional variations in marriage patterns in 1861 is that between rates of nuptiality and the proportion of women employed in domestic service: the greater the ratio of female domestics, the lower the levels of nuptiality. This raises the interesting possibility that part of the explanation for the rise in fertility rates during the late eighteenth and early nineteenth centuries may have involved a movement of women out of domestic service into less traditional types of employment, though proof that such a shift occurred is hard to provide (Anderson 1976).

It is, however, in Ireland that the effects on fertility of changes in the character of employment are most clearly seen. Following the Napoleonic Wars a combination of falling grain prices, the development of coastal steam shipping, rising British demand for livestock products and the repeal of the Cattle Acts encouraged Irish agricultural producers in the more fertile and prosperous eastern parts of the country to contract the acreage devoted to tillage and revert once again to pasture farming. As farms became larger and more expensive to acquire and stock and openings for wage labour declined, ages at marriage and proportions remaining unmarried rose and rates of fertility and population growth accordingly began to fall (Crotty 1966; Kennedy 1973).

Admittedly, the existence of a relationship between fertility and type of employment remains too crudely specified to be accepted unreservedly. The effect of changing employment conditions on marriage and fertility was not always consistent or continuous. Data from the 1841 census for Ireland, for example, suggest that the growth of occupational opportunities for single women in handicraft industries decreased rather than increased the attractions of marriage for females (Mokyr 1980). It is obviously dangerous to assume that increasing employment prospects *always* stimulated levels of marriage and fertility. The presumed stimulus to early marriage and fertility which came with the increased proletarianization of the labour force sits uncomfortably with a temporary downturn in rates of nuptiality during the earliest years of the nineteenth century when the number of propertyless wage-earners in England was rising rapidly (Wrigley 1983).

In any case, a distinction between attitudes to marriage among those who followed 'traditional' and 'non-traditional' occupations is not easy to identify. While the approach of wage labourers to marriage and child-bearing may well have differed considerably from that of large farmers and highly skilled, property-owning craftsmen and tradesmen, was it really all that different from that of handicraft workers employed as part of a long productive chain in the putting-out system, owning little if any of the means of production and as dependent on the vagaries of market forces as wage-earners? Were attitudes to marriage among agricultural labourers with their small cottage and garden radically different from those of the small peasant owner-occupier or tenant eking out a precarious living on a tiny property and often forced to rely on periodic work for others to supplement his income? It would be unwise to deny the potency of these reservations. The existence of a relationship between employment characteristics and rising rates of marriage and fertility remains to be proved. But surely it is equally unwise to assume that the synchronism between rising rates of nuptiality and fertility and a shift towards different types of employment for ever-larger sections of the population was entirely coincidental? Capitalist farming, manufacturing industry and the process of labour proletarianization were not unique to the second half of the eighteenth and first half of the nineteenth centuries. But they were certainly more extensive and developing more rapidly then than ever before.

THE EMPLOYMENT RATIO

Rising levels of nuptiality and fertility in the late eighteenth and early nineteenth centuries, it has been argued, also owed something to a steady increase in the proportion of women and children in gainful employment. Recently we have been reminded of the substantial and growing contribution of adult female earnings to family income in the late eighteenth century.[14] Conceivably, this played its part in encouraging earlier marriage and larger families though it is worth remembering that under certain circumstances the full-time employment of married women may actually have reduced levels of legitimate fertility (see pp. 114 for comments on the low level of fertility among women employed in cotton textile factories). Contemporary observers were in no doubt of the effects of economic growth on child labour and birth rates:

> Why have the inhabitants of Birmingham increased from 23,000 in 1750 to 30,000 in 1770? Certainly because a proportional increase of employment has taken place: wherever there is a demand for hands, there they will abound ... Thus where employment increases (Birmingham) the people increase: and where employment does not increase (Colchester) the people do not increase ... Away my boys – get children, they are worth more than they ever were (Young, A. *Political arithmetic,* London, 1774, p. 61).

To criticize this view on the grounds that children did not earn enough to cover the costs of their upbringing, and were therefore uneconomic, is misconceived. It was not essential for a child to yield a net profit in order to be considered worthwhile. In view of the strength of the natural desire to procreate, especially at a time when children were potentially useful supports to parental old-age, even a modest *reduction* in the net cost of child-rearing would have been sufficient to stimulate fertility rates. On the other hand, according to data on marital fertility trends in thirteen reconstituted parish populations, the regularity of child-bearing within marriage does not appear to have increased during the period of early industrialization, a difficult fact to explain if the growth of employment opportunities for children were acting as a stimulus to fertility (Wrigley 1983). Until, however, we have evidence on the behaviour of marital fertility rates over a much larger and more representative sample of communities it might be wise not to make too much of this criticism. The potential contribution of rising child (and female) employment ratios to the late eighteenth and early nineteenth century increase in fertility remains to be fully tested.

RISING PER CAPITA REAL WAGES

It is unlikely that the rise in fertility associated with the initial decades of the Industrial Revolution had any immediate or direct connection with a simultaneous increase in the level of real wages among adult males. When fertility rose between 1780 and 1810 the real earnings of adult males were relatively stable or even declining: when real wages recovered following the culmination of the Napoleonic wars rates of fertility decreased (Wrigley and Schofield 1981).[15] Possibly, however, the nature of the relationship between income and fertility has been misspecified. In a relatively unsophisticated age, marriage and fertility decisions among the labouring populations were more likely to have been determined by the more tangible and volatile fluctuations in levels of *money* wages and employment prospects than by an awareness of the amount of goods and services these would buy. Transferring the emphasis from *real* to *money* wage variations produces a better fit with fertility trends and a less 'strained' interpretation of the relationship between income and fertility than the 'delayed-response' thesis advocated by Wrigley and Schofield. Looked at in this way the rise in English fertility between the late eighteenth century and the conclusion of the Napoleonic Wars equates neatly with a simultaneous rise in levels of employment and money wages and the post-war decline in fertility with a general depression in employment and money wages. A similar interpretation holds good for Ireland. Contrary to Connell's view that the late eighteenth and early nineteenth century trend to earlier marriage merely represented a desperate search for personal satisfaction in the face of growing economic misery, it is now widely believed to have been a response to a steady improvement in employment prospects. Only after the Napoleonic Wars – with the onset of widespread industrial and commercial recession, the collapse of many of the country's handicraft industries, the switch from arable to livestock farming and the impossibility of further subdivision and reclamation – did employment opportunities and wage levels decline and nuptiality and fertility begin to fall.

If, as suggested, the rise in rates of legitimate fertility during the late eighteenth and early years of the nineteenth centuries should be seen primarily as a response to the forces of economic growth, why, from the later decades of the nineteenth century, when economic growth was common to all countries in the United Kingdom, did marital fertility begin a long period of secular decline?

Superficially, the answer to this apparent paradox lies in the fact that beyond a certain stage of economic development further growth produces a variety of circumstances and attitudes which are inimical to the continuance of the high fertility norms typical of more backward economies and which combine to counteract the positive effect of rising wages and employment levels on birth rates (Heer 1966, 1968). More specifically, however, it has proved extremely difficult to identify the precise circumstances and attitudes involved and to assign to each its relative weight. In part this is because the historian lacks direct access to the people whose fertility decisions he is attempting to explain. He cannot ask them why they behaved, or thought they behaved, as they did. For all the weaknesses inherent in modern personal survey techniques (Busfield and Paddon 1977), they afford distinct advantages over those which must rely on inference from historical events. In part the search for the causes of the fertility transition suffers from the lack of a clear theoretical model of the determinants of fertility behaviour.

On the whole, existing theories of fertility are either too selective or too crudely specified to take account of the full range and interrelationships of the factors dictating fertility decisions. They tend to overemphasize the influence of purely economic considerations by regarding procreation as a straightforward production function and children as merely another consumer good and fail to integrate, adequately, the influence of sociological and cultural forces.[16] And they have still to 'learn to compromise between the simplicity required for more manageable theories and the complexity of observed reality' (Liebenstein 1974, p. 470).

In view of the multiplicity of the processes shaping fertility decisions it is doubtful whether theory will ever manage completely to bridge the gap between the necessity for workable simplicity and the complexity of reality. Merely to list the processes involved illustrates how intricate any complete model of fertility determination would have to be. Among them would be included the effect of variations in income (its absolute level and its level relative to expenditure, parental income, the income of other social groups and expected standards of living); the extent of income inequality between different households and social classes; the material costs of child-bearing and child-rearing (including the direct costs of children themselves, parental income foregone by having children and the loss of goods which might have been purchased as an alternative to children); the social, cultural and psychological cost-benefit of child-bearing and raising; the degree of social mobility; the socio-occupational structure of a community; variations in expectations of what constitutes 'normal' family size and in the institutions and social arrangements which support this norm; levels of birth control technology and ease of access to it; standards of education; rates of infant and child mortality; relationships between rural and urban residence patterns; the ethnic composition, religious character, nationalistic zeal and historical situation of a population; the status accorded to women; employment ratios among married women; levels of fecundity; and purely demographic considerations – sex ratios, age structures, proportions married, migratory habits and the frequency of sexual intercourse.[17]

To make matters worse, no existing model has yet managed to grapple successfully with problems arising from the interconnectedness of the many forces responsible for shaping fertility norms or to determine, even theoretically, the relative importance which should be attached to each. Indeed, it is not always clear, even theoretically, in which direction the various determinants of fertility work. In one combination of circumstances a particular influence may work to stimulate rates of fertility, in others the same agency may tend to depress them. Such theoretical weaknesses, coupled with the practical difficulties historians face in securing sufficient historical evidence to meet the requirements of a rigorous model of fertility determination, explain why attempts to account for the late nineteenth century fertility transition have proceeded in a piecemeal and poorly specified fashion and why their findings remain vague and incomplete.

One of the factors which has undoubtedly played a part in the decline of marital fertility since the late nineteenth century is the increase in both knowledge of and access to effective means of birth control. Public appreciation of the value of contraception was considerably enhanced by the publicity given to the trial of Charles Bradlaugh and Annie Besant in 1877 for reissuing Knowlton's birth control pamphlet 'The Fruits of Philosophy' (Banks and Banks 1954). Never again would ignorance of the benefits to be derived from fertility control, and of the means for doing so, be as influential in maintaining high birth rates. To some extent also, and increasingly over time, the diffusion of new methods of birth control – synthetic rubber sheaths, diaphragms, syringes and chemical suppositories, made possible by the technology of modern industrialization – and the spread of retail outlets for the sale of contraceptive devices contributed to the growing practice of family limitation (Peel 1963–4; Shorter, Knodel and van de Walle 1971).

But we should be careful not to exaggerate the significance of innovations in birth control technology, particularly during the early decades of the fertility transition. In Ireland the decline in fertility was achieved principally by means of an increase in rates of lifetime celibacy and only partially through a reduction in the frequency of childbirth within marriage. In England/Wales and Scotland the new methods of birth control were adopted chiefly by upper and middle class sections of society. They were of little relevance to the working classes who continued to rely on traditional, more rudimentary birth control techniques – prolonged lactation, withdrawal, abortion, even infanticide – to reduce their fertility rates. For working-class women abortion had considerable advantages over the new forms of contraceptive technology: it was cheaper; better suited to the needs of families whose future income and employment prospects were difficult to predict and who, therefore, found long-term family-planning decisions irrational; imposed fewer requirements for privacy, preparation and perseverance; was necessary only when pregnancy actually occurred; did not depend on the cooperation of the male; was more appropriate for women who contributed significantly to the income of the household and thus had a greater awareness of the state of family finances and a greater responsiblity for decisions on family size; and was less unacceptable to women who suffered more from high rates of natural miscarriage and infant mortality and who were less likely to regard embryonic life as sacred (Knight 1977; McLaren 1977; Sauer 1978).

In fact, the labouring population was not merely indifferent to the new techniques of birth control but often positively hostile towards them. Some felt that those who advocated working-class adoption of the new birth control methods were attempting to divert the progress of social reform or rid the state of responsibility for the problem of poverty. Some saw birth control propaganda as a middle-class attempt to maintain social stability and inequality by preventing the labouring population from becoming too numerous. Many shared the view that 'artificial' methods of birth control were an affront to the natural laws of God, providence and nature. Others were repelled by the implication that the working classes lacked prudence and required help in achieving self-control over their sexuality. To the extent that the new techniques of contraception symbolized the triumph of individualism they ran counter to working-class belief in the family as the source of public morality and in the importance of individual self-sacrifice for family life and social cohesion. To those with a faith in God or the natural progress of reform and improvement 'unnatural' methods of birth control were selfishly irrelevant or, worse, a source of atheism and sexual immorality, a view fuelled by the fact that so many of the early advocates of the new methods were secularists who also advocated greater freedom in sexual behaviour.

Altogether, the working classes had too little faith in the motives of their upper- and middle-class 'superiors' to espouse, immediately, the birth control technology they promoted, even had this been better suited to their own circumstances.[18] By the inter-war period, it is true, much of the working-class hostility to 'artificial' methods of contraception had disappeared. Even so, traditional techniques of limiting births remained the principal means of controlling fertility within marriage: as late as 1970 a quarter of all birth control users practised the withdrawal method.[19]

Historians who stress the contribution of new birth control technology to the fertility transition are also apt to understate the extent of birth control in earlier ages. Not that it was practised everywhere.[20] When birth control was practised in pre-industrial Europe it was usually not of the parity-dependent type typical of modern societies, where it becomes more and more practised as the number of children already born to a couple increases, nor was it as extensive before as after the late eighteenth century except among a very narrow range of social groups (Knodel 1977; Flinn 1981). In Britain, before the onset of the fertility transition in the later 1870s, regional differentials in fertility owed much more to variations in levels of nuptiality than to differences in the frequency of child-bearing within marriage (Haines, 1977). Nevertheless, there is abundant evidence to show that birth control practices within marriage were common to many communities and social groups in pre-industrial times. They may not always have been regularly applied or always as effective as hoped and they certainly aimed at higher fertility norms than was to be the case from the late nineteenth century onwards. But of their widespread existence there is no doubt.

The concept of birth control in western Europe has been traced back to the late thirteenth and early fourteenth centuries (Biller 1982). Elizabethan cookbooks, herbal and medicinal manuals are replete with rudimentary, folklore birth control techniques – emetics and laxatives, blood-letting, genital baths and pessaries (Himes 1963; Schnuker 1975). Prolonged breast-feeding as a method of restricting conception was practised in sixteenth- and seventeenth-century England (McLaren, D., 1978, 1979). The practice of birth control has been noted among the peasants of Colyton (Devon) in the late seventeenth and early eighteenth centuries (Wrigley 1966b, 1978; Crafts and Ireland 1976a), gentry, craftsmen and tradesmen in three Lancashire parishes between 1650 and 1812 (Loschky and Krier 1969), the labouring populations of Moreton Say (Shropshire) in the late seventeenth and eighteenth centuries (Jones 1968), the inhabitants of Shepshed (Leicestershire) in the late eighteenth and early nineteenth centuries (Levine 1976b), early nineteenth-century cotton textile factory workers (McLaren 1977) and the British peerage of the early nineteenth century (Hollingsworth 1964). The frequency with which the Church denounced the practices of coitus interruptus, abortion and infanticide in late eighteenth-century England itself attests to their widespread existence (Langer 1975). At least part of the rationale of early nineteenth-century English birth control campaigners was the desire to wean the working classes away from what were regarded as dangerous and unethical methods of family limitation like abortion and infanticide towards less risky and ethically more acceptable techniques (McLaren 1976). That working-class attitudes to the 'new' methods were hostile cannot obscure the fact that the handbills and pamphlets published by the early birth control propogandists sold in their thousands (Langer 1975). Such interest surely reveals a population for whom family limitation was a meaningful issue.

On the Continent birth control was practised by many French peasants from the second half of the eighteenth century – though not, it would seem, by all,[21] by the French bourgeoisie of the late eighteenth and early nineteenth centuries (Blacker 1957–8), by the Genevan bourgeoisie from the second half of the seventeenth century (Henry 1956) and the French and Florentine nobility from the eighteenth (Levy and Henry 1960; Litchfield 1969). It was already widespread in five of the eleven provinces of the Netherlands by 1850 (Buissink 1971), in Sweden possibly by the last quarter of the eighteenth century and certainly by the second and third quarters of the nineteenth (Carlsson 1970; Flinn 1981; Lithell 1981), and perhaps in Hungary by the late eighteenth century (Andorka 1979).

Of course, the resort to birth control practices by married couples was far less common before the late nineteenth century than subsequently and opposition from the traditional opponents of working-class birth control like the Church and the medical profession was undoubtedly less stringent after the 1870s than it had ever been in earlier times.[22] But neither the concept nor the application of birth control practices within marriage were novel to the late nineteenth century. It follows that the fertility transition cannot be regarded as an innovation in sexual behaviour, especially if this is meant to imply that it was primarily a response to the availability of new methods of controlling births. Rather, it was merely an adjustment of fertility norms to lower levels, an adjustment which, for the majority of the population, was achieved largely through greater resort to long familiar techniques (Carlsson 1966). In Ireland this meant abandoning marriage altogether, in England/Wales and Scotland the wider and more intensive application of traditional mehods of curbing marital fertility. The development of new, safer and more reliable contraceptive devices no doubt played its part, and an increasing part as time went by. But, initially, their role was modest.

The question remains, why was this adjustment made? Why, beginning around 1876, did lower levels of marital fertility become so desirable? And why, in Ireland, was the method chosen to achieve them principally that of celibacy rather than the adoption of family limitation practices within marriage?

Sociological interpretations of the causes of family limitation usually place considerable stress on the significance of declining rates of infant and child mortality (Freedman 1961–2). When mortality in the early years of life is high, individuals have little room to exercise independent choice over the size of their families since both family and community well-being depend on the maintenance of relatively high fertility norms. Only when death rates in infancy and childhood are relatively low does a conscious, private choice in favour of lower fertility become possible (Wrigley 1978). Indeed, because higher survival rates impose additional strains on the material, social, cultural and psychological resources of the family, some reduction in fertility becomes inevitable.

At first sight the case for interpreting the fertility transition as a response to falling levels of infant and child mortality is attractive on several counts. First, socio-occupational class differentials in rates of infant and child survival correlate closely with those in levels of marital fertility: the higher the social group, the lower the level of mortality and the lower the rate of fertility. Second, a decline in infant and child death rates appears to be the only, immediately obvious, causal ingredient common to the many societies which underwent a decline in fertility during the late nineteenth or early twentieth centuries (Carlsson 1966). Third, falling mortality seems to be the only logical explanation for countries like late eighteenth- and early nineteenth-century France where the secular decline in fertility began long before the processes of economic modernization were fully under way (Camp 1961; van de Walle 1978).

Considered more closely, however, the association between rates of infant and child survival and marital fertility levels is less convincing. The very closeness of the fit between short-term fluctuations in child mortality and fertility in all regions in England and Wales since the quinquennium around 1876 is itself puzzling. If parents were taking into account the survival rates of their offspring before deciding whether or not to have additional children, variations in fertility rates ought to have lagged behind appropriate changes in levels of mortality. But they did not. Fluctuations in mortality and fertility appear to have occurred more or less simultaneously. This suggests that infant and child death rates were not the primary determinants of short-term variations in marital fertility: indeed, that both mortality and fertility were responding simultaneously, and independntly, to the influence of some other force or forces. Again, if the initial phase of the fertility transition was principally a consequence of falling mortality why between 1885 and 1898 and to a certain extent at other times too, when rates of fertility fell in all parts of England and Wales, did child death rates actually rise in some areas? (Brass and Kabir 1978).

There is no obvious relationship between the onset of fertility decline and the timing, extent or age-group distribution of the reduction in infant and child mortality in England and Wales during the late nineteenth and early twentieth centuries. Death rates in infancy (0–1), the age-group in which much the greatest percentage of deaths under the age of fourteen occurred, changed very little from at least the mid-1840s and did not begin their secular decline until the first decade of the twentieth century, thirty years after the decline in English and Scottish marital fertility rates had begun. And although the decline in mortality in the age-groups 1–14 pre-dated the fertility transition it was generally too modest to have caused such a dramatic alteration in fertility norms as took place: certainly, the difference between levels of infant and child mortality in the periods 1866–76 and 1876–86 was too small to be given the sole, or even the main, credit for the notable change in marital fertility schedules which occurred between the two periods.

Finally, for much of the initial phase of the fertility transition, the reduction in levels of mortality during infancy and childhood was concentrated between the ages five and fourteen. If parents were determining their fertility on the basis of child survival rates is it conceivable that they were prepared to wait for five to fourteen years before deciding whether or not to have another child? Given that the normal length of interval between births was two to three years it seems not (Banks 1981). Whatever the contribution of falling infant and child mortality to the persistence of the fertility transition in the generations after the First World War, and the *ultimate* significance of higher

113

survival rates to fertility control cannot be denied, its contribution to the initial stages of the transition to lower fertility norms should not be over-emphasized.

During the inter-war period, as a result of advances in economic and educational opportunities for women, girls began to enter married life with a greater sense of self-awareness and independence than ever before and marriage itself became a more equal partnership in which the wishes and interests of the wife were more likely to be respected. To the extent that this occurred it worked in favour of lower fertility norms (Gittins 1982). Before 1914, however, the relationship between falling levels of marital fertility and improvements in the status of women is less obvious. Working-class women had always exercised considerable influence on family fertility decisions. To suggest otherwise is to distort the nature of working-class family life and to impose erroneously upon it the type of relationship which prevailed between middle-class husbands and their wives.

It is difficult anyway to see an obvious association between the timing and pattern of fertilty decline in the period before the outbreak of the First World War and the attitudes taken towards married women. There is little sign of an improvement in the status of married women before 1914.[23] Not until the 1890s, and then guardedly, did the feminist movement openly espouse the cause of birth control – a delay explained partly by the fear of alienating 'respectable' public opinion, partly by a belief that the adoption of artificial means of birth control would increase, not decrease, the sexual demands of men on women, reduce the status of the wife to that of a whore and undermine the sancitity of family life, partly by a desire not to swim against the imperialist and eugenicist tide of pro-natalism, but perhaps most of all by the fact that the early feminists were more concerned with the lack of opportunities for unmarried women than with the problems of wives and mothers (Banks 1964; McLaren 1978).

Middle-class wives, increasingly emancipated from domestic chores and transformed from homemakers to ladies of leisure, became more, not less, dependent on their husbands. Few of the women in those socio-occupational groups which pioneered the transition to lower levels of marital fertility – the wives of army and naval officers, authors, editors, journalists, accountants, physicians, surveyors, medical practitioners, civil and mining engineers, painters, sculptors, artists, barristers and solicitors or of lower middle-class men in cities like Sheffield – can be considered in revolt against their husband's authority in sexual or other matters (Banks 1981). Among working-class families levels of fertility had long been influenced by the extent of employment opportunities for wives. The contrast between low rates of marital fertility in cotton textile communities and higher levels of fertility in coal-mining areas owed much to the fact that in the former a substantial percentage of married women were gainfully employed while in the latter married women rarely worked outside the home (Haines 1977; McLaren 1977).

Had employment ratios among working-class wives increased in the last quarter of the nineteenth century they might well have contributed to the decline in rates of marital fertility. But they did not. Except for a temporary rise during the years of the First World War, from the middle of the nineteenth century to the conclusion of the inter-war period the proportion of married women in gainful employment declined continuously, from 25% in 1851 to 13% in 1901, 12% in 1921 and 10% in 1931. Only since the Second World War has the trend been reversed. Married women did not turn to family limitation in order to protect opportunities for lucrative employment nor because employment gave them a greater influence in family fertility decision-making processes.

On the contrary, it is more plausible to argue that the *removal* of married women from the labour market, which was especially pronounced during the first decades of the fertility transition and which forced families to depend solely on the husband's earnings at a time when material and social expectations were rising steadily, was the principal motive for working-class wives to restrict their childbearing (Banks 1981). If this is true, working-class like middle-class wives were probably more, not less, dependent on their husbands at the beginning of the twentieth century than at the beginning of the nineteenth. There is, moreover, nothing in the historical record of the period before 1914 to indicate that this increase in economic dependency was offset by forces of a non-economic nature which worked to raise the status of married women relative to that of their husbands. The initiation of the trend towards smaller families, therefore, was not a phenomenon forced on men by increasingly independent wives. In reality, men were just as anxious as women to curb rates of marital fertility for reasons which, in the main, had little to do with any new sympathy they may have felt towards the problems of women subject to incessant childbirth.

It is often argued that high on the list of these reasons was the influence on fertility of increased opportunities for social mobility and a growing awareness of social status which came with the process of economic modernization.

> The industrial and agricultural revolutions carried with them a shift from settled, traditional ways of life, in which changes came slowly, to new ways of life in which changes were liable to be frequent and abrupt. The old settled ways of life, in which ties of family and community were strong, and in which most persons accepted the station into which they had been born, were passing. They were being succeeded by an intense competitive struggle in which the emphasis was increasingly placed on the individual rather than the community. Opportunities for 'getting on' were multiplied, but, at the same time, it became increasingly necessary to struggle to keep one's job and one's place in the community ... In general, it can be seen that as the nineteenth century advanced more and more people were being thrown into the struggle for security and social promotion (Royal Commission on Population, 1949, p. 39).

With its constantly changing demands for new technologies and skills and because it alters the criterion of social status from accident of birth or the influence of patronage to the requirements of talent and expertise achieved through education and training, modern economic growth considerably extends the possibilities for social promotion and demotion. By providing the masses with a range of consumer goods and services never before within their purchasing power, and promoting urbanization, it broadens the range of experiences and wants to which individuals are subject, thereby intensifying the urge for social emulation and advance. According to this interpretation, the spread of family limitation practices in the late nineteenth century reflected a more general desire to enhance or protect social status in an age when mobility was replacing immobility as a normal characteristic of the social ladder.

A typical argument is advanced to account for reduced fertility among the English middle classes during the last quarter of the nineteenth century. Middle-class fertility, the thesis runs, fell prey to a crisis of confidence which spread among middle-income groups when confronted by an apparent threat to their incomes and standards of living during the 'Great Depression' of the late Victorian era. To protect incomes and maintain, or increase, differentials in life style between themselves and the labouring population, whose incomes and standards of life were rising, the middle classes were required to adopt techniques of family limitation in addition to the control of fertility they had always exercised through delayed marriage (Banks 1954).

Whether such emphasis on social status and increased social mobility is justified is doubtful. In the first place, it is unlikely that the middle classes were any less confident of their relative status at the end than at the beginning of the Victorian era. Very few of those middle-class families who pioneered the way to lower fertility can be regarded as suffering a crisis of confidence during the decades of the 'Great Depression'. And the number of those who did was more than matched by the number of lower middle-class people for whom employment and incomes rose substantially and who cannot have resorted to family limitation out of fear of being overhauled by their social 'inferiors'.

More generally, it is by no means clear that either the interest in social status or the extent of social mobility was so much greater in the late nineteenth and early twentieth centuries that it had been previously.[24] Awareness of rank and jealousy of status were already deeply engrained in pre-industrial English society.[25] According to one authority the potential for upward social mobility actually fell between the 1870s and 1914.[26] And, anyway, how aware of the possibilities of social movement could late Victorians have been when nineteen in every twenty men were socially immobile? (Banks 1981). In the course of the inter-war period, not least because of the continued development of educational opportunities, the frequency of social mobility increased. Mid-twentieth century society was certainly more flexible than that of the late nineteenth.[27] Nonetheless, 'there were still more circles and grooves than ladders in the social hierarchy'.[28] Even in the 1960s the extent of social mobility was modest.[29]

To stress the contribution of urbanization per se to the fertility transition is similarly unwise. On the one hand, by raising the costs of children, affording easier access to birth control methods, intensifying the desire for social emulation and providing a wider range of attractive goods and services to compete with additional children in the allocation of family expenditures, urban living undoubtedly worked to decrease levels of marital fertility (Easterlin 1978). On the other hand, by allowing rural communities the alternative of shedding their surplus populations via migration to the towns and thus contributing to higher rates of infant and child mortality than would otherwise have prevailed, the rapidity of nineteenth century urbanization possibly delayed the coming of the fertility transition and moderated its initial impact (Friedlander 1969). Besides, the trend to urban living was not unique to the late nineteenth century. For urbanization to be regarded as the sine qua non of the transition to lower levels of marital fertility it ought to have begun its work much earlier in the century when the shift towards urban residence was most intense.

Much higher on the list of acceptable explanations of the fertility transition must come the effect of economic growth on levels of real income and patterns of consumer expenditure, on *desired* as opposed to *actual* standards of living and on the productive functions of the family and its individual members.

Real per capita consumer spending in Britain rose by a third between 1870 and 1913 and by a fifth between 1900 and 1945.[30] As consumer purchasing power increased, expenditure patterns altered in ways that had significant implications for levels of marital fertility. In low-income societies the proportion of income devoted to the purchase of goods and services essential to the maintenance of life is so high that little is left over for spending on less essential 'luxuries' and expenditures on additional children are less likely to be seen as an alternative to the purchase of 'luxuries', all the more so since the economy is not capable of generating an abundant supply of cheap 'luxury' products. The more incomes rise above basic subsistence and the more the technological and distributional innovations associated with modern economic growth provide a broader range of cheap consumer goods and services, the greater is the capacity for even the lowest income groups to extend the range of their expenditures and the more likely it is that children will be considered in competition with 'luxuries'. The assumption is that only from the later decades of the nineteenth century were real per capita incomes sufficiently high for a broad spectrum of society to exercise a genuine choice between children and 'luxuries'.

On the whole this assumption appears justified. While there was no dramatic alternation in the percentage of consumer expenditure devoted to non-food products and services before 1914, some change did nevertheless occur, albeit more towards expenditures on services like education, health and transport and leisure activities such as holidays, daytrips, music halls, gambling and organized sport than towards durable manufactured 'luxuries'.[31] The development of commercial retailing and of a mass entertainment industry in the late nineteenth century is proof enough of the consequences of rising income and technological innovation on consumer spending options.

Despite grievous levels of unemployment, the process continued unabated throughout the inter-war period. For those in employment real incomes and purchasing power continued to rise and the range of consumer spending continued to widen. Whereas the percentage of income spent on food changed little between 1903 and 1945, that on alcohol halved. The share of income going to the purchase of furniture, electrical goods and other consumer durables doubled between 1900 and 1937. Motor cars, a luxury in 1900, were more widespread by the 1920s. Leisure activities – the cinema, theatres, museums and art galleries, holiday resorts and the mass spectator sports of cricket, football, greyhound racing and speedway expanded at a frenetic pace.[32] Although babies are not entirely synonymous with consumer goods and services (Blake 1968), to the extent that levels of fertility are influenced by considerations of the material, social and cultural benefits foregone as a result of childbearing the rise of real incomes and the emergence of a mass consumer society from the closing decades of the nineteenth century played their part in reducing fertility norms. To the extent, also, that rising incomes were accompanied by a decline in the inequality of income between different socio-occupational groups, as may have been the case between certain sections of working- and middle-class society during the years of the 'Great Depression' (1873–96), the barriers to the spread of birth control practices were further lowered (Cook and Repetto 1982).

The modern decline in fertility, however, was as much a response to the effects of economic growth on *desired* as on *actual* standards of living. The higher the actual level of real income the higher the level of parental expectation for their own or their children's future standards of life, and the greater these expectations the more likely that parents will choose to sacrifice additional children in order to attain them, particularly if they have reason to suppose that the attainment of higher living standards is likely to be more difficult than ever before. Thus, confronted by an apparent threat to their *future* incomes during the depression of profits in the last quarter of the nineteenth century and by the fact that in the process of economic modernization children themselves were becoming increasingly costly to rear (see pp. 120–1 for the rise in costs of child-rearing), the English middle classes resorted to family limitation in order to ensure that their expectations for subsequent advance were actually met (Banks 1954). Events in post-Famine Ireland provide the best example of this influence at work.

As previously noted, the decline in Irish legitimate fertility rates during the late nineteenth and early twentieth centuries was chiefly the result of a widespread abandonment of marriage: the frequency of child-bearing within marriage altered little and rates of marital fertility remained relatively high. Since other European countries, with an equally high proportion of Catholics in their populations, had much lower levels of marital fertility than prevailed in Ireland, the preference of the Irish for celibacy rather than birth control within marriage can have been due only in part to the attitudes of the Catholic church towards procreation and the sanctity of family life.

Probably, the main reason lies in the selective effects of mass emigration overseas. A disproportionate number of those who chose emigration as an escape from economic hardship were people who were most likely to find the abandonment of marriage, and the lower material standards of life which came with regular child-bearing, unacceptable. By comparison those choosing to remain in the country were more conservative, more amenable to the exhortations of the Church against the restriction of births by 'artificial' means, less inclined to see celibacy as unbearable and less concerned about the effects of high levels of marital fertility on their own standards of living. Maybe, also, the preference of the Irish for celibacy was connected with a lack of opportunities for the employment of married women outside the home or a relative absence of social and recreational facilities in rural communities where children remained a mother's major source of satisfaction and status (Kennedy 1973).

Numerous reasons have been advanced for the growing tendency during the nineteenth and early twentieth centuries for Irish men and women to reject married life. These included a fear of repeating the extreme subdivision of landholdings which had given rise to the Great Famine; a new interest in the commercial exploitation of farms, encouraged in the later years of the century by land legislation which gave the peasant more chance of profiting from his labours and by the gradual transfer of landownership from large Protestant landlords to smaller, predominantly Catholic tenant farmers; a renewed emphasis on pasture as opposed to arable farming which, together with the spread of labour-saving technology, led to a rise in the average size of holdings; the substitution of an environment of labour shortage and land abundance by one in which labour was plentiful and land scarce; an alteration in the socio-occupational composition of Ireland's population, marked by a decline in the percentage of landless labourers and cottiers, among whom marriage was relatively early and widespread, and a rise in the percentage of farmers, who married later in life and less generally;[33] the replacement of multiple by single heir inheritance systems and the re-emergence of the peasant matchmaker and the 'arranged' marriage, both consequences of the changes which occurred in Irish agricultural life but adding their own impetus to the flight from nuptiality; rising life expectancy among farmers and the further delay this imposed on a son's inheritance of the family farm; from the 1880s falling rates of emigration, until then a ready alternative to celibacy; the general depression in agricultural prices between the mid-1870s and mid-1890s; and the lack of alternative opportunities for employment outside agriculture, particularly for males.[34]

But the influence with the greatest impact on nuptiality was the emergence in the second half of the nineteenth century of a new spirit of acquisitiveness among the Irish peasantry which brought with it a new commitment towards securing a higher material standard of life and a willingness to forego marriage in order to attain it. Nowhere was the difference between actual and desired standards of life as great as in late nineteenth-century Ireland. On the one hand, the expectations of the Irish peasant, shocked by the events of the Famine and renewed agricultural crisis in the west in the early 1880s and encouraged by the land legislation, rising standards of education and political awareness and a greater knowledge of conditions elsewhere spread through the medium of emigration, rose dramatically. On the other, constrained by low levels of agricultural productivity, falling agricultural prices, limited opportunities for labour in pasture farming, growing difficulties of acquiring a holding and a lack of employment outside agriculture, the actual conditions of his life, though better than in the years immediately preceding the Famine, remained among the poorest in the western world. More than any other single factor it was this difference between desire and reality, and the awesome difficulty of translating ambition into actual achievement, which prompted the rejection of marriage by so many Irish men and women (Kennedy 1973).

The coming of the fertility transition was also bound up with alterations in the productive functions of the family during the progress of economic modernization, alterations which particularly affected the status of children in the family. The trend away from domestic, family-based methods of production typical of the pre- and early industrial world towards the large-scale, capital intensive techniques of a modern economy, where labour requirements are met by hiring on the open market rather than through the family, considerably increased the real costs of child-bearing. It did so in two ways: first, by reducing the opportunities for child labour – a combined consequence of rising adult real incomes, which made the employment of children less essential to the welfare of the family, the increasing sophistication of industrial technology, which restricted the range of tasks children were able to perform, and of humanitarian opposition to child labour, reflected in the Factory and Education Acts;[35] second, by requiring greater expenditures on children themselves in order to fit them for effective participation in the more competitive, technologically complex productive functions of the modern world (Minge-Kalman 1978). As expenditures on infant and child health and, in particular, on education rose so, too, did the necessity for controlling rates of fertility (Banks 1981).

In essence this is a simplified variant of a more sophisticated family resource-flow explanation of the fertility transition recently advanced by Caldwell. In economies where production is largely family-based, adult males and the elderly, who dominate the productive and decision-making processes, inevitably attract a disproportionate share of wealth and emotional stocks generated within the family. Children, though an integral part of the labour supply, have relatively little responsibility for decision-taking and therefore, per capita, consume relatively little of the family's wealth and emotional supply. In modern, capitalist economies by contrast, where large-scale productive techniques based on a non-familial labour market have superseded family production, the direction of wealth and emotional flows within the family necessarily moves away from parents towards their children. In part this is because the employment of offspring outside the parental household lessens the influence of the father in family decisions: in part because of the need for greater material and emotional expenditures on the child in order to equip it for the more stringent requirements of the modern labour supply. Coupled with the loss of child earnings which came with a gradual withdrawal of children from gainful employment, the greater flow of resources towards the young, both materially and emotionally, made large families increasingly difficult to sustain (Caldwell 1981).

Apart from its contribution to the rising costs of child-bearing, there were several other ways in which the development of education from the later decades of the nineteenth century stimulated the adoption of family limitation practices. Firstly, the method chosen to assess educational achievement, based on the concept of the 'public examination', was possibly as significant a force in the trend to lower fertility norms as the costs imposed on parents by education itself. Examinations intensified the spirit of competitiveness, extended the belief that effort and 'sacrifice' brought inevitable reward and encouraged a faith in the virtues of planning and preparation for the future. Carried over into post-school life, these qualities enhanced the likelihood of an effective response to the demands of a changing environment for greater fertility control. Secondly, at least after 1914, rising standards of education were among the forces which gave women a greater influence in family decision-making processes and facilitated reduced fertility norms in the interests of their own and their children's welfare. Thirdly, the influence of education on fertility worked through its contribution to the increased authority and independence of the child in relation to his parents, a development which led parents to treat their offspring more as equals, to allow them more of an opportunity in determining their own futures and to take greater care in preparing them

121

for the future. Fourthly, education increased the perception of socio-occupational class inequality and the realization that family limitation could be utilized to lessen it. Higher standards of education may also have enhanced ambitions for improved life styles as an alternative to high fertility norms. Lastly, they helped to promote a modern sense of rationalism in place of the fatalism typical of less educated populations. Recognizing that difficulties are surmountable and that the future is to some extent controllable, educated man is much more inclined than his predecessors to countenance radical changes in behaviour. A decision to reduce fertility norms is more likely to be taken by men and women with reason to believe that it will make a fundamental difference to the quality of their life than it is by people so firmly resigned to life's difficulties that they regard family limitation as of little use or relevance. It may, then, be no coincidence that the introduction of mass compulsory education in the 1870s and 1880s equated in time almost exactly with the beginnings of the fertility transition (Wells 1975; Caldwell 1979, 1981; Banks 1981).

CONCLUSION

It would be naive to suppose that the forces responsible for the secular decline in rates of fertility which began in the last quarter of the nineteenth century have yet been clearly identified. In view of the myriad influences to which marriage and fertility decisions are subject this is scarcely surprising. The transition to lower fertility norms followed a variety of paths and was a response to a complex array of forces, the relative significance of each of which differed greatly from population to population and from group to group within the same population (Woods and Smith 1983).

Nonetheless, a review of the evidence relating to Britain and Ireland does point us towards certain agencies which appear to have been of special significance. In particular, it suggests that the long-term decline in fertility was, at root, a combined result of (i) the effect of rising real incomes on patterns of expenditure which, as never before, permitted consumers a realistic choice between additional children or alternative goods and services; (ii) widening differentials between actual and desired standards of life, differentials which exist only in societies where incomes are well above basic subsistence levels and the range of goods and services sufficiently broad to permit a reasonable expectation of higher standards of living; (iii) the substitution of family-based methods of production by large-scale arrangements of capital and labour and, through the latter's requirements for higher standards of worker education and training, the effect which these had on the real costs of raising children; (iv) the influence of education on competitiveness, rationalism, the independence of the child and the desire for a kind of life style which conflicted with regular child-bearing. Compared with such forces, the contribution to the fertility transition of increasing social mobility and a search for enhanced social status, improvements in the status of women, the availability of more efficient birth control techniques and the decline in rates of infant and child mortality were relatively unimportant.

NOTES AND REFERENCES

1. Defined as the physiological ability of men to impregnate and of women to conceive and bear healthy children.
2. **Morrow, R. B.** (1978), 'Family limitation in pre-industrial England, a reappraisal', *Economic History Review,* XXXI, 3; **Wrigley, E. A.** (1978), 'Marital fertility in seventeenth-century Colyton: a note', ibid.
3. A fall in fertility during periods of food shortage could as easily be explained by a reduction in the frequency of sexual intercourse at times of stress or by an increase in the extent of amenhorrea (the cessation of ovulation). **Menken, J., Trussell, J.** and **Watkins, S.** (1981), 'The nutrition fertility link: an evaluation of the evidence', *Journal of Interdisciplinary History,* XI, 3.
4. **Post, J. B.** (1971), 'Age at menarche and menopause: some medieval authorities', *Population Studies,* 25, 1; **Laslett, P.** (1971), 'Age at menarche in Europe since the eighteenth century', *Journal of Interdisciplinary History,* II, 2.
5. This is not to imply that variations in fecundity have had no influence on fertility rates. In Meiji Japan, for example, improvements in diet, medical care and standards of public health reduced the incidence of permanent sterility and the number of spontaneous abortions and stillbirths. **Mosk, C.** (1981), 'The evolution of the pre-modern demographic regime in Japan', *Population Studies,* 35, 1.
6. **Richards, E.** (1974), 'Women in the British economy since about 1700: an interpretation', *History,* 59.
7. At Portpatrick (Wigtownshire) during the second half of the nineteenth century for example, where rates of illegitimacy were very high, almost half of all illegitimates were born to women who had only one child out of wedlock and only 2.4% of all women who bore an illegitimate child had themselves been born outside marriage.
8. In the bondager system hinds or ploughmen were expected to provide able-bodied girls to work with them. Bothies were barracks attached to a farm where unmarried labourers were lodged with little or no supervision from their employer. Under 'chaumer' or 'kitchen' arrangements farm labourers were accommodated in the farm kitchen or in rooms in the farmhouse, again with little supervision of their relationships.
9. The north-east is defined as the counties of Aberdeen, Banff, Kincardine,

Moray and Nairn: the south, Roxburgh, Dumfries, Kirkcudbright and Wigtown: the north, Shetland, Orkney, Caithness and Sutherland: the north-east, Ross and Inverness.

10. **Woodward, D.** (1981), 'Wage rates and living standards in pre-industrial England', *Past and Present,* 91.

11. Connell 1950a and b, 1951: Crotty 1966; Johnson 1970; Kennedy 1973; Donnelly 1975; Mokyr 1981.

12. Chambers 1957.

13. In 1789 23.6% of the labour force was employed in manufacturing and mining: by 1831 38.4% and by 1851 42.9% (Armstrong 1965).

14. **McKendrick, N.** (1974), 'Home demand and economic growth: a new view of the role of women and children in the Industrial Revolution' in **McKendrick, N.** (ed.), *Historical Perspectives. Studies in English Thought and Society in Honour of J. H. Plumb,* London.

15. On real wage trends see **Flinn, M. W.** (1974), 'Trends in real wages, 1750–1850', *Economic History Review,* XXVII, 3; **von Tunzelmann, G. N.** (1979), 'Trends in real wages, 1750–1850, revisited', *Economic History Review,* XXXII, 1; **Lindert, P. H.** and **Williamson, J. G.** (1983), 'English workers' living standards during the Industrial Revolution: a new look', *Economic History Review,* XXXVI, 1.

16. Blake 1968; Simon 1969; Sweezy 1971; Schnaiberg 1973; Bhattacharya 1975; Terry 1975; Busfield and Paddon 1977; Beaujot, Krotki and Krishnan 1978; Easterlin 1978. In particular, existing theories of past changes in fertility schedules overemphasize the importance of general structural influences such as economic organization, socio-cultural arrangements and demographic and technological environments at the expense of the immediate motives for, and constraints upon, family decision-making processes – the behaviour context. They too readily assume that given structural alterations inevitably produce the same fertility response (Woods and Smith 1983).

17. Berent 1952; Becker 1960; Freedman 1961–2; Blake 1968; Easterlin 1968; Simon 1969; Namboodiri 1970; Sweezy 1971; Espenshade 1972; Willis 1973; Liebenstein 1974; Bhattacharya 1975; Terry 1975; Beaujot, Krotki and Krishnan 1978; Easterlin 1978; Wrigley 1978; Ermisch 1979; Flegg 1979; Zimmer 1981; Cook and Repetto 1982.

18. Langer 1975; Ledbetter 1976; McLaren 1976, 1978; Banks 1981.

19. **Van de Kaa, D. J.** (1980), 'Recent trends in fertility in western Europe' in **Hiorns, R. W.** (ed.), *Demographic Patterns in Developed Societies,* London.

20. It appears to have been largely absent in pre-industrial Germany, for example. **Knodel, J.** (1978), 'Natural fertility in pre-industrial Germany', *Population Studies,* XXXI, 3. See also Wrigley and Schofield 1983.

21. Contrast Camp 1961; Henry 1965; van de Walle 1974; Flandrin 1979 with Goubert 1968.

22. Campbell 1960–1; Peel 1964–5; Fryer 1965; McLaren 1978; Soloway 1978; Lewis, J. 1979.

23. **Thane, P.** (1981), 'Social history, 1860–1914' in **Floud, R.** and **McCloskey D.** (eds), *The Economic History of Britain Since 1700,* vol. 2, Cambridge.

24. **Perkin, H. (1969),** *The Origins of Modern English Society, 1780–1880,* London.

25. **Laslett, P.** (1965), *The World We Have Lost,* London.
26. **Thane** (1981).
27. **Goldthorpe, J. H.** and **Lockwood, D.** (1963), 'Affluence and the British class structure', *Sociological Review,* 11; **Goldthorpe, J. H.** (1969), *The Affluent Worker in the Class Structure,* Cambridge.
28. **Briggs, A.** (1981), 'Social history, 1900–45' in **Floud, R.** and **McCloskey, D.** (eds.), *The Economic History of Britain Since 1700,* vol. 2, Cambridge, p. 360.
29. **Ryder, J.** and **Silver, H.** (1970), *Modern English Society: History and Structure, 1850–1970,* London.
30. **Supple, B.** (1981), 'Income and demand, 1860–1914' in **Floud, R.** and **McCloskey, D.** (eds), *The Economic History of Modern Britain Since 1700,* vol. 2, Cambridge; **Briggs** (1981).
31. **Supple** (1981).
32. Briggs (1981).
33. The percentage of farmers with holdings of ten acres or more increased from 17% to 27% between 1841 and 1914 (O'Grada 1979).
34. Commission on Emigration, 1955; Ryan 1955; Connell 1958, 1961–2, 1968; Aalen 1963–4; Crotty 1966; Johnson 1970; Walsh 1970b; Cullen 1972; Kennedy 1973; Donnelly 1975; Chojnacka 1976; Dixon 1978; McKenna 1978; O'Grada 1979.
35. **Nardinelli, C.** (1980), 'Child labour and the factory acts', *Journal of Economic History,* XL, 4. In 1861 36.9% of boys and 20.2% of girls aged 10–15 were in gainful employment: by 1911 18.3% and 10.4% respectively. **Baines, D.** (1981), 'The labour supply and the labour market, 1860–1914', in **Floud, R.** and **McCloskey, D.** (eds), *The Economic History of Modern Britain Since 1700,* vol. 2, Cambridge.

Chapter 5

MIGRANTS AND THEIR MOTIVES

Reviewing the recent literature, Professor Gould has concluded that there is 'no agreement at all on the causes of (short-term) fluctuations in British emigration' to the United States during the nineteenth and early twentieth centuries. Whether because of inadequacies in the methodology adopted to identify the causes or because the causes themselves were so much more varied in the case of emigration from Britain than from other European countries, it is not yet known why, within the period between the mid-eighteenth and mid-twentieth centuries, the flow of emigration from Britain to the USA fluctuated so markedly from decade to decade (Gould 1979). Just as obscure are the causes of short-term variations in British emigration to destinations other than the USA, in the flow of Irish men and women overseas and in the levels of migration between and within the different countries of the United Kingdom itself.

Fortunately, the data on migratory movements summarized above raise a number of other issues which are more amenable to explanation (see pp. 37–43). Why, relative to population size and the rate of natural increase, was the extent of net outmigration so much greater in Ireland than anywhere else and greater in Scotland than England/Wales?[1] Why did the volume of overseas emigration decline everywhere during the inter war period? Why was the frequency of internal migration lower in nineteenth- and twentieth-century Ireland than in either England/Wales or Scotland?[2] Why were regional variations in rates of population growth in Ireland less dependent on inter-regional migration flows and more dependent on regional differentials in rates of natural increase and in the susceptibility of different regions to overseas emigration than was the case elsewhere in the UK? Above all, why did the processes of economic and demographic 'revolution' which began in the period between the mid-eighteenth and mid-nineteenth centuries have only a limited, immediate impact on the frequency and geographic pattern of human mobility? This is not to deny the occurrence of some increase in the extent of spatial mobility or of a striking alteration in the direction of migrant flows in the hundred years or so before 1850, both between the home countries and countries overseas and between and within the constituent countries of the British Isles: simply to suggest that, compared with what was to follow, the initial changes in migratory habits were very modest.

The volume of overseas emigration in the period between the mid-nineteenth and early twentieth centuries was unprecedented in its magnitude. Levels of migration between and within each of the home countries also rose to entirely novel heights in the later nineteenth and early twentieth centuries and, at least in England/Wales, the movement of people came to play a much more influential part in determining variations in regional rates of population growth than ever before. Internal migratory flows became increasingly less diffuse and more concentrated. And only from the very late nineteenth or early twentieth century was there any obvious increase in the distance normally travelled by people moving from one part of Britain to another. It is the main purpose of this chapter to explain why such dramatic changes in the levels and patterns of migration were so long delayed.

Although there is no sophisticated 'general framework or model within which the process of human migration can be conceptualized and investigated' (O'Rourke 1972, p. 263), the factors responsible for regional and temporal variations in the volume and pattern of migration must lie within one or other of the following broad sets of influences:

1. The strength of the *push* forces operating in the areas from which emigrants come. These include a wide range of social, political and demographic as well as economic circumstances such as levels of wages and employment opportunities and, also, the extent to which people are willing to consider moving from their place of birth and upbringing.

2. The strength of the *pull* forces from areas which attract immigrants; apart from the prevailing and perceived future economic, social and political conditions in receiving areas, these include variations in the extent to which their own populations are prepared to welcome, and able to absorb, newcomers.

3. The magnitude of the *differential* between social, political and, in particular, economic conditions and opportunities in sending and receiving areas.

4. The degree of *ease* with which movement from one area to another can be accomplished. This, in turn, involves the costs of migration, the amount of risk involved in the journey and the time it takes, the existence or otherwise of agencies willing to facilitate the process of migration, the depth of knowledge about conditions prevailing elsewhere and the extent to which migration requires a 'cultural' upheaval. In this last respect, ethnic, linguistic or other cultural similarities between sending and receiving communities, especially if accompanied by a willingness among receiving populations to

127

provide financial or other assistance for potential immigrants, are likely to generate higher levels of migration than in cases where the cultural traditions of sending and receiving communities are very different.

The problem, of course, has always been to identify the factor, or factors, in this list to which most responsibility for determining migrant flows should be given.

OVERSEAS MIGRATION

Differences in conditions and opportunities at home obviously go far towards explaining the marked regional variations in levels of emigration which existed between the mid-eighteenth and mid-twentieth centuries. Thus, Irish men and women contributed disproportionately to the stream of overseas migrants because economic and social conditions in Ireland were so much worse than elsewhere in the British Isles; and Scots were more prone than English to leave their native land because for so many more of them standards of life and prospects of betterment were poorer.

There is, however, no such ready correlation between the 'push' of poor domestic conditions and the vast upsurge in overseas emigration which occurred from all countries of the UK during the second half of the nineteenth and early years of the twentieth century. On the contrary, both in Britain and Ireland, the phenomenon of mass emigration in the fifty years or so before the outbreak of the First World War coincided with a general, if modest, improvement in income levels, employment opportunities and environmental conditions at home (Erickson 1972; Gould 1980b; O'Grada 1980). This is not to suggest that poor domestic circumstances played no significant part in determining individual decisions to emigrate. As John Murdoch, one-time editor of the 'Highlander', put it, many people remained disposed to emigrate 'in the way of hens which fly from the dogs', that is, only because they were forced to do so by circumstances.[3] Nor is it to deny the importance for the growth of emigration in the late nineteenth century of a growing awareness of the problems of deprivation at home: merely to point out that the great surge of overseas emigration which began around the middle of the nineteenth century and continued into the early twentieth cannot have been the result of a persistent deterioration of conditions in the motherland.

In only one respect, the willingness of people to consider emigration to distant lands as a solution to their problems and of philanthropists to help them do so, were 'push' forces more conducive to movement overseas during the later nineteenth and early twentieth centuries than ever before. Throughout the eighteenth and nineteenth centuries the debate persisted between those who saw emigration as a blessing for individuals, the motherland or the colonies and those who did not. In the early decades of the nineteenth century the virtues of emigration were as often pressed as its disadvantages were proclaimed in the later decades. In 1826, the Select Committee on Emigration from the UK advocated voluntary emigration as a permanent solution to the problems of excess labour at home and the needs of the colonies for labour and security from attack.[4] The Fenwick Emigration Society was typical of many private associations urging flight 'from the scene of destitution and distress' as a remedy for the 'fearful gloom (which) is fast thickening over the horizon of our country'.[5] The Reverend Coll McDonald of Portree (Skye) was one of numerous early nineteenth-century commentators advocating emigration as the sole means of combating overpopulation, of providing 'comfortably for a noble race of men', strengthening 'the hand of local government in the American colonies and' putting an end 'to the disaffection to the state in that quarter'.[6]

Most of emigration's earlier supporters, however, saw it merely as a short-term and partial solution to the country's problems. To have more lasting and extensive benefits emigration needed to be associated with measures to reduce rates of domestic population growth and promote education.[7] Nevertheless, that there was a considerable body of support for emigration as at least a temporary panacea for domestic ills in the first half of the nineteenth century is fully endorsed by the variety of public and private schemes designed to encourage it. Between 1815 and 1826 there were six separate ventures in state-aided emigration, involving roughly one in every nineteen emigrants leaving Britain.[8] Under the terms of the Poor Law Amendment Act of 1834 over 25,000 paupers, chiefly agricultural labourers from the south-east of England, had been assisted to emigrate by 1860 (Shepperson 1957). From 1840 to 1869, using funds from the sale of colonial land, the Colonial Land and Emigration Commissioners assisted the emigration of over 370,000 people to Australasia (Hitchens 1931). Out of an array of examples of private assistance for emigration we may note the help provided to their tenants by the Earl of Egremont and his son, Colonel George Wyndham, in the 1830s:[9] by Messrs Gurney and Matteaux from Norfolk, also in the 1930s:[10] by numerous large Highland landowners – the Dukes of Sutherland and Argyll, the Lords Selkirk and McDonald, Sir James Matheson, Colonel Gordon and Neill Malcolm – during the second quarter of the nineteenth century, often entirely from their own resources, sometimes in association with the Glasgow and Edinburgh committees for the relief of Highland destitution (Johnson 1913; Shepperson 1957): and by societies such as that for the Suppression of Juvenile Vagrancy (later the Children's Friend Society) (Johnson 1913;

Carrothers 1929), the myriad of usually short-lived emigration societies which sprang up around Glasgow and Paisley during the worst periods of depression in the handloom weaving trades and which relied heavily on charitable donations to assist the emigration of their members,[11] Caroline Chisholm's Female Colonization Loan Society (founded in 1848) and Sidney Herbert's Female Emigration Fund (begun in 1850) (Hammerton 1979).

The persistence of widespread opposition to emigration into the late nineteenth and early twentieth century is also indisputable. Its motives were varied: a belief that emigration would do little to solve the problems of the mother country or those parts of it like the Scottish Highlands, western Ireland and large urban communities where the evils of overpopulation, unemployment, pauperism or environmental squalor were greatest:[12] that it would retard the introduction of economic and social reform at home – a view especially prevalent among trade unionists and socialists:[13] positively endanger the long-term economic, political and social interests of the motherland,[14] or impose unfair burdens on countries which received what were often regarded as the dregs of our society:[15] that it was too extreme a measure for problems which were only temporary or partial in character,[16] of exaggerated value to the individual and, particularly where women and children were concerned, sometimes harmful:[17] and that it reduced the size of church congregations,[18] was unpatriotic and of little apparent benefit to those prepared to help finance it.[19] Ignorance and conservatism, fear of hardship, the material and emotional costs of moving vast distances and the expectation that conditions at home were bound to improve combine to explain why even those with good reason for leaving – the Highland crofter and the urban poor – were sometimes among emigration's staunchest opponents.[20] The difficulty many philanthropic emigration societies continued to face in attracting funds to carry out their work is ample testimony to the strength of the opposition which prevailed against emigration in many quarters until the turn into the twentieth century.

Despite this, support for emigration was immeasurably stronger at the end of the nineteenth century than at the beginning. Until after the Napoleonic Wars the cause of emigration attracted little sympathy, partly because a rapidly growing population was considered politically and economically desirable, partly because it meant the loss of skilled workmen and partly because, following the loss of the American colonies, overseas settlement was widely regarded as a fruitless, troublesome venture (Carrothers 1929; Wood 1964–5; Donaldson 1966). Most of the contributors to Scotland's First Statistical Account, compiled in the 1790s, commented on the absence of any widespread desire to emigrate among Highlanders and condemned emigration as a 'national evil'.[21]

One of the reasons for the passing of the 1803 Passenger Act, restricting the number of passengers in accordance with a vessel's tonnage, was the wish to reduce the loss of population in the interests of national power and prestige (Dunkley 1980). In the period between the culmination of the Napoleonic Wars and the mid-nineteenth century opponents of emigration continued to outnumber its supporters. To the majority of observers large-scale emigration was either unnecessary, irrelevant or positively harmful. Overpopulation was a local and temporary problem which could be overcome by the more efficient use and allocation of the plentiful resources of the motherland. 'It is a sorry pass if we, rich in capital, resources, ingenuity have to send the healthy, able-bodied overseas to get a living'.[22] The relief of destitution was better accomplished in other ways, all the more so since any reduction in population achieved by emigration would soon be made up by higher rates of population growth or immigration from Ireland.[23] By itself emigration would do little to solve the problems of destitution at home.[24] Many potential emigrants, it was felt, were spiritually or emotionally unsuited to life overseas,[25] while the mother country would suffer severely from the departure of its most useful and enterprising people.[26]

Such attitudes, together with a widespread feeling that emigration was a national, not merely a local, requirement and therefore the responsibility of government rather than of private charity,[27] go far towards explaining why the amount of philanthropic assistance available for it was disappointingly small.[28] Associated with understandable apprehension over the likely cost of state-aided emigration schemes and a fear that government sponsorship would lead to a decline in charitable donations to emigration or in the willingness of individual emigrants to finance themselves,[29] they also explain why state assistance for emigration was so spasmodic and limited in the decades following 1815 and why even the suggestion of the Horton committee of 1826–7, to assist emigration out of the poor rate (in England) or by voluntary contributions from landlords and their chief tenants (in Scotland) rather than from central government revenues, met with such fierce opposition (Carrothers 1929; Johnston 1972).

Until well into the nineteenth century the popularity of emigration continued to suffer from widespread anxiety about the hardships of life in colonial wildernesses, a reluctance to undergo the traumas of removal from country, family and friends and an assumption among 'respectable' people that emigration was fit only for criminals, paupers and others who had failed to make a success of life at home – an assumption which, though less common than it had once been, was kept alive by the policy of 'shovelling-out paupers' pursued by governments during the 1830s.[30] Only for Ireland, where problems of destitution were particularly severe, was the case for emigration viewed more sympathetically.[31]

Even so, long before the middle of the century support for emigration was increasing steadily. Encouraged by Malthusian fears of overpopulation, rural poverty, unemployment, urban squalor and overcrowding, emigration was increasingly seen as at least a partial solution to problems of destitution and a safety-valve against the possibility that these might spill over into revolution. A growing number of people came to regard emigration to the colonies as vital to the increase of markets for our manufactures, the supply of raw materials for our industries and the defence of the colonies themselves against foreign aggressors.[32] In 1831 it was reported that there had been a 'great increase in the desire for emigration from the UK':[33] in 1834 that the benefits of emigration to the working classes were now more widely recognized and that even Irish landlords were more disposed than ever to assist their tenants to move:[34] in 1836 that 'the interest taken by the gentry of England in favour of aiding their unemployed labouring population to transfer their industry and labour to these fine provinces (in Upper and Lower Canada) ... is on the increase'.[35] Five years later the Colonial Land and Emigration Commissioners informed Lord John Russell that 'never was there a time when there was greater anxiety for emigration in the three countries than now'.[36] At a meeting arranged by the Society for the Promotion of Colonization in 1848, Lord Ashley observed how the earlier prejudice of working men against emigration was beginning to disappear.[37] According to the Reverend Andrew Murray of Auchterderran (Fifeshire), in his contribution to the New Statistical Account, 'forty years ago emigration was thought of with great reluctance; now the predeliction for the native spot has diminished, and emigration is more readily embraced'.[38]

During the second half of the nineteenth century support for emigration, particularly that directed towards Britain's colonies, became still more vociferous and sustained. The burgeoning number of charitable societies providing financial and other forms of assistance to emigrants affords ample proof of emigration's increasing attractiveness. For all the continued opposition of working-class intellectuals and organizations, there is no doubt of the growing popularity of emigration among working-class men and women generally.[39] Despite the greater willingness of the charitable public to provide funds for emigration, almost without exception the various emigration societies received many more applications for assistance than they had funds to support.[40] By the early years of the twentieth century the enthusiasm for emigration among the labouring populations had reached unprecedented levels.[41] Partly as a result of the work of the emigration societies, the Emigrants' Information Office and government migration officers at home and abroad, and partly as a consequence of the growing demand for labour in the colonies and the assistance given to immigrants by colonial governments most of the suspicion of movement overseas previously harboured by the working classes had disappeared.[42] By 1900 emigration was widely regarded both as an acceptable and effective means of escaping from problems at home and as a way of ensuring the future unity and security of the Empire and the prosperity of British industry and trade.[43]

Generally, however, the influence of 'push' factors was a less significant cause of the upsurge in rates of emigration to the New World in the half century or so before the outbreak of the First World War than the 'pull' of opportunities in the New World itself. Until the later years of the nineteenth century the economies of New World countries were too underdeveloped and their political, social and cultural environments too primitive to attract immigrants in very large numbers. Significantly, most of the emigrants leaving the UK for the USA during the first half of the century were people with some capital or skill rather than the poorest, least skilled members of the community for whose services as labourers or domestic servants the American economy as yet had little to offer.[44] Until at least the middle of the nineteenth century the rudimentary nature of colonial life was a powerful disincentive to female emigration and its supporters (Hammerton 1979). Many early century commentators opposed emigration because they feared for the moral welfare of those who moved to countries which, in their view, lacked the necessary provision for educational and religious training.[45] The preference among the first Scottish emigrants to North America to go out in whole communities rather than as individuals itself reflects their apprehensions about the social and cultural desert to which they were going.[46]

Even in the twentieth century differences in the economic and environmental circumstances of receiving countries were important in determining the scale and direction of emigration from the British Isles. Irrespective of variations in the cost, time and risks of the journey, the relative absence of opportunities for employment and of so many of what were regarded as the essentials for a civilized life go far towards explaining why the colonies of Australasia and South Africa attracted fewer immigrants than North America. Charitable societies like the Liverpool Self-Help Emigration Society and the Church of England Waifs and Strays Society sent few emigrants to Australia, New Zealand and South Africa because 'of the few openings there'.[47] The Salvation Army avoided South Africa because cheap black labour allowed little opportunity for unskilled white workers, and Australasia partly because of the distance involved and partly because large numbers of immigrants were not wanted.[48] There was a particular reluctance to expose women and children to the more hostile colonial environments. Australia for instance, a less refined, more abrasive and less caring society, was considered less suitable for women and children than Canada.[49]

Throughout the period up to the First World War annual fluctuations in the number of emigrants despatched by philanthropic societies were principally determined by perceived levels of employment in each of the main receiving countries. Overall, however, as the economies of

133

overseas countries matured to offer greater opportunities for immigrants with few skills or little capital and as their social and cultural environments improved, the attractiveness of life overseas increased dramatically during the later years of the nineteenth and early twentieth centuries (Thomas 1954; Rubin 1958). In this simple fact alone lies much of the explanation for the timing of the phenomenon of mass emigration from the Old World to the New.

How far this vast exodus of human beings from European countries also depended on an increased willingness of overeas populations to welcome or positively encourage immigration is more difficult to assess. Attitudes to immigration varied considerably from one receiving country to another and from time to time within each receiving country – largely in accordance with levels of demand for labour, and were greatly influenced by the type of occupational skill possessed by potential arrivals. In the course of the second half of the nineteenth century receiving societies became more selective, in some respects, of the kind of people they were willing to accept. Pauper or destitute immigrants, defined as anyone whose passage was financially assisted by state or private charity, were regarded with growing hostility and by the early twentieth century normally admitted only if presumed to be healthy and industrious – and even then, as in Canada on the eve of the First World War, often only if they intended going into farm work, where labour was desperately needed.[50] Colony after colony passed legislation to exclude certain other classes of people whose immigration was felt to be undesirable: lunatics and idiots, the deaf and dumb, the blind and infirm, epileptics, anyone unable to read or write in a European language or thought likely to become a pauper once admitted, persons with 'loathesome' or contagious diseases, prostitutes and their pimps, and some types of criminal.[51] During the late nineteenth and early twentieth centuries the types of occupation welcomed by the major receiving countries, and still more so the types of occupation they positively encouraged to immigrate, became more and more restricted.

In the main, only farmers, agricultural labourers and domestic servants were assured of a consistently warm welcome and, invariably, were the only people who qualified for the free or reduced passages offered from time to time by colonial governments. Migrants intending to work in industry, teaching, clerical and general administrative or service occupations, where the demand for labour was more restricted, and whose arrival met with increasingly vociferous opposition from colonial trade unionists anxious to avoid a glut in the labour market, were less welcome.[52] Except, however, for those classified as undesirable under the terms of the colonial immigration laws no steps were taken to deny them access. And despite the growing selectivity of the colonies towards immigrants it is still true that their willingness to absorb newcomers was greater in the late nineteenth and early twentieth centuries than ever before, a fact which certainly contributed to the phenomenon of mass emigration to the New World in the decades before the First World War (Gould 1979).[53]

Of course, colonial attitudes to immigration were themselves primarily determined by economic conditions in the receiving countries, of which the state of the labour market was the most influential. In the final analysis it was the growth of opportunities for labour and capital overseas which was the critical factor pulling people from the Old World to the New. Not that more attractive economic conditions in the New World are alone sufficient to account for the upsurge in rates of emigration during the second half of the nineteenth and early twentieth centuries. In reality, as reflected in the statements and behaviour of charitable emigration societies, decisions on whether or not to emigrate were invariably based on a *comparison* of prospects in sending and receiving areas and therefore almost always involved both 'push' and 'pull' considerations (Duncan 1963–4; Gould 1979). What mattered was the *relative differential* between opportunites at home and overseas. However grim the circumstances at home, there was little point assisting emigration if prospects elsewhere were no better: and however attractive the opportunities elsewhere little incentive to consider emigration if conditions at home were equally satisfactory.

Societies like the Salvation Army, the Church Army, Barnardos, the Liverpool Self-Help Emigration Society, the South African Colonization Society and the Junior Imperial Migration Committee sent emigrants only to pre-arranged employment or, at least, only when they had reason to believe that their emigrants were *practically certain* to find work.[54] 'No emigrant should be sent out without prospect of employment', commented Miss Ashley, secretary of the Bristol Emigration Society, in her evidence to the Haggard committee.[55] In 1908, despite receiving large numbers of applications for assistance the Salvation Army refused to send more emigrants to Canada because of a temporary decline of employment opportunities in the colony.[56] The East End Emigration Fund delayed its appeal for donations in 1909 until improved prospects for labour in Canada coincided with poor employment prospects among London's general labouring population.[57] The Aberdeen Union of Women Workers steadfastly refused to emigrate females already employed in domestic service at home; the Church Army anyone in regular employment: Middlemore's no child who had a reasonable chance of succeeding in the motherland. The Church of England Emigration Society always distinguished carefully between those of its emigrants who were unemployed, who received financial assistance, and those who were in employment but merely wished to improve their prospects, who were given no financial aid.[58]

For individuals, as for emigration societies, decisions on emigration also usually involved a comparison between prospects at home and abroad. This is not to imply that either 'push' or 'pull' influences did not predominate in these decisions. As already noted, the fact that mass emigration was characteristic of the later rather than the earlier decades of the nineteenth century was itself due more to the attractions of the New World than the repellent qualities of the Old. It remains the case, however, that undue emphasis on 'pull' (or 'push') factors distorts and oversimplifies the *raison d'être* of the movement. It was not so much the growing attractiveness of life overseas which explained the timing of mass intercontinental migration as the fact that never before the later nineteenth and early twentieth centuries had the *differential* between opportunities in the Old World and the New been so great. In spite of their growing per capita prosperity, relatively overpopulated economies like the UK were unable to generate the same abundance of opportunity as the resource-rich and relatively underpopulated economies of the New World. It was this *comparative* circumstance more than any other which propelled people overseas (Galloway and Veddar 1971; Gould 1979).

The actual motives for emigration varied enormously from individual to individual. For many women the New World offered enhanced possibilities for marriage and a family (Hammerton 1979). To the promoters of child emigration it was a means of removing children from degraded surroundings and associations at home:[59] for others an avenue to higher earnings and improved standards of life.[60] But, as the statements of the emigration societies again show, emigration was essentially a quest for work – a flood of people escaping from countries where, for many, regular employment was at worst impossible, at best uncertain.[61] Above all, therefore, the phenomenon of mass emigration must be seen as the result of a unique intercontinental imbalance in the geographic distribution of the labour supply, an imbalance brought about by disparate rates of growth in the economies of the Old World and the New and which cried out to be corrected by a new alignment in the geography of the world's population (Tomaske 1971; Gould 1979). The efforts of the South African Colonisation Society to promote emigration as a means of ensuring 'a scientific distribution of population throughout the Empire in order to guarantee the differing labour needs of the Home Country and the various Dominions (and to ensure equality between the sexes)' are a perfect contemporary realization of its fundamental motivation.[62]

When, in the years between the world wars, the employment opportunity–differential between the Old World and the New narrowed, the tide of emigration ebbed. By the 1930s more people were returning from the New World than going to it. The adoption of legislation to restrict immigration by the USA and other 'receiving' countries contributed to the decline in emigrant flows.[63] But legislation was secondary to the fact that, in the midst of world economic depression, the countries of the New World were no longer able to absorb vast inflows of people. Significantly, the quotas set by the USA on immigration from Britain and Ireland were never filled. The fact was that the relative attractiveness of overseas countries had declined. Despite high levels of unemployment, conditions at home improved with the development of social security, insurance and pension schemes and a steady rise in real wages for those in work. In Ireland the replacement of Protestant landlordism by a class of predominantly Catholic small-owner farmers, state legislation in favour of better wages and working conditions for the landless, labouring population and the achievement of independence for the 26 counties of the republic lessened the necessity for Catholic emigration (Kennedy 1973). Prospects of employment and advancement were now little better in the USA and other overseas countries than in the UK. Temporarily, at least, the opportunity-differential was too small to make the upheaval of emigration worthwhile.

That differentials in opportunity were the main cause of the mass exodus of people from Britain and Ireland during the late nineteenth and early twentieth centuries is supported both by the geographic direction of emigrant streams and the relative contribution of each of the home countries to those streams. Between 1861 and the beginning of the twentieth century migrants to the USA and Canada outnumbered those to Australia by seven to one. In part this was due to lower transport costs, a speedier passage and a greater knowledge of, and affinity for, North American life. But it also reflected the greater opportunities for employment and advancement in North America than elsewhere. When, in the decade or so before the outbreak of the First World War, the preference of British emigrants increasingly turned from the USA towards Britain's colonies, especially Canada and Australia, the explanation lay chiefly in the narrowing of relative opportunity-differentials.[64] As the differential in opportunities between Britain and countries like Canada and Australia widened with the rapid growth of world demand for primary products, so that between Britain and the USA narrowed as a result of a growing scarcity of land in the USA, increasing opposition to immigration from the American labour movement and greater competition for unskilled work in the United States from immigrants from South and East Europe (Kelley 1965). For the first time the cost-benefit of migration to Canada and Australia equated relatively closely with that to the USA. Opportunity-differentials also go a long way towards accounting for variations in the relative extent of emigration from each of the different countries of the UK. Ireland, particularly, and Scotland contributed proportionately more than England to overseas emigrant flows simply because the difference between opportunities at home and abroad was greater for the inhabitants of Ireland and Scotland than England. The Irish and Scots had so much more to gain from emigration than the English.

This is not, of course, to imply that the greater the opportunity-differential the greater, necessarily, the rate of emigration. Apart from the will to leave, would-be emigrants also needed the resources to do so.

Without these emigration was impossible, however alluring the attractions elsewhere and however great the dichotomy between prospects at home and overseas. The point was recognized as long ago as the 1840s by the Reverend James Morrison of Kintail commenting on the attitudes of Scottish Highlanders to movement overseas:

> The love of country prevails most strongly; and they never think of emigration until, from poverty, they are unable to pay their passage and, under these circumstances, emigration is out of the question.[65]

Throughout the nineteenth century sheer poverty often ruled out emigration as an escape from misery. Material deprivation may have been the most powerful 'push' influence driving people overseas. But it could only work if the depths of hardship were not too extreme. The willingness of so many individuals to provide funds for the emigration of the poor, the supply of funds for emigration by poor law guardians, home and colonial governments, the vast amounts of money for emigration provided by relatives and friends already overseas,[66] and the proliferation of private charitable emigration societies amply demonstrate that large numbers of people were unable to respond to the lure of opportunities elsewhere because they lacked the personal resources to do so. The point is best illustrated by reference to Irish emigration.

Nowhere was the strength of domestic forces propelling emigration greater than in Ireland (Bovenkirk 1973; Kennedy 1973). The poverty which stemmed from an inability to keep rates of natural increase within the limits of resources, the backwardness of Irish agriculture and the restricted scope for employment in a poorly developed industrial sector are obviously an important part of the explanation for the scale of Irish emigration. Yet, significantly, regional and socio-occupational patterns of Irish emigration reveal that the worst extremes of poverty retarded as often as they promoted movement overseas. Until the 1880s aggregate levels of emigration from the poorest, western parts of Ireland were no higher than those from the more prosperous east. Only from the closing years of the nineteenth century, when material conditions in the west improved, did the absolute number of emigrants from the more backward areas come to exceed that from areas of greater prosperity.[67] Similarly, low rates of emigration from County Cork in the pre-Famine era were due to the presence of an unusually large population of landless labourers unable to meet the costs of movement. Only after the Famine, when levels of destitution declined, did emigration rates from Cork become the highest of all Irish counties (Donnelly 1975). In the Lower Roe Valley between 1831 and 1861 parishes where standards of agricultural practice and the size of farm holdings were relatively high had greater rates of emigration than those where agriculture was backward and holdings small: emigrants were by no means drawn from the ranks of the poorest in the county (Hunter 1971). Emigration from

County Derry in 1834 was dominated by small farmers and the better class of cottiers who could afford the costs of moving to North America (Johnson 1959). Until the final quarter of the nineteenth century movement overseas was at least as common from the more prosperous northern parts of the county as from its poorer south-eastern regions (Johnson 1970).

Conceivably, the official statistics upon which these conclusions are based understate the extent of emigration from the poorer parts of the country and overstate the role of extreme poverty as a factor in the restriction of emigration rates. Impediments to movement from areas of greatest hardship may as much have been the result of a greater willingness to accept poor standards of life, the easier availability of land or the longer continuance of traditional farming practices as of the influence of extreme poverty and an inability to finance movement (O'Grada 1978). Certainly, regional variations in rates of emigration from Ireland were the product of a more complex set of circumstances than relative poverty and backwardness alone, not the least important of these other circumstances being the geography of the domestic handicraft industry (Collins 1982). But it is difficult to deny entirely that in Ireland, as elsewhere, the worst extremes of hardship often impeded emigration. Only when deprivation was not too severe did poverty itself drive large numbers overseas. Rising incomes and expectations at home, coupled with the increase in assistance for emigration provided by philanthropic societies, governments, commercial companies and remittances from family and friends overseas, undoubtedly help to explain why the widening opportunity-differential between the Old World and the New which occurred between the mid-nineteenth century and the First World War was accompanied by such a dramatic transformation in the geography of the world's population.

This transformation was facilitated by advances in methods of international transport and communication which both increased popular appreciation of conditions and prospects overseas and brought them within easier reach. Reductions in the actual cost of overseas travel, however, were relatively unimportant. Most of the decline in ocean-going passage fares occurred in the early decades of the nineteenth century, before the great surge in emigration to the New World. From the 1830s onwards the cost of intercontinental travel altered very little and, for the vast majority of the population, emigration remained a very expensive matter.[68] Of greater importance than lower fares to the rise of overseas emigration was the improvement in the speed, comfort and safety of international travel which came with innovations in methods of transport (Gould 1979). The replacement of sailing vessels by steamships cut the time taken for the Atlantic crossing from six weeks in the mid-nineteenth century to a week on the eve of the First World War. By the end of the century Australia could be reached in a matter of weeks rather than months. With the reduction in time were

139

associated major improvements in the standards of comfort and safety of ocean travel which further lowered the barriers to long-distance human mobility.[69] The decline in the opportunity-cost of earning time wasted on board ship which came with the greater speed of passage was among the most important reasons for the considerable increase in the frequency of *temporary* movement between the Old World and the New during the later decades of the nineteenth century (Gould 1980a).

Ignorance of conditions in overseas countries and an understandable reluctance to venture into the unknown had been a powerful barrier to emigration during the early years of the nineteenth century.[70] As late as 1906 it was still believed that lack of information on colonial life reduced the desire for emigration among men and women of the working classes.[71] Nevertheless, by the close of the nineteenth century appreciation of the opportunities offered overseas was very much greater than ever before. The Emigrants' Information Office, founded in 1886 in response to growing demands for information on Britain's colonies,[72] was among the most significant of the new avenues for dispensing details of conditions in the New World, its widely circulated annual handbooks providing data on colonial life, the immigration regulations of colonial countries, the types of assistance given by colonial governments towards the cost of passage and settlement and the activities of charitable societies affording help to emigrants. Another was the work of the passenger agents of the various shipping companies which relied heavily on the revenue generated by emigrants and acted as influential recruiting and advertising agencies for the colonies.[73]

A third important source of information on colonial life was provided by the emigration societies. Some, like the Colonial Intelligence League, The Settlers' Emigration League and the Travellers' Aid Society, were almost solely concerned with disseminating information. But all regarded the supply of material on colonial conditions and opportunities as an integral and necessary part of their work. The quarterly journal of the Church of England Emigration Society, 'The Emigrant', had an annual circulation of between 20,000 and 25,000 and was especially important for the information it gave on places in Canada where immigrants would find cheap, temporary accommodation on arrival. The Society also published a handbook, 'The Church's Care for Emigrants', which included lists of overseas clergy and laity willing to advise and assist newcomers.[74] The Salvation Army publicized emigration's virtues by means of lectures in villages and towns throughout the country, posters from 'Lerwick to the Channel Islands,' periodical and newspaper articles and through its permanent offices in London, Bristol, Liverpool, Edinburgh, Aberdeen and Glasgow and from offices opened temporarily wherever emigration was thought essential. Its weekly periodicals, with a circulation of between 400,000 and 500,000, devoted regular space to emigration matters. In 1910 and 1911 2% of the total expenditure of the Army's Emigration Department went on advertising.[75] The South African Colonization Society regularly advertised its vacancies in the daily papers and, beginning in 1907, established local committees and correspondents throughout the UK to ensure adequate publicity of the opportunities for women in South Africa.[76] According to the Committee on Haggard, in the few years prior to 1906 public suspicion of emigration had been much reduced by the good work and propaganda of the Emigrants' Information Office and the leading emigration societies.[77] Facilitated by improvements in international postal services, probably the most important source for the growing knowledge of conditions overseas, however, was the increased flow of personal correspondence between relatives and friends in the UK and the New World. By the late nineteenth century, although variations in the availability of information on life overseas – in part related to the scale of previous emigration – continued to bear some of the responsibility for regional and national differentials in rates of emigration (Tomaske 1971; Gould 1980b), ignorance of opportunities elsewhere was no longer the formidable barrier to movement that it had once been.

In essence, then, the exodus of people from the UK to the New World during the second half of the nineteenth and early twentieth centuries must be seen as the consequence of a substantial and unique dichotomy in economic opportunities, a dichotomy which stemmed from a combination of higher rates of economic growth in the New World than the Old and the location of too high a proportion of the world's labour supply in areas where the rewards for labour were relatively meagre. Advances in methods of international transport and communications, the growing willingness of individuals and communities to regard emigration as a means to a better future and of 'receiving' countries to absorb immigrants, while adding their own impetus to migrant flows, were primarily a result of intercontinental differentials in economic opportunity.

But it is also important to stress the part played by rising levels of per capita real income in the UK itself. Without the modest rise in incomes which occurred in the half century or so before the First World War and which gave more people than ever before the capital to finance their own or others' emigration the flood of migrants to distant lands would have been greatly reduced. To see the age of mass overseas migration as the product of a continued *absolute* deterioration in the prospects for a decent life at home is to distort and misinterpret its true origins.

INTERNAL MIGRATION

Excluding seasonal mobility (that is, mobility which did not involve a change of 'permanent' residence), the pattern of migration in pre-industrial England was geographically diffuse and overwhelmingly short-distance. Except in the case of London, whose relative attractions in any case declined in the course of the eighteenth century,[78] and, to a lesser extent, other large urban centres there was little concentration in the direction of migrant flows. On the whole, migrants tended to scatter in many different directions, moving dispersedly around neighbouring towns and villages usually within a twenty-mile radius of their place of birth (Clark 1979). For most of the eighteenth century not even the newly industrializing regions of the North West (Lancashire and Cheshire), the North East (Durham and Northumberland) and the West Midlands (Warwickshire and Worcestershire) needed to attract disproportionately heavy flows of longer-distance migrants (Deane and Cole 1967). Even in Scotland, where the economy was poorer and less diversified and where periodic food and employment crises led to higher rates of longer-distance mobility in the search for life's essentials, short-distance movement predominated (Flinn 1977).

The diffuse and localized character of internal migratory habits in eighteenth-century England was the consequence of a variety of circumstances: low rates of population growth which, together with rising agricultural output and the growth of opportunities for employment in industry, lessened the need to migrate over long distances in search of food or work; the relative absence of devastating urban or regional mortality crises which would have created a demographic void that could only have been rapidly filled by large-scale in-migration; the stricter application of the laws of settlement and sterner legislation against vagrancy in the period following the Restoration which, coupled with the later emergence of more liberal forms of parochial poor relief, discouraged long-distance movement and encouraged residential stability (Clark 1979); low incomes; poor transport; ignorance of conditions elsewhere and a fear of the unknown among people with relatively little education and a limited range of experiences; and the importance of family and kinship ties in an age when the absence of adequate state provision in times of ill-health, unemployment or death of the breadwinner increased individual dependence on relatives, friends and the local community. But the main reason lay in the character of the pre-industrial economy. Until the emergence of large urban-industrial concentrations in the nineteenth century manufacturing industry, based on small-scale, domestic methods of production, was predominantly rural in location and widely scattered in its geography. Towns were usually small, commercial or administrative rather than industrial centres affording only limited opportunities for employment (Law 1972). Diffuse and localized migratory patterns were largely a consequence of the relative absence of urban-industrial complexes providing employment on a wholly dispro-portionate scale and of the wide spatial scatter of economic activity in which agricultural and industrial occupations were closely intertwined.

The initial progress of industrialization in Britain during the first half of the nineteenth century had only a moderate impact on traditional patterns of migration. Not until the second half of the century did the customarily diffuse and circular pattern of mobility give way to movement that was increasingly concentrated towards a relatively small number of highly specific regions: between 1851 and 1911 towards London, West Yorkshire, the North West, North East and Midlands of England, South Wales, Lanarkshire and Renfrewshire; after 1911, though the geography of migrant flows was noticeably more diffuse than in the second half of the previous century, towards the English South East and parts of the Midlands and South West. Not until the last quarter of the nineteenth century was there any substantial increase in the frequency of internal migration and only in the twentieth century any marked rise in the average distance travelled by migrants (see pp. 42–3 for further details).

It is not difficult to explain why migratory patterns altered so little during the early decades of the nineteenth century. Firstly, many of the traditional barriers to mobility – low incomes, poor standards of education, reliance on family and friends in times of misfortune and inadequate methods of transport – remained more or less as severe as they had always been. Secondly, in spite of these hindrances to mobility, human migration was already commonplace in the centuries preceding the Industrial Revolution, so commonplace that not even the further progress of economic and social modernization in the later nineteenth and twentieth centuries could be expected to have had any *dramatic* effect on its extent (see pp. 41–2). While pre-industrial society lacked the same means and opportunities for movement that exist in more advanced economies, its inhabitants, confronted by periodic food shortages and more limited, less diversified chances for employment, often had a greater necessity to migrate, a necessity which forced the majority of them to overcome the barriers to mobility at some stage or other in their lives. Thirdly, regional differentials in rates of population growth, income and employment opportunities in the first half of the nineteenth century were not as extreme as they were later to become and therefore were less likely to affect changes in migratory habits.

In absolute terms, employment in rural areas increased, particularly where handicraft industries continued to thrive. As a result, there was less need to look for employment elsewhere while the range of areas offering work, and thus attractive to migrants, remained relatively diffuse. And because the population of rural communities continued to expand there was no need to cast over a wider area in search of a marriage partner. Finally, the relative stability of traditional migratory patterns through the first half of the nineteenth century reflected the gradual, evolutionary nature of the process of early industrialization itself. Large-scale methods of industrial production emerged only slowly. Before the middle decades of the century large manufacturing complexes were the exception rather than the rule and their demands for labour were modest. And still, in the early nineteenth century, the majority of factory industry was located in areas where there was a well-developed range of handicraft industries and an abundant population with a high rate of natural increase. Consequently, most of the early industrial centres were able to rely on nearby populations for their labour supply and did not require to disturb unduly the traditional patterns of short-distance migration.

Only from the later decades of the nineteenth century were economic and social conditions so different from the past as to have a more radical impact on established migratory habits. Improved methods of public transport – railways, paved highways, the bicycle and the motor bus – made movement over longer distances easier and less expensive.[79] Shorter working hours and better standards of health gave people more time and energy to travel longer distances between home and place of work and increased the opportunities for social and recreational contact which extended the geographic range of marriage horizons. Higher standards of literacy and education enhanced the employment flexibility of the labour force and, through the media of letter writing, the rise of local newspapers and the contacts promoted by friendships made at school, raised both the individual's awareness of opportunities elsewhere and his ability to respond to them. Rural depopulation, enhanced by agricultural depression in the last quarter of the nineteenth century, reduced the size of village communities and forced people more often to look for employment and marriage partners further afield. Rising real incomes not only lessened the financial constraints on mobility and made it easier for society to cope with the needs of migrants for housing and social services but also intensified the desire to live in less crowded, physically and aesthetically more acceptable environments than those usually found around the workplace. The twentieth-century trend towards suburban living mirrors well the growing division between place of work and residence which economic growth encourages and makes possible.

Above all, the increase in the frequency and distance of internal migration since the later years of the nineteenth century reflects the substantial widening of regional disparities in rates of economic growth which is a normal corollary of the process of economic modernization. To some extent, this is a result of regional variations in the pace of technological obsolescence and innovation and their effects on employment prospects; to some extent, of the development in particular localities of hitherto neglected or underutilized natural resources and of the declining utility of the resource allocations of other areas. But it is also a legacy of the trend towards regional product specialization which occurs in modern economies and the growing division between areas of prosperity and depression which this causes. In earlier times, when the spatial division between agricultural and manufacturing activities was less pronounced, the geography of prosperity and depression was more localized and intertwined and patterns of migration, therefore, more short-distance and circular in character.

With the growth of regional specialization, the size of the areas subject either to prosperity or depression widened and migration perforce became longer in distance and more concentrated in direction (Perry 1969; Parish 1972–3; Lewis, G. 1979). During the second half of the nineteenth century this was mirrored in the flow of migrants towards the prosperous textile, coalmining, iron and steel and shipbuilding industries of the North West, North East and Midlands of England, West Yorkshire, South Wales and South West Scotland. When towards the end of the century and, particularly, during the interwar period the fortunes of Britain's staple industries declined it was these areas which suffered most from migrational loss. Instead, migrants came to focus on regions like the South East and parts of the Midlands whose economies were geared to the production of 'new' consumer goods for which demand was rising.

In Ireland the frequency of internal migration, whether short or long distance, was always markedly lower than elsewhere in the UK. To some extent this was due to the relative lack of employment opportunities outside agriculture. But it was also due to the particular attractions for the Irish of *seasonal* labour migration to Britain. To many Irishmen, for much of the nineteenth century, temporary mobility in search of employment was a more attractive choice than permanent movement.

Seasonal movements of labour, of course, were common to many parts of the UK. Originating in the decades following the Restoration, possibly as an alternative to the decline in the frequency of long-distance permanent movement, and already well-established by the end of the eighteenth century (Clark 1979), they rose to a peak during the third quarter of the nineteenth century before falling to negligible levels by the early twentieth. Urban workers flowed into summer agricultural employment in the Fens and the East Riding and in the orchards and hop gardens of Kent, Surrey, Herefordshire and Worcestershire. Streams of rural labourers moved backwards and forwards from one farming system to another where peak demands for labour varied in their timing – from pasture to arable, hill to vale, light to heavy soil areas, north to south and between areas of small, subsistence farming and large-scale, capitalist agriculture. But it was Scottish Highlanders and the Irish who dominated seasonal migrant flows.

The predominance of Scottish Highlanders and the Irish in seasonal movements of labour and the particular popularity of seasonal migration during the first three-quarters or so of the nineteenth century were the product of a variety of closely-related factors: overpopulation, poverty and the absence of local opportunities for employment outside agriculture;[80] the development of railways and steamships which made temporary departures easier; and the fact that seasonal migration could be achieved at less real cost than the alternative of permanent movement, an especially important consideration in areas where incomes were low. To some extent the popularity of seasonal migration during the first three-quarters of the nineteenth century also reflected a unique association of circumstances in the areas to which temporary migrants were attracted. First, there was a growth in occupations which required labour of a specifically seasonal type – agriculture and fishing, domestic service, railway construction and the building industry. Second, the general decline in the price of many agricultural products made the flexibility afforded by labour of a seasonal type especially attractive to employers anxious to contain their costs. Third, in the absence of labour-saving technology, reliance on seasonal labour was often the only way of filling the void created by the decay of the traditionally close links between agricultural and industrial occupations and the loss of agricultural labour to full-time industrial work.

Already by the closing years of the nineteenth century, however, the impulses for specifically seasonal movement were beginning to weaken. Depopulation and an easing of the worst problems of under-employment and poverty in areas like Ireland and the Scottish Highlands, together with growing opportunities for full-time emloyment in non-agricultural work, reduced the supply of temporary migrants while the onset of agricultural depression in the last quarter of the century and the spread of labour-saving agricultural machinery eroded demand for them. At the same time, fostered by rising standards of income and education, improved methods of long-distance transport and communications and a greater willingness to depart permanently from relatives, friends and homeland, seasonal movement was increasingly replaced by emigration overseas as the means to a better future. By the beginning of the twentieth century temporary migration was both less feasible and less necessary than it had been for much of the nineteenth.[81]

NOTES AND REFERENCES

1. Net outmigration is defined as the numerical balance between emigrants and immigrants.
2. Internal migrants are identified only as those who changed their place of 'permanent' residence. 'Seasonal' labour migration is treated separately. See pp. 145–6. In reality, the distinction between a 'seasonal' and a 'permanent' migrant is not easy to make.
3. Report from the Select Committee on Colonization, 1890, p. 273 in Reports from the Select Committees on Colonization, 1889–91, *Emigration,* 9, Irish University Press, Shannon, 1969.

4. Report from the Select Committee on Emigration from the U.K., 1826, *Emigration,* 1, Irish University Press, Shannon, 1968, pp. 3–4, 10.

5. Minutes of the Fenwick Emigration Society, 1839, with a note by **George Neilson,** *Scottish Historical Review,* 17, 1919–20, p. 221.

6. *New Statistical Account of Scotland,* Edinburgh, 1845, XIV, pp. 231, 236.

7. See **Reverend Robert McPherson** of Inverness, First Report from the Select Committee on Emigration, Scotland, 1841, p. 195, in *First and Second Reports from the Select Committee on Emigration, Scotland,* BPP, 1841, VI, and **Reverend Archibald Clerk** of Skye, *New Statistical Account,* 1845, XIV, p. 345.

8. Johnston 1972; see also Johnson 1913; Carrothers 1929; Shepperson 1957; Guillet 1963; Donaldson 1966; Glass and Taylor 1976.

9. BPP, 1836, XL, pp. 4, 6; BPP, 1840, XXXIII, p. 71; *The Times,* 15 April 1833, 29 April 1834.

10. BPP, 1837–8, XL, pp. 13–14.

11. Carrothers 1929; Donaldson 1966; *The Times,* 20 August 1842; BPP, *Accounts and Papers,* XXXI, 1842, pp. 6, 15–16.

12. See **Malcolm McNeill, Charles Lucas, Robert Giffen, Reverend William MacRae, Sir Baldwin Leighton, William Redmond, Angus Sutherland, R. M. Fergusson,** *Select Committee on Colonization, 1889–91,* pp. 20, 25, 28, 30, 34–5, 44, 72, 75–6, 233, 236, 248, 321, 440–1, 449, 459–65; **H. Lambert, F. Morris, Ernest Aves, J. H. Richardson, C. S. Loch, C. W. Cohen,** *Report of the Departmental Committee appointed to consider Mr Rider Haggard's report on agricultural settlements in British colonies,* BPP, 1906, LXXVI, pp. 561, 646, 669, 672, 690–7, 700–3, 756, 771; a Mr Johnson at a public meeting to discuss the formation of a Federated Council of Emigration, *The Times,* 27 January 1870; the National Association for Promoting State-directed Colonization, *Select Committee on Colonization,* 1889–91, pp. 94–5, 99–100.

13. *Haggard,* 1906, pp. 690–7, 716, 777, 803; *The Times,* 12 October 1908; Royal Commission on the Natural Resources, Trade and Legislation of certain portions of His Majestry's Dominions, *First Interim Report, Part I, Migration,* BPP, 1912–13, XVI, pp. 149, 173.

14. See **John Murdoch,** *Select Committee on Colonization,* 1889–91, pp. 290–1, 296–7, 304–6; **Herbert Samuel, Herbert Grange, W. Crooks, J. G. Legge,** *Haggard,* 1906, pp. 559–60, 677, 740, 742, 846; **Lady Knightley, Mrs Joyce, D. Lamb,** the South African Colonisation Society, the British Women's Emigration Association, **Sir C. Kinloch-Cooke, W. Baker, Sir Albert Spicer, Earl Grey,** the Royal Colonial Institute Standing Committee on Emigration, the British Passenger Agents' Association, *Natural Resources,* 1912–13, pp. 141, 149, 153, 165, 191–3, 223–4, 226, 239–42, 244, 251, 259, 284–6, 337; *The Times,* 12 July 1871; *Hansard,* VIII, 1911, pp. 25–7, XXIX, 1911, pp. 635–7, 640.

15. **E. Gates, E. Aves, J. H. Richardson, H. R. Maynard,** *Haggard,* 1906, pp. 632, 669, 672, 690–7, 700–3, 744–5; **E. Gates,** the British Passenger Agents' Association, *Natural Resources,* 1912–13, pp. 195, 251; **Sir Baldwin Leighton,** *Select Committee on Colonisation,* 1889–91, p. 253.

16. **Herbert Samuel,** *Haggard,* 1906, pp. 559–60; **Earl Granville** and **Lord Overstone,** *Hansard,* CXCV, 1869, pp. 954–6; *Select Committee on Colonisation,* 1889–91, pp. ix–vi.

17. BPP, 1875, LXIII, p. 274ff; **Charles Lucas,** *Select Committee on Colonisation,* 1889–91, pp. 72, 75–6; Hammerton 1979, p. 12.
18. **W. P. Edward,** *Select Committee on Colonisation,* 1889–91, pp. 225, 228.
19. **Reverend William MacRae,** *ibid,* pp. 233, 236; *The Times,* 22 July 1869; **Reverend W. Carlile,** *Haggard,* 1906, p. 639.
20. *Ibid,* p. 671; **J. Murdoch, A. MacKenzie, J. H. Richardson, Bolton Smart,** *Select Committee on Colonisation,* 1889–91, pp. 260, 262–3, 269, 273, 275, 290–1, 296–7, 304–6, 700–3, 740, 742.
21. **Grant I.** and **Withrington, D. J.** (eds) (1977), *Sir John Sinclair, The First Statistical Account of Scotland, 1791–9,* East Ardsley, XII, pp. 188–90.
22. **R. Montgomery Martin, Philip Halliwell,** Report from the Select Committee on Handloom Weavers' Petitions, 1834–5, *Industrial Revolution, Textiles,* 7, Irish University Press, Shannon, 1968, pp. 73–4; First, Second and Third Reports from the Select Committee on Emigration from the UK, Third Report, 1827, pp. 14–41, *Emigration, 2,* Irish University Press, Shannon, 1968; *Select Committee on Emigration from Scotland,* First Report, pp. 28–9, 37; **Reverend James Wilson,** *New Statistical Account,* 1845, X, pp. 226–7; **Reverend John Munro,** *ibid,* XIII, p. 177.
23. **Thomas Kennedy, Henry Drummond, Alexander Campbell,** *Select Committee on Emigration from the UK,* Second Report, pp. 24, 27, 150–1, 154–5, Third Report, pp. 14–41, BPP, 1826–7, V; **E. McIver, A. MacKinnon, D. Shaw,** *Select Committee on Emigration from Scotland,* First Report, pp. 125, 157–8, 200–1, BPP, 1841, VI; *The Times,* 27 November 1827; **Reverend James Morrison,** *New Statistical Account,* 1845, XIV, p. 177; **Reverend David Duff,** *ibid,* X, p. 470.
24. **Mr Gregorson, Reverend Robert McPherson,** *Select Committee on Emigration from Scotland,* First Report, pp. 43, 195.
25. **Reverend Norman McLeod,** *ibid,* pp. 71–2, 83, 86; **Alexander Beith,** *New Statistical Account,* 1845, XIII, p. 136.
26. **Robert Graham,** *Select Committee on Emigration from Scotland,* First Report, p. 39; **Alexander Campbell,** *Select Committee on Emigration from the UK,* Second Report, pp. 150–1, 154–5; **R. Montgomery Martin,** *Select Committee on Handloom Weavers' Petitions,* p. 73.
27. **Alexander Campbell,** *Select Committee on Emigration from the UK,* Second Report, pp. 150–1, 154–5.
28. *Ibid,* pp. 6–7; *Select Committee on Emigration from Scotland,* First Report, pp. 28–9, 37; Colonial Land and Emigration Commissioners, *General Report,* BPP, 1844, XXXI, p. 12.
29. **H. Baillie,** *Hansard,* LVI, 1841, pp. 514–5; BPP, 1831–2, XXXII, p. 3.
30. Hammerton, 1979. A Colonial Office grant of £3,000 towards the emigration of women to Australia between 1832 and 1836 provoked revulsion at the thought of 'respectable women going to live among convicts'. *Ibid,* pp. 54–5.
31. *Select Committee on Emigration from the UK,* Second Report, pp. 6–7, Third Report, pp. 14–41.
32. Carrothers 1929; Shepperson 1957; Glass and Taylor 1976; Hammerton 1979; **A. C. Buchanan, D. Gurney,** BPP, 1836, XL, pp. 16–18; **V. Smith,** *Hansard,* XC, 1847, p. 838.
33. BPP, 1831–2, XXXII, p. 20.

34. BPP, 1835, XXXIX, p. 7.
35. **A. C. Buchanan,** BPP 1836, XL, p. 4.
36. BPP, 1840, XXXIII, p. 55.
37. *The Times,* 12 July 1848.
38. *New Statistical Account,* 1845, IX, p. 173.
39. Charles Lucas, secretary of the Emigrants' Information Office, contrasted the attitudes of individual working men, who generally favoured emigration, with those of trade union leaders, who were usually indifferent or hostile to it, *Select Committee on Colonisation,* 1889–91, p. 75.
40. *Ibid,* pp. 163–4, 194; *Haggard,* 1906, pp. 549–52, 556, 584, 617, 632, 637, 639–41, 646, 650, 662–3, 701, 756, 778–9, 793, 797–8; *Natural Resources,* 1912–13, pp. 102, 137, 141–2, 153, 160, 185, 205–6, 260–2; *The Times,* 26 May 1869, 26 January 1870, 2 July 1870, 26 April 1882, 2 February 1886, 6 March 1886, 31 January 1905, 23 February 1906, 8 May 1906, 27 April 1907, 4 December 1907, 10 December 1907, 6 January 1908, 10 February 1908, 28 February 1908, 22 July 1908, 25 January 1909, 23 December 1909, 27 December 1909, 11 June 1914; *Hansard,* VIII, 1911, p. 39.
41. *Haggard,* 1906, p. 749; *The Times,* 19 February 1907, 9 April 1912.
42. *Haggard,* 1906, pp. 549–52, 556.
43. *Ibid,* pp. 716, 750, 767, 771; *Natural Resources,* 1912–13, pp. 124, 141–2, 148, 153, 165–7, 173, 179–80, 191–3, 195, 198, 225–7, 245–7, 339–40; Royal Commission on the Natural Resources, Trade and Legislation of certain portions of His Majesty's Dominions, *Second Interim Report,* BPP, 1914, XVIII, p. 149; *The Times,* 13 April 1869, 27 January 1870, 8 February 1870, 29 April 1870, 6 March 1886, 31 January 1905, 3 August 1906, 15 January 1907, 16 July 1907, 24 May 1909, 23 April 1913; *Hansard,* CXCIX, 1870, p. 1016, CCCIV, 1886, pp. 587–94.
44. Johnson 1959; Cousens 1960; Hunter 1971; Donnelly 1975; O'Grada 1978; Erickson 1981.
45. **Reverend Alexander Beith,** *New Statistical Account,* 1845, XIII, p. 136.
46. **E. McIver, A. Scott,** *Select Committee on Emigration from Scotland,* First Report, pp. 125, 148.
47. *Haggard,* 1906, pp. 650, 782.
48. *Natural Resources,* 1912–13, p. 174.
49. *Ibid.*
50. BPP, 1833, XXVI, pp. 39–40; BPP, 1837–8, XL, pp. 11–12; Colonial Land and Emigration Commissioners, *General Report,* BPP, 1870, XVII, pp. 4–9; Emigrants' Information Office, *Report,* BPP, 1888, LXXIII, p. 5; *Haggard,* 1906, pp. 583, 650, 657, 659, 729–30, 777, 790–2; *Select Committee on Colonisation,* 1889–91, pp. 50, 52, 56–7; *Natural Resources,* 1912–13, pp. 127, 131, 181, 203, 207; *The Times,* 23 February 1906, 16 February 1907.
51. See the acts passed by the governments of New Zealand (1882, 1899), Cape Colony (1902, 1904), Southern Rhodesia and Natal (1903), Victoria (1865), Tasmania (1885, 1898), South Australia (1891), New South Wales (1893), Western Australia (1892, 1897), the Commonwealth of Australia (1901), Canada (1886, 1906, 1907, 1910), Ontario and Manitoba (1897), and Quebec (1989). The details are contained in the various Statutes and General Handbooks published annually by the Emigrants' Information Office.

52. On colonial attitudes to immigration see *Select Committee on Colonisation,* 1889–91, pp. 57, 75, 252; *Haggard,* 1906, pp. 583, 654, 692, 694, 756, 790–2; *Natural Resources,* 1912–13, pp. 173, 180, 194–6, 225–6, 245–7; *The Times,* 3 July 1885, 12 October 1908, 24 May 1909.

53. *Select Committee on Colonisation,* 1889–91, pp. 50, 56–7; *Haggard,* 1906, pp. 654, 729–30, 790–2; Emigrants' Information Office, *Report,* BPP, 1906, LXXVI, p. 654.

54. *Haggard,* 1906, p. 779; *Natural Resources,* 1912–13, pp. 160, 163, 176, 180, 340, 343; *The Times,* 20 August 1891, 30 March 1909.

55. *Haggard,* 1906, p. 900.

56. *The Times,* 25 January 1909.

57. *Ibid,* 30 March 1909.

58. *Haggard,* 1906, p. 754; *Natural Resources,* 1912–13, p. 161; Emigrants' Information Office, *Emigration Statutes and General Handbook,* No. 12, 1903, HMSO, 1903, p. 76; Middlemore's Birmingham Children's Emigration Homes, *Eighth Annual Report,* Birmingham, 1881, pp. 4–5, *Fifteenth Annual Report,* Birmingham, 1888, p. 4.

59. *Haggard,* 1906, pp. 650–1, 653; Manchester and Salford Boys' and Girls' Homes and Refuges, *Third Annual Report,* Manchester, 1873, pp. 16–17, *Twenty-fifth Annual Report,* Manchester, 1895, *Twenty-ninth Annual Report,* Manchester, 1899, p. 41; Birmingham Children's Emigration Homes, *First Annual Report,* Birmingham, 1873, p. 4, *Tenth Annual Report,* Birmingham, 1883, p. 6, *Twenty-seventh Annual Report,* Birmingham, 1900, p. 3, *Thirty-sixth Annual Report,* Birmingham, 1909, p. 4; Liverpool Sheltering Homes, *Second Annual Report,* Liverpool, 1874, p. 4, *Ninth Annual Report,* Liverpool, 1882, pp. 23–4, *Fourteenth Annual Report,* Liverpool, 1887, p. 11; **Ross, J.** *The Power I pledge,* Glasgow, 1971, p. 59; **Edmondson, W.,** *Making Rough Places Plain: Fifty Years Work of the Manchester and Salford Boys' and Girls' Refuges and Homes, 1870–1920,* Manchester, 1920, pp. 88, 91–3.

60. Hammerton 1979, pp. 150, 153–4; *Haggard,* 1906, p. 663; *Natural Resources,* 1912–13, pp. 142, 148; *The Times,* 12 July 1848, 8 February 1870; Manchester and Salford Boys' and Girls' Home and Refuges, *Third Annual Report,* Manchester, 1873, p. 16.

61. The relief of unemployment was the overwhelming motive for societies concerned with the emigration of adult males but was also a major consideration for those involved with female and child emigration, whose motives were generally more varied. *Haggard,* 1906, pp. 634, 644, 653–4, 715, 717, 793, 896–7; *Natural Resources,* 1912–13, pp. 148, 165–7, 180, 703; Brighton Emigration Society, *Fifth Annual Report,* p. 175; *The Times,* 26 May 1869, 6 April 1883, 13 November 1883, 16 February 1910. Levels of employment and unemployment were the main determinants of *short-term* fluctuations in rates of overseas emigration during the period between the mid-nineteenth century and 1914 (Gould 1979).

62. *Natural Resources,* 1912–13, p. 339.

63. In the USA the 1921 Quota Act restricted annual immigrants from any one country to 3% of the number born in that country and enumerated in the census of 1910. The 1924 Immigration Restriction Act reduced the quota to 2% of the number of a country's nationals resident in the USA in 1890. Further restrictions were imposed by the Nationals' Origins Quota Act of 1929. By the early 1930s only persons with substantial financial

resources were admitted. Canada introduced an Immigrant Restriction Act in 1923, in 1929 withdrew the £10 ocean passage rate previously offered to immigrants and from 1931 admitted only close relatives of existing residents. By the early 1930s, too, Australia offered assisted passages only to the families of existing settlers.

64. The change in the direction of emigrant flows from the USA to Britain's colonies also reflected the growing propaganda in favour of emigration to the colonies rather than to 'foreign' countries in the interests of the economic and political well-being of the Motherland and its Empire. The strength of its influence is shown by the refusal of emigration societies to grant financial aid to emigrants who went to other than British colonies.

65. *New Statistical Account,* 1845, XIV, p. 177.

66. Remittances, which averaged £1m a year between 1848 and 1900, paid for three-quarters of all Irish emigration to the USA during the period (Kennedy 1973).

67. Cousens 1960, 1961-2, 1963, 1963-4, 1965.

68. Steerage fares to the USA fluctuated between £3.50 and £5 throughout the second half of the nineteenth century. Steerage to Canada cost £5 or £6 in the 1820s and five guineas at the end of the century. The basic fare to Australia varied between £15 and £20 from the 1830s to the outbreak of the First World War. Between 1870 and 1914 steerage to New Zealand was between £15 and £21 and the basic, third class fare to South Africa remained twelve to fourteen guineas. At the opening of the twentieth century the average man could expect to pay a third of his annual income to emigrate himself, his wife and two children to Canada. Emigration to Australia, New Zealand or South Africa required a single adult to devote between a quarter and a fifth of his yearly income to the costs of passage and men with families considerably more than their annual income.

69. On transport improvements see Coleman 1974; **Dyos, H. J.** and **Aldcroft, D. H.**, *British Transport: an Economic Survey from the Seventeenth Century to the Twentieth,* Leicester University Press, 1969.

70. *Copy of Reports from the Commissioners of Emigration to the Secretary of State for the Colonial Department,* BPP, 1831-2, XXXII, p. 3.

71. *Haggard,* 1906, pp. 690, 695, 701, 885.

72. *Memorandum on the History and Functions of the Emigrants' Information Office,* BPP, 1907, LXVII, pp. 457-70; *The Times,* 18 January 1886; *Hansard,* CCCIV, 1886, pp. 587-94.

73. 'Every shipping agent's office is a living advertisement of colonial opportunities', commented the representative of the British Passenger Agents' Association in 1912, *Natural Resources,* 1912-13, pp. 161, 340-2.

74. *Haggard,* 1906, p. 750; *The Times,* 14 March 1914.

75. *Natural Resources,* 1912-13, pp. 163, 340-2.

76. *Ibid,* p. 339; *The Times,* 9 November 1907.

77. *Haggard,* 1906, p. 550.

78. Clark 1979; **Wareing, J.** (1980), 'Changes in the geographical distribution of the recruitment of apprentices to the London companies, 1486-1750', *Journal of Historical Geography,* 6, 3; **Wrigley, E. A.** (1967), 'A simple model of London's importance in changing English society and economy 1650-1750', *Past and Present,* 37.

79. Care should be taken not to exaggerate the effect of economic and social

modernization on patterns of migration, however. The influence of transport improvement on migratory habits, for example, is less clear-cut than sometimes supposed. On balance, the spread of the railway network in nineteenth-century Britain undoubtedly increased human mobility. Directly or indirectly, the railways provided the basis for prosperous new regional economies; facilitated the import of overseas food supplies and the diffusion of labour-saving agricultural machinery, which contributed to the flight of rural labourers to the town; and made migration more attractive by allowing those who moved to remain in regular contact with the friends and relatives they left behind. In other respects, by contrast, the railways discouraged migration. By allowing speedy access to markets for perishable foodstuffs they increased employment opportunities in those areas able to turn to dairying, fruit-growing and market gardening as an escape from the competition of overseas grain and livestock products. By making it easier to commute daily from home to place of work they reduced the necessity for short-distance migration. By facilitating long-distance travel they may have encouraged seasonal movement at the expense of permanent migration. It was the introduction of the railway (and the steamship), for instance, which enabled nineteenth century Irishmen and Scottish Highlanders to choose the option of seasonal rather than permanent migration in search of work and thus to remain in their home communities for longer and to a far greater extent than would otherwise have been the case.

80. The great increase in temporary migration from the Scottish Highlands in the half century after 1815, for example, owed as much to the decline of the kelp fishing and illicit whisky distilling industries and the disappearance of military employment as to the fall in cattle prices (Devine 1979).

81. On seasonal migration see Johnson 1959, 1967; Douglas 1963; Cousens 1965; and especially O'Grada 1973; Collins 1976; Devine 1979.

Chapter 6

POPULATION GROWTH AND THE ECONOMY

To a greater or lesser degree all economies are subject to the influence of their demographic circumstances. At every stage of economic development variations in the size and rate of growth of a population, in age, sex and marital structure, in the size and composition of households and families, in levels of fertility, mortality and the volume and net balance of migration have some effect on the size, growth rate, flexibility and productivity of the labour supply, the extent and character of demand for goods and services and levels of saving, investment and inventiveness. Generally, the economic consequences of demographic conditions are more pronounced in low-income, labour-intensive economies than in economies based on capital-intensive methods of production with higher per capita real incomes, in which population trends have only 'very secondary effects on possibilities for economic growth' (Maillat 1978, p. 77). To some extent this is because advanced economies have a greater capacity for substituting technology for manual labour and for controlling their own rates of population increase: to some extent because, at higher levels of income, variations in demand and in the ability to save and invest are more dependent on fluctuations in real income and consumer taste which occur independently of demographic change.

This generalization apart, however, theorists have always disagreed violently both about the *direction* of the economic influence exerted by demographic variables and the *significance* of this influence relative to that of other, non-demographic determinants of economic change. Such empirical testing as has been attempted of their hypotheses has done little to resolve the disagreement. There is almost as much dispute about the economic consequences of demographic change among present-day scholars as there was in the eighteenth and nineteenth centuries when the issue of population dynamics and their effects first entered the arena of public debate.

In part this lack of consensus reflects the complexity of the influence of demographic variables themselves. Although, in theory, it can be

153

assumed that the more gradual the alteration in the components of demography the less dramatic their economic effects and the easier it will be for an economy to adjust to them, in practice it is extremely difficult to determine what the optimum pace of demographic change should be. All too often the economic impact exerted in one direction by one of the demographic variables is countered by the influence of another working in the opposite direction. From time to time even the same population variable may have very different effects on the economy. In the long term, for instance, a decline in fertility will reduce the size of the available labour force. In the short term however, through its influence on the age structure of a community, it may increase the proportion of the population in employable age-groups.

But the main cause of disagreement stems from the fact that population is only one of a complex array of mutually inter- related forces which together decide the fortunes of an economy. Neither the quantity and quality of the workforce, the supply of capital, invention and innovation nor the level and composition of effective demand are solely, or often even mainly, determined by demographic circumstances. And both the direction and extent of demography's economic effects depend, fundamentally, on the nature of the non-demographic environment within which population change occurs. A given set of demographic circumstances may produce one kind of economic response in one society and quite the opposite response in another where the relationship between existing demographic and material resources and the non-demographic determinants of economic development are altogether different; hence Schumpeter's remark that the 'economic response to population growth may range from stagnation to innovation'.[1]

POPULATION AND THE BRITISH INDUSTRIAL REVOLUTION

Though on the whole careful not to overstate the independence of the demographic contribution, explicitly or implicitly and with varying degree of emphasis, most historians accord the dynamics of population change some role in the conception, gestation and birth of Britain's Industrial Revolution. Their interpretations of the way in which demographic trends worked to foster industrialization, however, vary considerably. Specifically, there is a sharp distinction between those who stress the value of relatively high and rising rates of population growth and those who emphasize the fact that rates of demographic increase were relatively restrained.

Numerous scholars regard demographic decline or stagnation as a major part of the explanation for the mediocre aggregate performance of the British economy during the fourteenth and fifteenth and late seventeenth and early eighteenth centuries. Incentives to adopt and maintain productivity-generating 'institutional arrangements' diminished or disappeared during periods when the stimulus of population growth on the price of marketable goods and factors of production was removed (North and Thomas 1970). High rates of mortality caused by the recurrence of bubonic plague in seventeenth-century towns damaged urban economies and delayed the onset of sustained economic growth (Dyer 1978). For much of the late seventeenth and first half of the eighteenth centuries labour shortages and unusually low grain prices, both the product of demographic stagnation, seriously restricted the amount of capital available for productive investment and the absolute size of the effective market for manufactured goods and commercial services; the former because high wages and a preference for leisure among the workforce raised costs of production and cut employers' profit margins, the latter because the main source of demand for non-agricultural products came from the sellers of foodstuffs whose own propensity to consume depended on high food prices (Chambers 1957; Deane and Cole 1967).

Obversely, periods of demographic increase were equated with higher aggregate rates of economic growth and the disproportionately rapid adoption of technological and organizational innovations which acted as bases for subsequent economic progress. Through its effects on the size and location of markets and relative product and factor prices, population growth during the twelfth and thirteenth and sixteenth and early seventeenth centuries made it worthwhile to devise new 'institutional' arrangements – rights of private property ownership, a system of patent law, formal commercial contracts, free labour, larger and more durable trading organizations, insurance, banking and capital-raising facilities – which increased both the desire and ability to raise levels of productivity and thus aided *long-term* economic advance. Until the coming of a third sustained phase of population increase, in the second half of the eighteenth and nineteenth centuries, these productivity-generating institutions were insufficiently embedded in the economic system to permit a continuous rise in output and income per head. The result was that, towards the end of the thirteenth and sixteenth centuries, population growth outran the capacity of the economy to generate adequate supplies of material resources. In the periods of demographic decline or stagnation which followed some of the productivity-raising institutions fell into decay or disappeared altogether. But not all were lost. Some survived to provide a platform on which others could be established when population once more began to increase.

Accordingly, by the late seventeenth and early eighteenth centuries, the economy was better able than ever before to cope with the periodic tendency for pre-modern populations to overshoot the supply of resources essential for their survival. By the time a third cycle of population growth began in the second half of the eighteenth century productivity-generating institutions were so widespread and secure on mainland Britain that the persistence of high rates of demographic increase no longer seriously threatened to outrun the capacity of the economy to provide the basic essentials for life. Institutional innovation, and the incentives to productivity which arose from it, at last made it possible to achieve that sustained increase in per capita output which was required to break out of the traditional Malthusian trap (North and Thomas 1970, 1973a).

The increase in rates of population growth after 1750, these same scholars argue, provided the final demographic ingredient necessary to trigger-off industrialization. To begin with it solved the problem of labour shortage which had so impeded the aggregate growth of the economy in the earlier years of the century, providing employers not only with a labour force that was cheaper in real terms and, faced by increasing competition for employment, more inclined to work harder and more efficiently but also with a labour force which was geographically more mobile than in the past, an important consideration given the localized nature of early industrial development. In doing so it reduced real costs of production, thereby increasing the size of the potential market, and raised employers' profit margins, thereby stimulating rates of investment and innovation.[2] On the realistic assumption that there was no serious decline in per capita real incomes between 1750 and 1850,[3] the acceleration in rates of population increase also contributed *directly* to rising levels of demand which played their own part in fostering proft accumulation and higher rates of productive investment (Chambers 1957; Habakkuk 1963b, 1971).

To some scholars rising demand was achieved primarily through the effect of population growth on the incomes and purchasing power of farmers and landlords, who prospered from higher food prices and rents and who remained the principal source of demand for industrial products and commercial services (Deane and Cole 1967). To others it stemmed from the effects of population growth and changes in the age structure of the community on rates of migration which redistributed the population from areas of low- to higher-income employment and increased the pace of household and family formation (Lee 1979). To yet others it was a straightforward consequence of the increased number of bodies demanding food, clothing and shelter, the basic necessities without which life cannot be sustained and for which, so long as incomes do not plummet disastrously, there is always an effective market. It has been suggested, for example, that it was the needs of a growing population which underlay the development of handicraft industries, which themselves provided many of the pre-requisites for subsequent industrialization (Mendels 1972; Lee 1979; Pollard 1981). Through the pressure it placed on natural resources, the growth of population also worked to promote the spread of innovations designed to economize on the use of existing resources and to extend the resource base (Habakkuk 1963b, 1971). Improvements in methods of transport, too, owed much to the greater density of population which came with demographic increase and added their own impetus to the expansion of the market (Habakkuk 1963b, 1971; Engelmann and Wanner 1969).

As Habakkuk once observed:

> I am not arguing that the effects of population growth were simple or straightforward or that they were invariably favourable. But I find it difficult to interpret the eighteenth century without supposing that, on balance, population increase was a stimulus to the development of the economy (Habakkuk 1971, p. 48).

It is hard to dissent radically from this view. In an age when the bulk of consumer demand was for the essentials not the luxuries of life, and assuming no observable decline in average per capita consumer purchasing power, the increase in the size of the market which occurred in the late eighteenth and early nineteenth centuries must have been at least partly due to the growth of population alone. So too, at a time when the capacity for devising labour-saving technology was limited and manual labour the fundamental basis of production, substantial increases in output were very dependent on an increase in the quantity of human labour. Historically, it is no accident that rates of innovation in technology and methods of production were always greater in periods of population growth than population decline or stagnation.[4] Most innovations were devised, not to save labour directly but, in a context of rising demand, either to economize on natural resources or to overcome bottlenecks in existing methods of production and supply which prevented producers from capitalizing on this demand.

Of course, the rise in output which occurred during the late eighteenth and first half of the nineteenth centuries could not have been achieved merely through the addition of more and more workers relying on traditional techniques. New technologies and methods of organizing labour for production, which minimized the additional amounts of labour required, were obviously crucial to the rise in output which occurred during the Industrial Revolution. Nevertheless, in absolute terms, the productive innovations of the first Industrial Revolution called for a much larger labour supply than ever before and could not have been widely adopted without it. The process of early industrialization does not *necessarily* require large additional inputs of labour. But in the British case, where the transformation from labour- to capital-intensive methods of production was gradual and partial, it undoubtedly did (Weaver 1974). While some improvement in the quality of the labour supply, notably its greater geographic flexibility

157

and willingness to work harder and more regularly, was also essential to successful industrial 'take-off', a simple increase in the absolute number of people available for work mattered much more (Tranter 1981; Kenwood and Lougheed 1982).

For all this, the contribution of population growth per se to the British Industrial Revolution should not be overstated. In the first place, the fact that higher rates of population growth in late eighteenth- and early nineteenth-century Britain were on balance beneficial to the economy was only due to the presence of a society capable in all other essentials of generating sustained economic advance, not least through its ability to ensure a rise in agricultural output sufficient to avert any threat to real incomes and thus to levels of demand for industrial goods which would otherwise have arisen from the effect of population growth on food prices. Some, at least, of the scholars who stress the advantages of demographic acceleration to the British Industrial Revolution underplay the significance of the context within which population growth occurred and therefore overstate the independent importance of demography's contribution to economic growth. Depending on the context, a growing population can as easily lead to institutional arrangements which impede economic progress as to those which promote it. In addition, productivity-generating institutions themselves are by no means always the consequence of demographic increase and its effect on the relationship between population and the availability of basic food and raw material resources (Ringrose 1973; North and Thomas 1973b; Field 1981).

Quite apart from the influence of the environment within which it occurs, the effect of population increase per se on the potential for economic development is itself contradictory. On the one hand, rising rates of population growth in the late eighteenth and early nineteenth centuries tended to reduce average per capita incomes and, because falling incomes divert expenditures from manufactures to foodstuffs, the demand for industrial products. On the other, by depressing wages and raising land rents, they worked to lower the price of manufactures relative to agricultural products and thus, to the extent that expenditures on food were elastic, encouraged the purchase of manufactures rather than foodstuffs and stimulated industrial production. Faced by such contradictory tendencies, in practice the net effect of population growth on levels of effective demand for industrial commodities is very difficult to assess (Lee and Schofield 1981). Perhaps this explains the difference of opinion which exists between those who see population growth as vital to the increase in demand for manufactures between the mid-eighteenth and mid-nineteenth centuries and one recent commentator who suggests that it accounted for only 10% or less of the total rise in the output of non-agricultural products (Mokyr 1977).

To date, the hypothesis that rising rates of population growth made a significant contribution to the coming of the Industrial Revolution has received little empirical testing. In the one case where this has been attempted the findings will be disappointing to its supporters. Such alterations as occurred in the ratio of dependents to producers as a result of demographic change in eighteenth-century England were too slight to have had more than a marginal impact on levels of saving and investment (Lee and Schofield 1981). Again, the late eighteenth and early nineteenth century rise in fertility, and the more youthful age structure of the population which stemmed from it, reduced rather than increased the ratio between producers and consumers and, proportionately, decreased the productive capacity of the economy (Wrigley and Schofield 1981).[5] Clearly, more empirical work is needed to assess the validity of assumptions concerning the benefits of higher rates of population increase to the growth of the economy in pre- and early industrial England.

In two other respects, also, undue emphasis on the economic advantages accruing from relatively high and rising rates of population growth incompletely and inaccurately specifies the contribution of the demographic variable to early British economic development. First, it fails to make adequate allowance for the fact that even at their peak rates of population growth were moderate both compared with what is theoretically possible and with levels actually prevailing in many underdeveloped societies of the present day. Second, it ignores the positive value to long-term economic advance of periods of demographic stagnation or decline.

The overall moderacy of rates of population increase in pre-industrial England, a product of relatively high ages at marriage and low levels of marital fertility, contributed to the secular development of the economy in two significant ways. By easing the pressure of population on natural resource supplies, it protected real incomes and, therefore, levels of effective demand for manufactured products. By ensuring relatively high proportions of the population in the productive age-groups, it raised levels of per capita productivity and increased the capacity for saving and investment (Spengler 1968; Chambers 1972).

Some authorities also suggest that it was low rates of population growth which account for the introduction of many of the most crucial innovations in technology and methods of production during the eighteenth century. The resulting shortages of labour, they argue, forced employers to pay higher wages than they were either willing or able to pay. Inflated wages raised the purchasing power of the wage-earning sections of the community and boosted levels of demand for industrial goods, thereby encouraging risk-taking investment. And because wages were by far the largest component in production costs, high wages intensified the search for labour-saving technologies and methods which, once adopted, were a vital ingredient in the long-term rise of productivity and per capita output (Crouzet 1967; Pentland 1972).

Arguably, the Pentland–Crouzet thesis goes too far. In the first place, it exaggerates both the importance of labour-saving as a motive for innovation and the ability of the economy to generate labour-saving methods and technologies. Secondly, it too readily assumes that variations in the purchasing power of the wage-earning sections of the population were the principal source of changes in the level of demand for the manufactured products upon which the Industrial Revolution was based. If this was so, why did aggregate demand for manufacturers rise most rapidly in the late eighteenth and earliest years of the nineteenth century, when adult male per capita real wages rose relatively slowly, if at all? One possible explanation is that the effect of any decline in male incomes was offset by increases either in the absolute number of consumers or in the contribution of female and child earnings to family purchasing power. Another is that the principal source of demand for manufacturers continued to come from sectors of the community other than the labouring population – farmers, landlords, the urban middle classes and skilled workers whose own incomes and purchasing power depended more on high than low rates of population growth. Thirdly, the Pentland–Crouzet thesis errs in assuming that falling profits were a greater incentive to productive innovation than rising ones. Although reduced profit margins frequently underlay the adoption of cost-reducing innovation in the first half of the eighteenth century, levels of investment and innovation were nonetheless greater in the second half of the century, when the share of profits in national income was rising not falling. In general, advances in technology were more common at times when rates of population growth were high and were more usually a response to rising demand, shortages of raw materials or deficiencies in methods of distribution, all of which were positively correlated with rates of demographic increase, than to shortfalls in the labour supply.

To overstress the contribution of low rates of population growth to the increase in aggregate output, therefore, is unwise. Even so, emphasis on the importance of moderacy in rates of demographic increase does remind us that the coming of the Industrial Revolution may have been seriously retarded had rates of population growth been much higher than they were. It is significant that on those occasions in pre-industrial times when rates of English population increase exceeded 0.5% per annum the productive system was unable to maintain customary levels of per capita output. By the late eighteenth century the ability of the economy to generate the resources necessary to cope with higher rates of population growth was undoubtedly greater than it had ever been before, but only marginally so. Not until the nineteenth century was the economy able to meet the material needs of a growing number of consumers without serious strain (Wrigley and Schofield 1981).

Perhaps the most significant contribution of periods of demographic stagnation or decline to long-run economic development lay in their effects on the composition of output. Habakkuk once wrote that

... the slow population increase and low grain prices of the 1730s and 1740s produced one type of economic growth and the rapid increase and rising grain prices of the later eighteenth century a different type; and both types of growth, in the order in which they occurred, were necessary for the Industrial Revolution (Habakkuk 1971, p. 48).

The details of this argument were elaborated subsequently by Chambers. By themselves, neither periods of population growth nor population stagnation or decline were sufficient to facilitate sustained economic development. Carried too far and for too long both demographic increase and demographic retardation would have deterred the long-term growth of the economy. What mattered was that, for purely fortuitous reasons, long periods of population growth in the pre-industrial era alternated in strict sequence with equally long periods of demographic stability or decline. It was only because of the accidental sequence of alternating cycles of population growth and stagnation that the role of demography in early industrialization was positive rather than negative.

During times of demographic upswing the combination of growing numbers and high incomes among farmers and landlords, a result of population pressure on food and land resources, led to abnormally high rates of growth of total output, focussed on the narrow range of commodities essential to the maintenance of life. In the intervening periods of demographic downswing, as the pressure of population on supplies of food and land lessened, income was diverted from the producers of essential goods to the wage-earning masses who bought them. As a result, while *aggregate* output rose relatively slowly, the increased ability of the labouring population to purchase less essential, 'luxury' goods enabled the economy to diversify the *range* of its products. Indeed, confronted by depressed levels of demand for essentials, producers were positively impelled to extend the breadth of their activities. Rising real incomes among the population at large may also have widened the social basis of saving and investment, a tendency which went some way towards alleviating the depressive effect on investment of falling profits among the producers of essentials and helped maintain levels of productivity. By raising the ability of wage-earners to purchase 'luxuries', widening the range of output and the potential sources of capital for productive investment and promoting the adoption of more efficient methods of production to cope with falling prices, demographic retardation made it easier for the economy to respond to the different challenges and opportunities which emerged when rates of population growth once more increased (Chambers 1972).

Wrigley and Schofield, too, emphasize the significance of demographic stagnation between the mid-seventeenth and mid-eighteenth centuries to later industrial 'take-off'. Like Chambers, they argue that high per capita real income among the labouring population,

161

through its effect on the structure of demand, boosted the output of commodities other than those basic to the maintenance of life, thereby encouraging sectors of the economy whose development was critical for successful industrialization. But they place particular emphasis on the economic advantages which accrued from changes in the age structure of the population during periods of demographic stagnation. Because of relatively low fertility the population of late seventeenth- and early eighteenth-century England contained a smaller proportion of people in the dependent age-groups than it would after 1750 when fertility rates were higher.[6] This had two consequences. First, it raised the ratio of producers to consumers, thus increasing the productive potential of the economy. Second, because an older population devotes a lower proportion of its income to agricultural products than a more youthful one, it reinforced the growing demand for manufactures already arising in response to a reduction in the pressure of population on basic food resources and improvements in the ratio of producers to consumers (Wrigley and Schofield 1981). The result was a broader and firmer basis for subsequent economic development than would otherwise have been the case.

Admittedly, some of the gains to the economy conveyed by demographic stagnation in the decades before 1750 were eroded in the second half of the century when rates of fertility and population growth began to rise, once more to test the community's ability to generate sufficient of the basic essentials for life. To some extent rising food prices and falling money wages, by reducing per capita purchasing power among adult male wage-earners, worked against continued growth and diversification in the economy. It is conceivable that the requirements of the Industrial Revolution for labour, capital and markets would have been more easily met had rates of population increase in the first half of the eighteenth century been *marginally* higher than they were. On the other hand, the erosion of such economic benefits as were bequeathed by demographic stagnation in the period before 1750 does not appear to have been serious. In part this was because any decline which occurred in the per capita purchasing power of adult male wage-earners was more than offset both by an increase in their own numbers and by rising incomes in other classes of the population (see p. 160): in part because the acceleration in rates of population growth after 1750 was itself only moderate and, therefore, the pressure on food and other essentials less intense than it might have been: in part because the labouring population was willing to work harder and longer to protect the taste for 'luxuries' acquired in the first half of the century and was given the opportunity to do so by the effect of higher rates of population growth on demand for labour in agriculture and other basic industries. But, principally, it reflected the extent to which the economy had already grown and diversified by the middle of the eighteenth century.

There is abundant evidence in the first half of the century of a notable increase in the ratio of manufactured to agricultural output and of a widening in the range of products within both the industrial and agricultural sectors of the economy, trends which were accompanied by a significant advance in the efficiency of production methods (John 1961, 1965; Jones 1965).

What happened in agriculture was especially critical for industrial 'take-off' in the closing decades of the century. The need to cut costs of grain production, together with new opportunities for livestock and dairy farming, fruit growing and market gardening, improved the sectoral balance of British agricultural output and raised yields per unit area of land. In the period before 1750 the average size of farms increased, working relationships between landowners and their tenants improved and a system of mixed farming emerged in which the integration of arable and livestock cultivation endowed agriculture with a new responsiveness to changes in market demand and a capacity for achieving simultaneous long-term increases in both arable and livestock output.

True, not all parts of the country shared in these advances. Innate conservatism, fragmented holdings, lack of capital, the rigidities of open field methods, problems of drainage on heavy, clay soils or remoteness from markets prevented many farmers from responding effectively to the shifting pattern of demand which came with demographic stagnation. But on the lighter soils of southern and eastern England and in areas bordering on large, urban communities innovation and rising productivity were the order of the day. It was this which ensured that the output of food in the second half of the eighteenth century more or less matched the acceleration in rates of population growth and, therefore, that even low-income consumers retained at least part of their income for expenditure on the manufactured products upon which industrial 'take-off' was based (Eversley 1967).

That manufacturing industry already had a significant place in the economy well before the accepted period of industrial 'take- off' is amply demonstrated by recently compiled statistical data which show that British manufacturing output in the 1770s was almost twice as great as previous estimates had suggested.[7] The existence of a well-developed industrial base, and the supply of capital, labour and entrepreneurial skill which flowed from it, goes a long way towards explaining why an Industrial Revolution occurred only in Britain towards the end of the eighteenth century. It also explains why historians now view the Industrial Revolution as a less revolutionary adjustment to the traditional economic order than was once supposed.[8]

The role of demographic change in the birth of the Industrial Revolution was by no means straightforward. On balance, however, its influence was undoubtedly beneficial. In part this was because of a fortuitous alternation of cycles of demographic growth and stagnation (Chambers 1972). Partly it was because rates of population increase, and

163

fluctuations around the norm were moderate and avoided the extremes which prevailed in certain other societies and which were so much more difficult to cope with. But, in the main, it reflected the nature of the environment wthin which population change occurred – an environment embracing all the other necessary ingredients for economic advance, not least the capacity for keeping levels of fertility within the bounds of available resources. In other contexts, similar demographic patterns may well have hindered long-term economic advance.

POPULATION AND THE BRITISH ECONOMY, 1850–1940

Until recently it was generally accepted that demographic trends had exercised a considerable influence on the performance of the British economy during the period between the mid-nineteenth and mid-twentieth centuries and that, in an economy with the capacity for ensuring that supplies of basic resources exceeded the growth of numbers (Grigg 1980), the nature of their influence was strongly positive: that is to say, the continued growth of the British and international economies in the later nineteenth century owed much to the persistence of high rates of population increase, while the decline in rates of population growth in the twentieth century contributed significantly to the economic ills of the inter-war years.

According to one contemporary observer, whose views were widely supported, population growth was the key to the development of international trade and the international economy during the second half of the nineteenth century. The increase of population in Europe raised levels of demand for the food and raw material resources of primary-producing countries in the New World, in turn enabling these latter to expand their consumption of European manufactured goods. In the case of free trade Britain the availability of an abundance of cheap overseas food supplies boosted real incomes and purchasing power among wage-earners at home and enhanced the size of the domestic market for industrial products and commercial services. Simultaneously, the mass migration of people from Europe to the New World, unimaginable without the prior growth of European populations, provided primary-producing economies with essential labour and eased the problems of surplus labour in many European countries, thus ensuring a more efficient international allocation of labour resources. When, during the inter-war period, rates of European population growth slumped these stimuli to economic development disappeared, with disastrous consequences.

In the pre-war period we adjusted our commercial and industrial machinery to provide for an annual increase of about 2 per cent in our total food supplies, and this necessitated an annual increase of about 5 per cent in our imports of foodstuffs. Between 1911 and 1926, however, our total consumption of foodstuffs increased by less than $\frac{1}{4}$ per cent per annum, and the highly complicated commercial and industrial machinery which we set up on the basis of requiring an increase of 5 per cent per annum in our imported food supply is only required to produce an annual increase of less than 1 per cent. This simple fact seems to me to be at the bottom of many of the world's economic troubles ... If we could have taken more foodstuffs and raw materials from the rest of the world in the past few years, not only would our own exports have been better maintained, but the international trade of other countries would, in turn, have been improved (Snow 1935, p. 259).

The post-war Royal Commission on Population was only a little more circumspect in its emphasis on the economic impact of demographic trends. While acknowledging the *potential* dangers inherent in unduly high rates of population growth, its authors were in no doubt that, *in practice,* the rapid increase in population in the decades before the First World War had been beneficial to the economy just as lower rates of demographic growth after the war were detrimental to it.

It is reasonable to expect that a radical change in a factor of such fundamental importance as the trend in population must exert far-reaching repercussions on the workings of the economic system. The development of that system, since the beginnings of the industrial revolution, has been associated with rapidly growing populations in Great Britain and throughout the western world (Royal Commission on Population, 1950, p. 3).

Population increase and the migration of people to the New World in the late nineteenth and early twentieth centuries were fundamental to the development of overseas trade and investment, the emergence of London as the world's banker and insurer, the prosperity of Britain's principal industries – shipbuilding, cotton, coal, iron and steel and engineering, all of which relied heavily on export markets, and the supply of foodstuffs and raw materials so essential for rising standards of living at home. Together with the efflux of goods and capital which accompanied it, the flow of people from Europe to the New World played a major part in establishing that intricate international division of labour which was the cornerstone of the Victorian economy's success. Although recognizing that the economic depression of the inter-war years chiefly stemmed from non-demographic causes, the authors of the Royal Commission were convinced that the decline in rates of population growth greatly intensified the problems of the age. Had population grown more quickly the world glut of foodstuffs and raw materials, originating primarily in the spread of technological innovation, would have been less severe and the international exchange of goods and services less seriously restricted (Royal Commission on Population 1949, 1950).

Perhaps, too, higher rates of population increase would have enabled the domestic economy to respond more successfully to the changed circumstances of international economic relations in the inter-war years. During the nineteenth century, by facilitating the continuous growth in the size of markets, high levels of population increase gave businessmen and investors the confidence necessary for the pursuit of risk-taking innovation. They also guaranteed the existence of a labour supply sufficiently large and flexible to ensure that new enterprises were not hampered by labour shortages. By contrast, lower rates of population growth during the inter-war period, which appeared to threaten the future growth of demand and the availability, adaptability and vitality of the workforce, supposedly undermined the willingness to invest and innovate and reduced the productive potential of the economy. At precisely the time when the collapse of international trade demanded urgent structural adjustments to the British economy, demographic retardation made such adjustments more difficult to achieve.[9]

On the whole, more recent commentators are less impressed by the contribution of demographic trends to the performance of the British and international economies between the mid-nineteenth and mid-twentieth centuries and less inclined to accept the existence of a close, positive relationship between rates of population growth on the one hand and of economic growth on the other. Only in regard to the influence of overseas migration on the growth of the international economy and to that of seasonal migration within Britain on the flexibility of the domestic economy do their conclusions continue to conform with traditional interpretations.

Evidence on the timing of emigrant flows and the geographic origins and occupational composition of British migrants to the USA and Britain's colonies shows that, in the main, those who emigrated were surplus to the requirements of the domestic economy. Their departure eased rather than intensified the periodic and regional strains to which the domestic economy continued to be subject. In acting as a safety-valve for unemployment, poor prospects and low incomes, overseas migration was a decided asset to the British economy in the decades between the mid-nineteenth century and the First World War (Thomas 1954; Duncan 1963–4; Erickson 1981). It also contributed significantly to the growth of Britain's exports and helped to provide the food and raw material imports which did so much to raise standards of living among those who remained at home. Before 1914, the flow of emigrants was equally valuable to the economies of the countries receiving them. It increased levels of demand, particularly for essential public utilities and social overheads, thereby encouraging the productive use of savings; reduced the real cost of labour to employers (in part because the costs of upbringing and initial training were met by the sending societies) and thus lowered the price, and increased the marketability, of products; and, partly because immigrants were more than usually conscientious in their work habits and adaptable in their responses to new ideas and techniques, stimulated levels of invention and the capacity of the labour force to adapt to innovation. In addition, through the stimulus it gave to improved methods of international transport and communication and inter-continental flows of capital and technology, emigration assisted that reduction in inter-country differentials in the availability and cost of the various factors of production which underlay the pre-1914 global rise in levels of per capita output and income.[10]

By helping to iron out structural and geographic imperfections in the agricultural labour supply – imperfections which had become steadily worse as rural populations drifted to the towns, seasonal movements of labour within the United Kingdom made an important contribution to the rise in the output of British agriculture during the nineteenth century. Because seasonal workers required little expenditure by employers on accommodation or other social services, and could be dispensed with easily at times of the year when labour was less required, they were ideally suited to those sectors of the economy like agriculture in which employment was heavily labour-intensive, the demand for labour most variable and wages relatively low. Given that the pattern of relative factor costs and prices favoured the saving of land and other resources rather than labour and also that farming was biased towards labour-intensive crops and techniques, reliance on seasonal labour was unlikely either to have seriously reduced earnings and employment prospects among full-time workers or to have seriously retarded the pace of technological advance.

There were, of course, occasions when the availability of seasonal workers inhibited technological innovation. But to the extent that seasonal labour weakened existing social constraints against the use of labour-saving machinery it as often hastened technological advance as delayed it. Significantly, the adoption of threshers, horseshoes, barn and harvesting machinery came earliest and most extensively to areas where dependence on seasonal labour was greatest. In sum, the flow of temporary migrants was essential to an efficient distribution of the agricultural labour supply in an age when there were frequently serious social barriers to wholesale mechanization and when, in any case, mechanization was often technically difficult (Collins 1976).

Seasonal migration was likewise of benefit to the economies of those regions from which it originated. In the short-term, perhaps, it prolonged the survival of inefficient, traditional forms of economic organization by lessening the pressure of population on resources and thus the necessity for change. But in the long-term, temporary migration was advantageous to the economies of areas like Ireland and the Scottish Highlands, easing the burdens of overpopulation, raising income and standards of life, intensifying the desire for material and cultural improvement and, by broadening the range of individual experiences and eroding the barriers of cultural, ethnic and linguistic difference, making it easier for people to espouse permanent movement.[11]

The economic value of *permanent* migration between the different regions of mainland Britain is more debatable. True, through its contribution to the gradual erosion of urban-rural wage differentials after the middle of the nineteenth century and by shifting people from low to high wage areas, it contributed to the general increase in aggregate levels of effective demand. And, during the inter-war period, rising levels of internal mobility went some way towards alleviating whatever detrimental effects lower rates of demographic increase and the accompanying ageing of the population may have had on the geographic flexibility of labour supplies and the regional availability of labour. On the other hand, certainly before 1914, regional variations in demands for labour were met much more by regional differentials in rates of natural increase than by inter-regional migration flows. Labour migration was unable to override the influence of non-demographic determinants of regional differences in the quantity and quality of the labour supply and did little to diminish the great disparities in the price of labour which persisted well into the twentieth century (Hunt 1973; Pollard 1978).

Otherwise, in complete contrast to earlier interpretations, demographic variables nowadays rarely figure among the factors most influential in determining the fortunes of the British economy since the mid-nineteenth century: and when they do, again in contrast to previous views, the tendency is to stress the disadvantages rather than the advantages of high rates of population growth before 1914 and the advantages rather than the disadvantages of lower rates of population increase during the inter-war years.

To the extent, for instance, that the increasing technological sophistication of the economy called for higher standards of education among the labour force the persistence of high levels of fertility and population growth before 1914 made these more difficult to achieve. In contrast, lower rates of fertility and the steady decline in the numbers of children reaching school age which occurred during the inter-war period made it easier to provide a decent education for the young and therefore raised the overall quality and efficiency of the labour supply. Possibly, too, lower levels of fertility and population growth in the decades before 1914 would have raised the level of purchasing power within the domestic market without seriously diminishing the contribution of population growth to the development of primary-producing economies overseas or the international flow of people, goods and capital. It is, however, concerning the presumed relationship between population growth and the pace of technological progress at home that some recent historians have expressed the gravest reservations.

According to Habakkuk, one of the chief reasons for levels of technological innovation and labour productivity being higher in the USA than Britain during the second half of the nineteenth century was the differing labour endowments of the two countries. In the USA, for much of the century, labour, especially unskilled labour, was in shorter supply than in Britain. As a result, the costs of labour relative to the costs of capital were higher in the former than the latter and the differential between the wages of skilled and unskilled workers noticeably lower. It follows that American employers had greater incentives and opportunities to introduce capital-intensive, labour-saving technology than their British counterparts who found it less necessary and less economical and who, in any case, were more likely to meet opposition from organized labour. Once begun, the impetus for labour-saving innovation was maintained even into the later decades of the century when labour became more plentiful. In part this was because American employers continued to believe that the costs of labour were always inclined to rise more rapidly than the costs of raw materials and capital: in part because technological advance in one sector of the economy inevitably created pressure for innovation in another.

The consequence was an economy with relatively high levels of technology and output per worker and a considerable potential for long-term economic progress. By comparison, in Britain, an abundant labour force, so necessary to the success of early industrialization and, according to earlier observers, so important to the continued prosperity of the economy in the second half of the nineteenth century, impeded the long-term rate of economic advance (Habakkuk 1962, 1963a).[12]

The Habakkuk thesis has aroused considerable debate. To some it assumes too easily and probably erroneously that American technology of the late nineteenth and early twentieth centuries was generally superior to British.[13] To some it exaggerates the role of labour shortage in technological advance.[14] To others it errs in suggesting that the *real* costs of labour relative to other factors of production were greater in the USA than Britain.[15] On the other hand, there are those who have found evidence in support of the case for higher American real labour costs[16] and who argue that at least part of the relatively rapid rise in American labour productivity during the nineteenth century was due to the effects of technological innovation arising from labour shortage.[17]

The controversy provoked by Habakkuk remains unresolved. But whatever the outcome it reminds us that earlier writers may have been premature in equating British economic growth in the late nineteenth century with the increase in the size of the labour force which came with population growth. If Habakkuk is correct, the economy would have been better served by the kind of technological advance provoked in the USA by labour shortage. If he is incorrect, relative labour endowments were of little significance to the pace of technological innovation. Should subsequent research prove the contention that in the nineteenth century 'both relatively abundant and relatively limited supplies of labour (were) consistent with rapid technological diffusion' (Kenwood and Lougheed 1982, p. 95), the emphasis placed by earlier observers on the economic advantages of a rapidly growing labour supply will prove to have been unwise.

There are also grounds for querying the significance of declining rates of population growth to Britain's economic ills during the inter-war period. The problems of the international economy in the 1920s and 1930s, from which Britain suffered severely, stemmed from the chronic overproduction of food, raw materials and basic manufactures which came with the widespread adoption of innovations in productive methods. Falling rates of population increase merely aggravated the imbalance between supply and demand. In fact, long before the twentieth-century decline in rates of population growth the smooth flow of international trade was beginning to give way to tariff protection and incipient economic nationalism in the face of an increasingly desperate struggle for markets. The competitive weaknesses of many of Britain's staple export industries were already apparent by 1914. Whatever the cause or causes of late Victorian or Edwardian economic 'retardation' – entrepreneurial failings, deficiencies in scientific and technical education, imperfect capital markets or peculiarities of demand structure – falling rates of population growth cannot be included.[18] On the contrary, it was the persistence of *high* rates of population increase which reinforced Britain's commitment to the import of foodstuffs and export of staple manufactured products, to overseas investment and international banking, insurance and carrying services and which thus delayed those changes in the structure of the economy that were to become so necessary in the changed world of the inter-war years.

It is also by no means clear that low rates of population growth in the 1920s and 1930s weakened the ability of the economy to respond to the difficulties arising from the collapse of international trade. In view of the mass unemployment of the inter-war decades it is absurd to suggest that the economy was constrained by labour shortages; even in areas of prosperity the workforce was always large enough to meet the demands placed upon it, partly because in absolute terms population continued to grow, partly because of immigration from areas of depression and partly because falling fertility was accompanied by a rise in the proportion of the population in the productive age-groups, 15–64. Although average annual increments to the labour supply were smaller than before 1914, they nevertheless exceeded the demands of the economy for additional labour inputs.[19] To the extent that falling fertility permitted higher levels of per capita expenditure on the education of the young significant improvements were also achieved in the quality of the annual increments to the workforce during the inter-war period.[20]

In addition, falling fertility and low rates of population growth during the 1920s and 1930s contributed to a change in the structure of consumer demand which helped smooth the transition of the economy from its dependence on depressed staple industries directed at overseas customers towards 'new' industrial products – housing and household appliances, motor cars, electrical and chemical goods – geared to domestic consumers. Even allowing for the tragedy of mass unemployment, per capita real wages rose by almost 1% a year throughout the inter-war period.[21] By raising the ratio of producers to consumers and reducing the real cost of essentials like food, demographic retardation, together with improving terms of trade and an increase in the ratio of salaried employees in the working population, undoubtedly contributed to the growth in income per head.[22]

In the century after 1850 demographic variables continued to play a role in shaping the fortunes of the economy of mainland Britain. But, as expected in a more sophisticated economy where production and consumption are less dependent on the absolute number of hands and mouths than on levels of technology, real incomes and consumer tastes, their economic significance was more limited than in earlier times. Certainly, population trends were less vital to British economic development between 1850 and 1940 than most contemporary or near contemporary observers supposed. To the modest degree that demographic factors did affect patterns of economic growth in the late nineteenth and first half of the twentieth centuries their influence was probably benign. Though their effects were never consistently in one direction or another, on balance, high rates of population growth in the second half of the nineteenth century and lower rates of population growth in the years between the world wars promoted rather than retarded economic progress.

POPULATION AND THE IRISH ECONOMY

In the case of Ireland the economic impact of population trends since the mid-eighteenth century has been very different. Whether because the Irish economy was less developed or because Irish society lacked the same capacity for keeping its fertility within the bounds of available food resources, the economic consequences of demographic change have been greater and more prolonged and less obviously beneficial than elsewhere in the British Isles. By the opening years of the nineteenth century the persistence of high rates of population growth had become a major barrier to further Irish economic development. After 1850 the net effect of demographic trends is more contentious. Overall, their influence was probably beneficial: but only marginally so and less

171

clearly than in the case of England/Wales and Scotland. In many respects demography continued to pose major problems for the long-term development of the country's economy.

Whereas in England and Scotland the acceleration in rates of population growth during the late eighteenth and early nineteenth centuries helped produce an Industrial Revolution in Ireland it led to immiseration (Razzell 1967). Initially, the renewed growth of population which followed the period of demographic stagnation in the second quarter of the eighteenth century stimulated economic progress. Aided by rising per capita incomes, it boosted demand for agricultural and industrial commodities and was a major part of the explanation for the notable growth and diversification of the economy which occurred in the decades after 1750 (Cullen 1972).

Unfortunately, the further surge in rates of population increase which began towards the end of the century and persisted throughout the years of the Napoleonic Wars was instrumental in destroying much of this progress. Falling rates of population growth following the culmination of the wars came too late and too slowly. From the late eighteenth century to the outbreak of the Great Famine in 1845 too fast an increase in population was among the principal causes of Ireland's economic problems. It was a leading factor in the decline in the average size of landholdings, the rise of a landless, underemployed proletariat, the failure of Irish agriculture to transfer quickly enough from arable to livestock and, generally, in the growing impoverishment of an ever-larger proportion of the community. Coupled with the effects of competition from British manufactures, it was the poverty induced by overpopulation which brought about the widespread collapse of domestic handicraft industries upon which so many had come to depend for their basic livelihood. By itself, the availability of a plentiful supply of cheap labour was not sufficient to offset the fall in demand for handicraft products which came with the sharp decline in per capita real incomes induced by too high a rate of population increase.[23]

In view of the calamitous effects of late eighteenth- and early nineteenth-century population growth, enshrined forever in the Great Famine of the later 1840s, the absolute decline of Ireland's population throughout the second half of the nineteenth and early twentieth centuries was in many ways a blessing. Immediately, and increasingly over time, it eased the worst pressures on land, food resources and employment opportunities. Slowly, in the decades following the Famine, the average size of farms rose and, in response to technological innovation (partly to combat labour shortage) and the spread of more commercial methods of production, the efficiency of Irish agriculture improved.[24] Agricultural output switched from arable to livestock products for which demand was more buoyant and an abundant labour supply less necessary. Incomes, dietary standards and general living conditions among the peasantry gradually rose. In time the increased purchasing power of the rural population came to be reflected in a steady rise of industrial output and exports, an increasing scale of industrial enterprise and the emergence of an extensive and sophisticated domestic commercial system.[25] For all of this the persistent decline in population can be given some of the credit.

It is possible, however, that the decline in population proceeded too far and lasted too long. Even Cullen, among the leading advocates of the economic advantages of demographic decline, acknowledges that there were times, in the 1930s for example, when the Irish economy would have benefited from the larger domestic market that population growth might have ensured. In addition, high rates of emigration and low rates of marriage may have lessened that individual inclination for hardwork and innovative enterprise which is so essential for economic progress. Perhaps, also, the productivity of the economy suffered from the unusually low proportions of the population in the productive age-groups, 15–64. The very absence of the pressure of population on natural resources itself may have removed one of the principal incentives for productive effort (Ryan 1955; Commission on Emigration 1955; Meenan 1958). On the whole, these disadvantages of population decline did not outweigh its advantages. They did, nevertheless, go some way towards modifying them, and it is conceivable that the benefits of demographic decline would have been more pronounced had the reduction of population been less dramatic or less sustained.

That the economic consequences of demographic trends were less benign in Ireland than on mainland Britain was the result of two circumstances. First, variations in rates of population growth have always been more extreme in Ireland than elsewhere and the very extremity of their behaviour imposed strains which the more moderate demographic vagaries elsewhere did not. Second, Ireland's economic and social system was itself less able than that of the mainland to adjust to the pressures arising from population change. High rates of population increase in the late eighteenth and early nineteenth centuries would have been easier to manage had Ireland possessed an economic, social and political environment more conducive to rapid growth of output. As it was, the capacity of the economy for sustained advance was hampered by a variety of non-demographic factors: paucity of natural resources, lack of investment, absentee landlordism, British tariff policy and competition from British manufacturers, the divisiveness produced by religion and the vast inequalities of wealth between rich and poor, the communal nature of so much of Irish agriculture, and the preference for leisure and lack of interest in material accumulation among the rural population (Hutchinson 1970; Grigg 1980). Faced by such problems, many of which continued unabated into the second half of the nineteenth century, the response of the economy to the pressures imposed by extreme demographic changes was less successful than it would otherwise have been.

NOTES AND REFERENCES

1.   Quoted by **G. Ohlin**, 'Historical evidence of Malthusianism', in Deprez 1970, p. 4.

2.   Chambers 1953, 1957, 1972; Habakkuk 1963b, 1971; Loschky 1972; Bowen 1976; Lee 1979. Whether or not the agricultural enclosure movement also played a part in supplying labour to manufacturing industry is once more a matter of dispute. Contrast Chambers 1953 with **Baack, B. D.** and **Thomas, R. P.** (1974), 'The enclosure movement and the supply of labour during the Industrial Revolution', *Journal of European Economic History,* 3, 2; **Crafts, N. F. R.** (1978), 'Enclosure and labour supply revisited', *Explorations in Economic History,* 15, 2; **Crafts, N. F. R.** (1980), 'Income elasticities of demand and the release of labour by agriculture during the British Industrial Revolution', *Journal of European Economic History,* 9, 1.

3.   **Lindert, P. H.** and **Williamson, J. G.** (1983), 'English workers' living standards during the Industrial Revolution: a new look', *Economic History Review,* XXXVI, 1.

4.   **Deane, P.** *The First Industrial Revolution,* Cambridge U.P., 1965; **Lilley, S.** (1965), *Men, Machines and History,* London, 1965 **Lilley, S.** (1973), 'Technological progress and the Industrial Revolution' in **Cipolla, C. M.** (ed.), *The Fontana Economic History of Europe,* vol. 3, London, 1973; Chambers 1972; **Rostow, W.** *How It All Began,* London, 1975.

5.   To some extent, the influence of rising fertility on the dependency ratio may have been offset by higher labour participation ratios in the adult male age-groups or by an increasing trend towards female and child employment.

6.   The age-groups 0–14 and 60 and over.

7.   **Harley, C. K.** (1982), 'British industrialization before 1841: evidence of slower growth during the Industrial Revolution', *Journal of Economic History,* XLII, 2.

8.   *Ibid;* **Lindert, P. H.** (1980), 'English occupations, 1670–1811', *Journal of Economic History,* XL, 4; **McCloskey, D.** (1981), 'The industrial revolution, 1780–1860: a survey', in **Floud, R.** and **McCloskey, D.** (eds), *The Economic History of Modern Britain Since 1700,* vol. 1, Cambridge U.P., 1981; **Crafts, N. F. R.** (1983), 'British economic growth, 1700–1831: a review of the evidence', *Economic History Review,* XXXV, 2.

9.   Keynes 1937; Hansen 1939; Titmuss 1942; Royal Commission on Population 1949. Strictly speaking, contemporary or near-contemporary observers were not so much concerned about lower rates of population growth as about the spectre of an absolute decline in population in the future. Many of them believed that the problems associated with slower rates of population increase could be overcome so long as appropriate action was taken. A few felt that lower rates of population growth actually offered opportunities for economic and social progress. The majority, however, was convinced that demographic retardation in the decades after the Great War were at least partly responsible for the economic ills of the age.

10.   United Nations 1953; Thomas 1954, 1958; Lebergott 1964; Kelley 1972; Gould 1979; Kenwood and Lougheed 1982.

11. Douglas 1963; Johnson 1967; O'Grada 1973; Devine 1979.
12. See also **Rothbarth, E.** (1946), 'Causes of the superior efficiency of USA industry as compared with British industry', *Economic Journal,* 56.
13. **Saul, S. B.,** *Technological Change: the United States and Britain in the Nineteenth Century,* London, 1970.
14. To many scholars labour shortage was only one, and among the least important, of many causes of such American technological superiority as existed. **Burn, D. L.** (1935), 'The genesis of American engineering competition, 1850–70', *Economic History,* LV; **Sawyer, J. E.** (1954), 'The social basis of the American system of manufacturing', *Journal of Economic History,* XIV; **Woodburn, R. S.** (1960), 'The legend of Eli Whitney and interchangeable parts', *Technology and Culture,* I; **Rosenberg, N.** (1963), 'Technological change in the machine tool industry, 1840–1910', *Journal of Economic History,* XXIII; **Rosenberg, N.** (ed.) *The American System of Manufactures: the Report of the Committee on the Machinery of the US in 1855 and the Special Reports of George Wallis and Joseph Whitworth, 1854,* Edinburgh 1969; **Rosenberg, N.** (1972), 'Factors affecting the diffusion of technology', *Explorations in Economic History,* 10, 1; **Murphy, J. J.** (1966), 'Entrepreneurship in the establishment of the American clock industry', *Journal of Economic History,* XXVI, 2; **Ames E.** and **Rosenberg, N.** (1968), 'The Enfield arsenal in theory and history', *Economic Journal,* LXVIII; **Cain, L. P.** and **Paterson, D. G.** (1981), 'Factor biases and technical change in manufacturing: the American system, 1850–1919', *Journal of Economic History,* XLI, 2.
15. **Temin, P.** (1966), 'Labour scarcity and the problem of American industrial efficiency in the 1850s', *Journal of Economic History,* XXVI; **Rosenberg, N.** (1967), 'Anglo-American wage differentials in the 1820s', *Journal of Economic History,* XXVII, 2; **Adams, D.** (1970), 'Some evidence on English and American wage rates, 1790–1830', *Journal of Economic History,* XXX, 3; **Adams, D.** (1973), 'Wage rates in the iron industry: a comment', *Explorations in Economic History,* 11, 1; **Earle, C.** and **Hoffman, R.** (1980), 'The foundations of the modern economy: agriculture and the costs of labor in the United States and England, 1800–60', *American Historical Review,* 85; 5; **James, J. A.** (1981), 'Some evidence on relative scarcity in nineteenth century American manufacturing', *Explorations in Economic History,* 18, 4.
16. **Zabler, J. F.** (1972), 'Further evidence on American wage differentials, 1800–30', *Explorations in Economic History,* 10, 1; **Zabler, J. F.** (1973), 'More on wage rates in the iron industry: a reply', *Explorations in Economic History,* 11, 1; **Brito, D. C.** and **Williamson, J. G.** (1973), 'Skilled labour and nineteenth century Anglo-American managerial behaviour', **Explorations in Economic History,** 10, 3; **David, P.** *Technical choice, innovation and economic growth,* Cambridge U.P. 1975.
17. **Uselding, P. J.** (1972), 'Factor substitution and labor productivity growth in American manufacturing, 1839–99', *Journal of Economic History,* 32, 3.
18. For the debate on the timing and extent of the 'failure' of the British economy before 1914 see **McCloskey, D.** (1970), 'Did Victorian Britain fail?', *Economic History Review,* XXIII, 3; **Floud, R.** (1981), 'Britain, 1860–1914: a survey', in **Floud, R.** and **McCloskey, D. (eds),** *The Economic History of Britain Since 1700,* vol. 2, Cambridge U.P.; and compare with

Kennedy, W. P. (1974), 'Foreign investment, trade and growth in the UK, 1870–1913', *Explorations in Economic History,* 11, 4; Crafts, N. (1979), 'Victorian Britain did fail', *Economic History Review,* XXXII, 4; Nicholas, S. (1982), 'Total factor productivity growth and the revision of post 1870 British economic history', *Economic History Review,* XXXV, 1.

19. Baines, D. (1981), 'The labour supply and the labour market, 1860–1914' in Floud, R. and McCloskey, D. (ed), *The Economic History of Britain Since 1700,* vol. 2, Cambridge U.P., 1981; von Tunzelmann, G. N. (1981), 'Britain, 1900–45: a survey' in *ibid.*

20. Baines, D. (1981), in *ibid.*

21. von Tunzelmann, G. N. (1981) in *ibid.*

22. Between 1911 and 1938 the number of producer units rose by 27% and of consumer units by only 18%. Pollard, S. *The Development of the British Economy, 1914–63,* London, 1963, p. 292.

23. Bourke 1965; Crotty 1966; Cullen 1972; Donnelly 1975.

24. On the extent of commercialization in Irish agriculture before and after the Famine see O'Grada, C. (1975), 'Supply responsiveness in Irish agriculture during the nineteenth century', *Economic History Review,* XXVIII, 2; Nicholas, S. J. and Dziegielewski, M. (1980), 'Supply elasticities, rationality and structural change in Irish agriculture, 1850–1925', *ibid.* XXXIII, 3; O'Grada, C. (1980), 'Supply elasticities in Irish agriculture: a reply', *ibid.*

25. Thomas 1958; Crotty 1966; Cullen 1972; Donnelly 1975; O'Grada 1978, 1980; Fitzpatrick 1980.

Chapter 7

SOME SOCIAL IMPLICATIONS OF POPULATION CHANGE

Much of the recent work on the social implications of demographic change since the middle of the eighteenth century has focused on those aspects of society most susceptible to quantitative techniques of analysis – its age and sex composition and the size and structure of its households and families. As a result, we have a reasonable understanding of the extent to which these features of the social system varied over time and from place to place in response to changes in rates of population growth and in the mechanisms of nuptiality, fertility, mortality and migration responsible for them.

To date, much less attention has been devoted to the evaluation of the *significance* of these aspects of social structure. Worst still, with only rare exceptions, no sustained attempt has yet been made to advance the work of earlier scholars on the implications of demographic change for those many other, less tangible and less easily quantifiable characteristics of the social order which are equally vital in determining the character of community life. These include: the influence of demography on international politico-military status and ambition; the structure and stability of domestic political systems; the frequency and pattern of social mobility and the nature of the interaction between different socio-occupational groups on cultural life and the provision of social and recreational services; the status accorded to sub-groups in the population, and the ease or otherwise with which newcomers to the community are assimilated. It follows, then, that our appreciation of the social consequences of demographic trends in modern times is seriously imbalanced and incomplete and, on certain matters, extremely confused. A rounded account of the contribution of demography to social change remains a long way off.

177

AGE AND SEX STRUCTURE

Variations in age structure are determined largely by changes in levels of fertility: when fertility rates are high, age structures are relatively youthful: when fertility falls, the average age of a population rises.

Historically, fluctuations in age structure over time and from one place to another have often been substantial. In England, for example, between the mid-1670s (when fertility rates were relatively low and the average age of the population relatively high) and the mid-1820s (when fertility was at its peak and the population most youthful) the proportion of infants and young children (0–4) in the population rose by about a third, of children and juveniles (5–14) and mature adults (25–59) by a quarter, while the ratio of young adults (15–24) remained roughly constant and that of the elderly (60 and over) fell by a third. Throughout the first three-quarters of the nineteenth century, with fertility remaining high, the age structure of England's population altered little.[1] Thereafter, however, declining rates of fertility led to an ageing of the population unique in both its rapidity and extent. In the short space of forty years between 1891 and 1931, though the proportion of the population in the age-groups 15–44 stayed constant, that aged 0–14 declined by almost a half while that in the age-groups 45–64 and 65 and above rose by more than a half. It was the sheer pace of the ageing process which caused contemporaries so much concern.

In Scotland, where there appears to have been no increase in fertility during the late eighteenth and early ninetenth centuries, the age structure of the population varied little until the closing decades of the nineteenth century. Then, though more gradually than in England where the decline in fertility was more pronounced, the average age of the population also began to rise. By 1931 the proportion of the population aged 0–14 was a third smaller than in 1891 and that aged 45–64 and 65 and over roughly one half larger. Only in the age-groups 15–44 was there no real change (Flinn 1977).

There are no data on the age composition of Ireland's population until 1821 and the 1821 figures themselves are highly suspect. On the eve of the Great Famine, as a corollary of relatively high fertility and high rates of emigration among young adults, the ratios of the Irish population in the age-groups 0–14 and 65 and over were greater than in England/Wales and Scotland and in the productive ages 15–64 lower. The economic and social burdens of dependency were clearly greater in pre-Famine Ireland than elsewhere in the UK. The Famine marked the onset of a sharp decline in the proportions aged 0–14 and 65 and over and an increase in the proportion of the population aged 15–64, eventually resulting in an age structure closer to that in England and Scotland. Even so, during the period between the late nineteenth and mid-twentieth centuries, there were several notable differences in the age composition of Irish and British populations. First, because the decline in fertility was more gradual in Ireland than in England or Scotland, the reduction in the proportion of the population aged 0–14 was relatively modest.[2] Second, the rise in ratio of elderly people began much earlier in Ireland than elsewhere. Between 1855 and 1891, under the influence of falling birth rates and high levels of emigration, the percentage of Ireland's population aged 65 and over increased by more than three-quarters. In England/Wales and Scotland it changed barely at all. By 1936/7 the proportion of elderly people in the Irish community was almost half as large again as in 1891. Third, the increase which occurred between 1891 and 1936/7 in the percentage of Ireland's population aged 45–64 (14%–15%) was very much smaller than in England or Scotland. By the inter-war period the most significant differences in the age structures of the constituent countries of the British Isles were the unusually high proportion of elderly people in Ireland and the relatively low ratio of infants and young children (0–4) in England and Wales, the latter a consequence of markedly lower birth rates than elsewhere. In other respects, national differences in age composition were slight.

TABLE 10   Age structures (both sexes), England/Wales, Scotland 1821–1931, Ireland 1821–1936/7. Per cent.

	0–14			15–44			45–64			65 and over		
	E/W	S	I	E/W	S	I	E/W	S	I	E/W	S	I
1821	48	38	41	29	–	49	16	–	9	7	–	1
1841	36	37	43	46	46	42	13	13	7	4	4	8
1851	35	36	36	46	46	46	14	14	14	5	5	4
1861	36	36	33	45	44	46	15	15	17	5	5	5
1871	36	37	35	45	44	42	15	14	17	5	5	6
1881	37	37	35	45	44	43	14	14	16	5	5	6
1891	35	36	33	46	45	44	14	15	17	5	5	6
1901	32	33	30	48	47	46	15	15	17	5	5	6
1911	31	32	30	48	47	45	16	16	15	5	5	10
1921	28	30	–	47	46	–	19	18	–	6	6	–
1926	–	–	29	–	–	43	–	–	19	–	–	9
1931	24	30	–	47	46	–	22	2–	–	7	7	–
1936/7	–	–	28	–	–	44	–	–	19	–	–	10

Sources: England/Wales, Armstrong 1965 (1821), Mitchell and Deane 1961 (1841–1931); Scotland, Flinn 1977; Ireland, Vaughan and Fitzpatrick 1978 (1821), 15 and under, 15–50, 50–70, 70 and over: 1841, under 17, 17–45, 46–55, 56 and over.

Variations in rates of population growth and in the demographic mechanisms responsible for them seem to have had little differential effect on the secular behaviour of sex ratios in each of the countries of the UK. Taking all ages together, the number of males per hundred females in England/Wales was probably lower by the inter-war period than at the beginning of the nineteenth century: in Scotland and Ireland somewhat higher. These differences were due to a combination of factors: the greater excess of male over female emigration from England than from either Scotland or Ireland: the decline in Scottish and Irish seasonal labour migration (chiefly a male phenomenon): and the relatively rapid improvement in English life expectancy, from which females benefited more than males. But, generally, secular trends in sex ratios were much the same from one country to another.[3] So, too, was the actual level of the ratios between the sexes. Despite their divergent demographic experiences, throughout the nineteenth century the sex ratios of all the home countries were very similar[4]. In the twentieth century, the sex structures of England/Wales and Scotland remained practically identical. Only Ireland was exceptional. There by the 1930s, thanks to the excess of females over males in the flow of emigrants overseas, males exceeded females in the resident population.

TABLE 11 Males per hundred females (all ages), England/Wales, Scotland, 1801–1931, Ireland, 1821–1936/7.

	England/Wales	*Scotland*		*Ireland*
1801	92 (97)	85		
1811	92 (98)	84		
1821	95 (98)	89		97
1831	95 (97)	89		96
1841	96	90		97
1851	96	91		95
1861	95	90		96
1871	95	91		95
1881	95	93		96
1891	94	93		97
1901	94	95		97
1911	94	94		100
1921	91	93	[1926]	100
1931	92	92	[1936/7]	102

Sources: England/Wales, Mitchell and Deane 1962; Scotland, Flinn 1977; Ireland, Vaughan and Fitzpatrick 1978. The figures in brackets are for England only and take account of the number of men serving in the armed forces and merchant navy who are excluded from the official census returns (Wrigley and Schofield 1981).

What were the social consequences of the trend towards a more youthful population in England in the decades leading up to the early nineteenth century? What were the social implications of the process of demographic ageing which began in the late nineteenth and early twentieth centuries, particularly in England and Scotland where it was most marked? How did Irish society cope with its relative 'burden' of child- and old-age dependency in the years before the First World Famine and with an unusually large percentage of elderly people during the inter-war period? What particular social and psychological responses were generated by the unique excess of males over females in twentieth century Ireland?

To date these questions have attracted little scholarly attention. Wrigley and Schofield have recently concluded that the social implications of the changes which occurred in the age structure of the English population between the late seventeenth and early nineteenth centuries 'warrant further investigation' (Wrigley and Schofield 1981, p. 449). Much the same could be said of the social consequences of high dependency ratios in pre-Famine Ireland. There has been a good deal of discussion about the *theoretical* implications of declining ratios of children in the twentieth century for educational services, standards of child care, the nature of family life and the like, and much *supposition* about the requirements of an ageing population for health and other social services and about the effects of ageing on attitudes and practices towards the elderly. But little empirical work has been done to test their *actual* consequences. In twentieth-century Ireland there is no doubting the contribution of the excess of males over females to the abnormally high rates of lifetime celibacy which prevailed among men. And it has often been argued that low marriage rates were among the principal reasons for the existence of an unsettled and discontented community in which individual self-sacrifice in the common interest was less well developed than in societies where family life was more widespread (Commission on Emigration, 1955). There has, however, been little empirical effort to test the veracity of this contention and little discussion of other possible social implications arising from Ireland's peculiar sex ratio. Until more work is carried out it is difficult to say anything very positive about the social consequences of the changes which have taken place in the age and sex structures of the populations of Britain and Ireland since the middle of the eighteenth century.

HOUSEHOLD AND FAMILY

Between the mid-sixteenth and beginning of the twentieth centuries the mean size and composition of the English household altered little. The typical household unit contained between 4½ and 4¾ residents and was made up predominantly of members of the nuclear family (man, wife and their offspring.[5] Drastic changes in household size and structure did not come until the first half of the twentieth century. By 1951 the mean size of the English household had fallen to around 3¼ (Laslett 1969, 1970; Nixon 1970). Accompanying this decline were pronounced modifications in composition. Compared with its predecessor, the mid-twentieth-century English household was more often composed of single persons living alone, more likely to include parents without resident offspring and, generally, had fewer children, servants, relatives and 'lodgers'.[6]

Even during the period from the sixteenth to the nineteenth centuries there was, of course, some variation in household size and structure from area to area, from one socio-occupational class to another and, less obviously, from time to time. Households were larger and more complex in their composition in urban than rural communities and in communities whose populations were growing relatively rapidly. Mean household size (MHS) varied positively with the socio-occupational status of the household head: the wealthier the household the more servants it could afford and, because of lower mortality and a lesser need for its offspring to find employment, the more resident children it contained.[7] Recent comparisons of the periods 1650–1749 and 1750–1821 (or the nineteenth century generally) show little change over time in the mean size of the household or of the sibling group within it, in the percentage of households headed by married couples, the percentage containing two generations or in the composition of resident kin. On the other hand, inter-community differentials in MHS, in the size of resident sibling groups and in the proportion of households which included servants and married people became less pronounced after the middle of the eighteenth century, while community differentials in the percentage of households with resident kin and *male* servants widened. There was a moderate rise in the number of households containing resident kin and in the percentage spanning three generations and a more noticeable increase in the number headed by single persons and in the percentage of resident offspring they contained. By contrast, the frequency of very small households, the proportion of households headed by females and the percentage of resident servants declined. Overall, the nineteenth-century English household was slightly more complex in its structure than that of the seventeenth and eighteenth centuries (Laslett 1969, 1977; Wall 1978).

Much less work has been done on regional and chronological variations in the size and structure of the Scottish household. So far as one can tell its fundamental characteristics were very similar to that of England.[8] In nineteenth- and early twentieth-century Ireland, on the other hand, MHS appears to have been larger than in England and Scotland, though the differential was not startling.[9] In the counties of Cavan, Meath, Fermanagh, King's and Galway in 1821 MHS was 5.45, mean family size 5.05, the mean number of servants per household 0.40 and of 'inmates' 0.23. Generally, the Irish household of 1821 was larger in the poorer western than more prosperous eastern parts of the country, though the range of variance, from 5.26 to 5.60, was modest (Carney 1978).[10] Between 1841/1851 and 1911 the size of the Irish household fell from 5.55/5.21 to 4.70. In England and Wales, where a secular decline in the size of the household did not begin until the early twentieth century, households contained an average of 4.73 residents in 1851 and 4.36 in 1911 (Fitzpatrick 1983).

The larger size of the Irish household was due to the greater number of resident kin it contained, itself a consequence of the relative prevalence in Ireland of households of the stem family type (households embracing three related generations). Although more frequent in western than eastern areas, the stem family was common everywhere. Only after 1911 did its significance decrease (Fitzpatrick 1983).[11] According to one authority, stem family residence patterns originated in the years immediately following the Famine as a response to the transition from subsistence to commercial agriculture, from arable to livestock farming, partible to single-heir inheritance practices, irregular to regular seasonal or permanent emigration and from an environment in which marriage could be contracted without land to one in which it was possible only when a holding had been obtained (Connell 1961–2). Kennedy, on the other hand, dates its diffusion only from the 1880s when a new desire for improved standards of life among the peasantry accelerated the trends towards emigration, later marriage and celibacy and farmers increasingly delayed retirement in order to retain the unpaid labour services of offspring and kin (Kennedy 1973). In fact, the data for 1821 suggest that kin co-residence and stem family living arrangements long pre-dated the Famine.

The prevalence and survival of the stem family household owed much to three conditions of the country's demography: large-scale emigration, which afforded a ready outlet for those who did not inherit land; high rates of celibacy among non-inheritors; and high levels of marital fertility, which increased the competition for land and thus the bargaining power of those who held it (Fitzpatrick 1983). But its actual origins lay elsewhere. In part it reflected the dominance of small peasant farms where home and workplace were integrally associated and which depended for their economic viability on the cheap labour provided by offspring and kin. Moreover, for as long as parents retained control over the means of production and for as long as there was a general desire to maintain holdings within successive generations of the same family, parental authority over their offspring remained strong and children were less likely to leave the family home, all the more so since the stunted development of the non-agricultural sectors of the economy provided few opportunities for those who chose to stay in Ireland to find work away from the parental farm. In part it reflected the wish of the household head to keep open his choice of who might be best suited to inherit his holding. Possibly, too, it owed something to the emphasis placed by Catholicism on the virtues of family life. The matter certainly requires further investigation.

The factors responsible for such changes as occurred in the size and structure of the English household during the later eighteenth and nineteenth centuries also need to be more thoroughly investigated. Regional differentials in MHS and structure, in particular, require further study. Perhaps the rise in the percentage of households containing resident offspring reflected the increase in the relative size of the infant and child age-groups which came with higher levels of fertility or the spread of urban living which offered greater opportunities for children to live with their parents than in rural communities where the likelihood of proximate employment was more restricted. The decrease in the ratio of households headed by females may have been due to a reduction in the percentage of widows in the population concomitant upon the general decrease in the relative numbers of elderly people. Lower ratios of resident servants in nineteenth-century households reflected a decline in the number of live-in male servants and a growing tendency for servants to be female and to concentrate on purely household chores. With the increasing commercialization of agriculture, live-in farm servants gave way to more flexible and economical wage labour hired for specific tasks and living away from the farm. At the same time, in industry, the emergence of factory methods of production and the erosion of the household as an independent productive unit reduced the numbers of live-in male apprentices.

Rising levels of kin co-residence in the nineteenth century may be accounted for in various ways: by population growth and the decline of handicraft industries in rural areas which intensified pressures on accommodation and forced those who were unemployed or underemployed increasingly to rely on relatives for succour and support[12]; by urbanization which aggravated housing problems and increased the necessity for shared accommodation; by the vast influx of immigrants, many of them teenagers and young adults, into urban areas; by the increasing reliance on the elderly as childminders in areas where opportunities for the employment of married women were growing; or by the rise in the proportion of households headed by single persons with more space and more to gain in terms of combating loneliness or sharing accommodation costs from taking in kin or 'lodgers'.

On the face of it, however, it is surprising that the economic and demographic upheavals of the late eighteenth and nineteenth centuries did not have a more obvious impact on the size and structure of the English household. There are, perhaps, two main reasons for this.

Firstly, the pace of economic change in the late eighteenth and first half of the nineteenth centuries was less dramatic than is sometimes supposed. The transformation in methods of production which the

Industrial Revolution began was a gradual, not a revolutionary, process.[13] As late as 1851 the majority of the labour force was employed in occupations whose basic character had altered remarkably little.[14] The family as a work unit was not immediately destroyed. Indeed, even in the early factories, it often survived as a means of raising and disciplining labour.[15] Unmarried daughters continued to find employment in the kind of work that had long been traditional and, when they lived away from home, continued to remit part of their earnings to their parents. Patterns of employment among married women, by and large, stayed much the same as in pre-industrial times. The family as a productive unit largely survived the early stages of industrialization and so did the tradiional structures and concepts around which it was organized. The fact that there was no *major* transformation in either the size or composition of the English household in the late eighteenth and nineteenth centuries is testimony to the gradualness of the changes which were taking place in economic and social life (Scott and Tilly 1975).

Secondly, there is no reason to suppose that demographic change always has a major influence on household and family structures. And if there is a relationship between the behaviour of the population variables and the size and composition of the household it is by no means a straightforward, easily predictable one. At Portpatrick (Wigtownshire), St Just and Camborne (Cornwall) and North Cardiganshire, MHS was largest when the size and rates of growth of population were greatest (Lewis 1979; Brayshay 1980; Tranter 1980). Yet the average size of the English household in the late eighteenth and nineteenth centuries, when rates of population increase were relatively high, differed little from that of the seventeenth and early eighteenth centuries, when the population was much smaller and growing only slowly. In one case, North Cardiganshire, population decline was accompanied by an increasingly simple household structure: in another, Portpatrick, by an increase in its complexity (Lewis 1979; Tranter 1980). Regional variations in Irish household structure in 1911 bore little obvious correlation with regional differentials in rates of fertility, mortality or emigration (Gibbon and Curtin 1978). To suggest, as some have,[16] that the nuclear family predominated in pre-industrial western societies because high rates of mortality made it impossible for people to achieve the large household unit to which, ideally, they aspired overlooks two awkward facts: (i) that MHS in traditional societies was often larger in areas of high mortality than in areas where death rates were relatively low; (ii) that the twentieth-century decline in MHS occurred despite the trend towards lower mortality.

This is not to imply that demographic influences played no part in determining regional and secular variations in the size and composition of the household group. Declining rates of fertility may go some way towards explaining the reduction in household size which began in

Northern France and Belgium around the time of the French Revolution (Harris 1974). The relatively large size of pre-Famine Irish households may have had something to do with unusually high rates of marital fertility and population growth. Lower MHS in western than eastern Europe no doubt owed much to the relatively high age at marriage among western women, a fact which restricted the number of children they bore and the number of relatives who might require support (Mitterauer and Sieder 1982).

Nevertheless, the simulation exercises undertaken by Wachter and his colleagues clearly demonstrate that the principal determinants of household size and structure in pre- and early industrial times lay outside the realm of demographic behaviour. Secular and regional differences in the size and complexity of the co-resident domestic group were not so much a function of population variables as a matter of choice exercised by men and women in response to the nature of the economic, social and cultural environment within which they lived. Behavioural rules rather than demographic constraints were the key forces underlying patterns of household and family formation (Laslett 1977; Wachter, Hammel and Laslett 1978). Any influence demographic conditions may have had on the structure of the household was largely determined by the context within which they occurred: hence the absence of a consistent relationship between population trends and household types.

It follows, then, that we should be careful not to interpret the twentieth-century decline in MHS too readily as a response to the transition to lower levels of marital fertility and family size which began in the later years of the nineteenth. Admittedly, the decline in net reproduction rates which occurred in western societies, at varying dates, between 1881 and 1911 was everywhere followed, some twenty years later, by the onset of a long-term decrease in MHS and some of the responsibility for the smaller households of modern times must be accredited to this transformation in fertility norms. But it is surely significant that the mean size of the English household continued to fall after 1931, when net reproduction rates were actually rising (Laslett 1972). In any case, some of the central ingredients in the reduction of household size – the decline in the number of resident servants and kin and the increase in the number of solitary-person households – were less obviously linked with fertility than the decline in numbers of resident offspring.

The disappearance of the domestic servant from the household, which had begun as early as the late eighteenth century but was essentially a twentieth-century phenomenon, is easily explained. In part, for women especially, it reflected the emergence of better paid, more attractive alternative employment opportunities in the industrial and service sectors of the economy: in part an erosion of the respectability of servanthood in the face of a growing awareness of individual independence, status and equality: and, in part, the decline in the number of people who could afford servants and the spread of labour-saving household gadgets and smaller, more easily managed houses which made domestic chores take up less time and physical effort.

The recent disappearance from the household of kin and 'lodgers' and the growth in the frequency of solitary-person and 'empty-nest' (childless) households require a more complex explanation. The increase in parental life expectancy and the development of state social services has reduced the numbers of orphans, the elderly, sick and unemployed needing the assistance of kin.[17] Higher incomes have made it easier for individuals to cope with temporary problems of ill health and unemployment, to provide for their old age and to set up their own households earlier in life. They have also reduced the number of people for whom sharing a home with kin or 'lodgers' was financially essential.[18] The greater availability of housing, better transport and communications, labour exchanges and the wider advertisement of employment vacancies and higher standards of education are among the many other factors which have lessened the necessity for people to rely on others for assistance and made it easier for individuals to live alone. At the same time, falling mortality has prolonged the period of life in which one or both parents live without children in the household.

As long as the family retained a direct productive function, the household was likely to be headed by married rather than single people and to contain relatively large numbers of children, kin and 'lodgers' to meet its needs for labour. So long as the task of preparing children for adulthood remained a matter for the family, the household continued to include numerous offspring. As large-scale, capitalist methods of production gradually eroded the economic functions of the family and the institution of formal schooling came to take over much of the responsibility for the socialization of children, the size and structure of the household began to change. Without the same economic compulsion to fill the roles of both husband and wife households could more often be headed by the unmarried. As individuals increasingly came to earn their living outside the home the rationale for remaining within the parental household lost its force. Generally, too, the process of economic and social modernization has tended to compress the number of years over which indiviuals begin work, marry and establish their own household; and by the twentieth century this cluster of events occurred earlier in life than ever before. To some extent this process was the result of an extension of the period of compulsory education: to some extent of better opportunities for early marriage which came with rising real incomes. In part, it reflected the adoption of more effective techniques of family limitation which curbed child-bearing and lessened the material and cultural 'sacrifices' which children involve.

Whatever the explanation, the consequence has been that twentieth-century parents are less likely to share their home with grown-up offspring. Finally, as if to compensate for the loss of its productive functions, the nature of family life itself has altered in ways that are less conducive to the presence in the household of individuals other than the offspring of its head, and fewer even of these latter. Greater equality and attachment between husbands and wives and between parents and their children, coupled with an enhanced concern for the well-being and future of the child, has intensified both the desire for privacy on the part of the conjugal family (parents and their unmarried children) and the willingness to sacrifice parental and kinship interests in favour of those of the child. The new 'discreteness' of conjugal family life left less emotional room for sharing with relatives, married offspring or 'lodgers' at precisely the time when economic modernization made it easier for these to maintain their own independent households (Flandrin 1979; Anderson 1980; Mitterauer and Sieder 1982).

To go beyond a discussion of trends in household size and structure, and their possible causes, to an analysis of their social impact is a still more hazardous exercise. Present work on household structures in past times has been subjected to many criticisms. All too often it has failed to establish a consistent and unambiguous definition of the term 'household' or co-resident domestic group (Berkner 1975; Bradley and Mendels 1978). In its anxiety to define the characteristics of household size and composition over long periods of time and between whole communities or nations, it has tended to understate or ignore the existence of significant short-term temporal, regional and socio-occupational variations in household structure – a weakness with particularly serious implications for the period before the introduction of civil census enumerators' books when the paucity of private listings of inhabitants, and their bias in favour of small, relatively homogeneous and settled communities, makes it difficult to assess their representativeness and the degree of variance around the supposed norm (Armstrong 1972; Harris 1974; Anderson 1980). By focusing on the size and structure of the household at single, specific points in time it has neglected both variations in the composition of the household over the life cycle of its head and the crucial analysis of the life courses of its individual members which aims to determine the points at which individuals radically altered their relationships to the co-resident domestic group.[19]

Above all, it is charged, its bald, summary statistics tell us little about relationships between individuals within the household or between each household and the wider networks of kin and community. Matters such as the role, reputation and authority of individuals, individual isolation and interdependence, sexual and age subordination within the household or the significance of kinship relationships for the socialization of the individual cannot be assessed on the basis of numerical studies of census-type documents alone. They require considerable complementary work on parish and civil registers, personal diaries, poor law records, wills and other legal documents. With only rare exceptions (Chaytor 1980), this remains to be done.[20] It is, therefore, much too premature to attempt a discussion of the social consequences of secular, regional and social class variations in household formation. All that can be said with any certainty is that the size and structure of the English household appears to have altered remarkably little over the last three hundred years despite major changes in the attitudes and functions of its individual members and their relationships to each other. In view of this, the importance attached to work on the size and composition of the co-resident domestic group may well have been misplaced.

OTHER SOCIAL IMPLICATIONS

Of the impact of demographic variables on other facets of social order and behaviour, even less can be concluded with any precision. The treatment of the implications of population change for the international political and military influence of the state or the stability of the social order and its potential for progress may be taken as illustrations of the general confusion which prevails.

On the one hand there is the view that a growing population is a significant, possibly even an essential, requirement for political and social progress. The writings of John Cary in the late seventeenth century, Josiah Tucker in the mid-eighteenth, Simon Gray, James Grahame, George Ensor and Archibald Alison in the nineteenth are typical of the many earlier commentators who assumed that population growth was a force for betterment in forms of social organization, standards of political and social equality, public morality and industry.[21] This view was expressed with particular vehemence during the inter-war period by the many writers who were concerned about the dangers of declining rates of fertility:

> ... in the event of a war similar to that which we have just experienced, what would happen to us with a greatly reduced birth-rate? Surely all we have would be taken and we must become slaves – as we should be today if we had entered on the struggle with Germany without adequate manpower. Moreover, what would happen to our Empire? ... All those enormous lands, with their countless native races, we hold with under 60 millions of white people, of whom 45 millions dwell in these little islands. But, unless we add to our numbers, for how long shall we be able to fulfil our obligations in the face of recent developments of race and ambitions? (National Birth Rate Commission, 1920, p. lxxii).

Twenty years later similar sentiments were expressed by Mrs Hubback:

> A Britain with a much smaller population would no longer be an important influence in world affairs, either in peace or war; she would lose her status and power, with all that implies as regards the welfare of the Commonwealth and of the world (E. M. Hubback, *The Population of Britain*, London, 1942, p. 139).

Declining fertility threatened the end of social progress, even social degeneration. Because the initial decrease in fertility had been more pronounced among the upper and middle than the lower classes the community was in danger of being stripped of the very people most responsible for its past achievements and the most likely source of future glories. Race suicide, it was believed, would be the result. Artificial methods of contraception would lessen society's capacity for moderation and self-control and promote immorality. The refusal to accept 'reasonable' burdens of parenthood would damage the moral fibre of the race, encourage individual selfishness, endanger the happiness of the home and stunt the personal development of parents. So strong was the fear of the social imbalance that might arise from class differentials in fertility that many on the political right fiercely opposed the provision of social welfare services for the working population; and so strong the fear of population decline that many on the political left feared the collapse of social democracy, for the survival of which a growing population was considered vital (Winter 1980).

Mass emigration to the New World in the decades before the First World War drew equal opprobrium from those who were convinced of the need for rapid population growth at home. Many felt that the quality of society would deteriorate with the emigration of its most active and enterprising people, especially since they left behind them a disproportionately large residue of the elderly, the sick and the least energetic.[22] Trade union and socialist opinion often opposed emigration on grounds that it diminished the likelihood of domestic economic, social and political reform by removing those with the greatest reason to support the reformist cause.[23] To many, emigration was unpatriotic, a national evil which lessened our capability in war, increased the power of our enemies and bred restlessness and discontent among those who remained behind.[24] Emigration and demographic decline in Ireland after the Famine have frequently been accused of contributing to the supposed shortcomings of modern Irish social life: poor marriage prospects; individual selfishness, cynicism, irresponsibility and a growing spirit of unease and discontent; looser ties of community and family solidarity; a loss of pride and confidence in the nation; undue constraints imposed by parents and priests on social intercourse between the sexes; and the existence of a community more than usually conservative and conformist in its attitudes, little interested in material or cultural advancement and less inclined than most to adopt the ideal of small family size in order to achieve it.[25]

On the other hand, there is an equally long-standing belief which sees population growth as a source of political and social decay. Sir William Petty, the Reverend Thomas Malthus and his many followers are typical of numerous earlier commentators who saw the increase of population as a potential agent of individual and social degeneration.[26] Against the tide of inter-war opinion Harold Cox declared that

> the growth of population with the resulting desire for economic expansion is a necessary cause of war ... Each race as it grows in numbers, and finds increasing need of fresh outlets, seeks those outlets by invading any other territory that is attractive to it. (H. Cox, *The Problem of Population,* London, 1922, pp. 72, 78).

Matossian and Schafer have recently argued that periods marked by high rates of population growth, as between 1750 and 1850, were associated with an increase in political instability and violence, intra-family tension and the incidence of aggression between people and nations (Matossian and Schafer 1977). Greater rates of geographic mobility which often come with higher rates of population growth have also been seen by some as a force for social instability.[27] Many of those contemporaries who favoured emigration from the British Isles during the nineteenth and early twentieth centuries did so out of a conviction that too large and too rapidly growing a population caused serious social as well as economic problems. Emigration was a necessary, albeit a temporary, palliative for unemployment and poverty and, as such, fulfilled a useful function in removing people likely to become the social derelicts of the future.[28] It eased the moral dangers stemming from an excess of women at home and the likelihood of urban populations being overrun by the lower stratas of society;[29] acted as a general safety-valve for misfortune and discontent;[30] and enabled the working classes to make better provision for their old age, to cultivate the habits of prudence so essential for ensuring the improved mental and spiritual education of their children and to wean themselves away from the grip of vice and immorality.[31] Rapid population growth in Ireland during the late eighteenth and early nineteenth centuries has often been held at least partly responsible for the increasing proletarianization of Irish society, characterized by a disproportionate rise in the number of poor cottiers and landless labourers, and for the increasing divergence between standards of material and non-material life among the different socio-occupational classes in the community.

In sharp contrast, emigration and demographic decline in the years following the Famine were paralleled by a steady reduction in the population of landless labourers and small peasant farmers and a narrowing in the disparities of life styles between the various socio-occupational groups.[32] To the extent that *seasonal* migration from Ireland in the second half of the nineteenth century worked to reduce the extent of *permanent* emigration overseas and thus to moderate the pace of demographic deline, in the short-term at least, it may have delayed the final demise of an increasingly anachronistic social order and hindered the forces of social and cultural change (Douglas 1963; O'Grada 1973).

This conflict of opinion over the political and social consequences of population growth stems essentially from two factors: the absence of a detailed, theoretical model of the role of demographic variables in political and social development; and the sheer complexity of the relationship between demography and the various aspects of political and social change, together with the practical difficulties involved in trying to separate the influence of population from that of the many other, highly interdependent, determinants of political and social behaviour. Until methods of theoretical and empirical analysis are improved, little can be done to clarify the confusion. For the time being, therefore, only two general conclusions can be reached with any certainty.

The first is that most of the current literature attaches too much prominence to the part played by demography in political and social development since the middle of the eighteenth century. In earlier ages, when, in the face of the largely uncontrollable vagaries of mortality, rates of population growth fluctuated wildly and populations lacked the technology, organization and resources to cope with such extremes, the politico-social consequences of demographic change were often considerable. Successive visitations of bubonic plague in the fourteenth century had profound effects on standards of education, architecture, morality, religious belief and the role of the church (Ziegler 1969). In the sixteenth and seventeenth centuries outbreaks of plague in urban communities promoted irrationality and social conflict and weakened social and administrative structures (Dyer 1978). Since the middle of the eighteenth century, however, only in Ireland, where demographic fluctuations have been relatively extreme, have the social consequences of population trends approached the magnitude of earlier times, and even here their role should not be exaggerated.

Generally, the less volatile secular pattern of modern population change and the existence of more sophisticated forms of economic and social organization have moderated the significance of demographic variables for the process of political and social evolution. To accord variations in the size and rate of growth of population more than a marginal role in the rise and fall of Britain as an international power over the last two hundred years, for example, is clearly untenable. Throughout human history, and especially in recent times, a country's political and military status has been more a matter of its economic and technological capability than its population size. As expressed by C. V. Drysdale, secretary of the Malthusian League:

> The fear of a disproportionate increase of population in other countries is in many cases a most fallacious one. The great battles of the world

from Marathon and Salamis to the Chino-Japanese and Russo-Japanese wars have most frequently been won by the smaller nations and armies ... even in war, quality counts more than quantity. Wealth and national reserves also probably count as much (National Birth Rate Commission, 1917, pp. 99).

Or, as J. M. Robertson observed:

... a relatively large population in one country, and a small population in another, does mean relative disadvantage to the small populated country, but the country that limits its population from the point of view of comfort of the family would, in the end, be as strong as the country which increased its population from a point of view of military needs ... I do not deny that the commonsense fact that a population of 100,000,000, properly and thoroughly organized, is stronger for military purposes than a country of 50,000,000, but in the cultivation of more numbers you must lose an element of strength ... I consider that a large population of a low level of intellectual life, comfort, education etc., means a relatively lower military efficiency (National Birth Rate Commission, 1920, p. 113).

Few would interpret the acquisition by Britain and other European countries of vast territories in tropical or subtropical parts of the globe in the late nineteenth century as an *immediate* response to the pressures created by overpopulation for new sources of food or raw materials or new outlets for people and resources redundant at home. And none would claim that Britain's dominance of international affairs during the nineteenth century depended on the size or rate of growth of its population. It was the ability of a relatively small country to devise and adopt the technology of the modern age earlier and more extensively than other nations which guaranteed its primacy just as it was the decline of Britain's economic supremacy, rather than lower rates of population growth, which led to the erosion of its standing as an international power in the twentieth century.

Similarly, to concentrate on the contribution of emigration and population decline to changes in the character of Irish social life in the decades following the Famine is to underplay the arguably more important influence of non-demographic circumstances. Among these were the effects of economic change and land legislation on inheritance and marriage practices, attitudes to property and individual and socio-occupational class relationships. But with them, also, would have to be grouped the effects on marital fertility and community behaviour which stemmed from the relative lack of employment, cultural and recreational opportunities for married women, the persistence of small family farms dependent on the unpaid labour of children and the emphasis given by the Catholic church to the virtues of family life (Kennedy 1973).

193

The second general conclusion is that, whatever the relative significance of demographic trends for political and social conditions, the direction their influence takes is determined wholly by the character of the environment within which they occur. Depending on the context, the consequences of both population growth and population decline may be either beneficial or detrimental.

Very largely, the social and political implications of demographic change are decided by the effect of the latter on the delicate relationship between numbers of people and the supply of food and other essential resources. In early nineteenth-century Ireland, where the balance between population and resources was already strained, the continued growth of numbers intensified material problems and promoted social and political discontent and instability. In early nineteenth-century England, also, the growth and geographic re-location of population aggravated social tensions and created problems that were novel in magnitude, if not in character, compared with those of the past.

By contrast, the persistence of high rates of population growth in England throughout the second half of the nineteenth century did not result in any further deterioration in social and political conditions. On the contrary, all the indications are that society slowly came to terms with the new environment created by industrialization and that the worst of the political and social tensions of the early decades of the century were disappearing. In the course of the century standards of public and personal health improved. Levels of drunkenness, which rose to a peak around the mid-1870s, declined steadily thereafter.[33] Rates of suicide, crime and homicide, other reasonable proxies of levels of social welfare, also remained stable or declined. The real incidence of suicide altered very little from the mid-sixteenth century.[34] During the period 1858–1910 suicide rates were lower among urban-industrial populations than in rural communities and lower in large urban-industrial centres than in small, non-industrial towns.[35] Suicide cannot be regarded as a particular product of industrialization. Whereas the incidence of serious crime rose during the first half of the nineteenth century it declined steadily in the second half, partly because of an improvement in the efficiency of policing but chiefly because rising standards of prosperity made resort to crime less necessary.[36] Homicide was twice as frequent in the sixteenth century as in the mid-Victorian period and twice as frequent then as in the 1960s: the long-term trend in rates of homicide has clearly been downwards.[37] Even if rapid population growth and urbanization in the early years of the nineteenth century undermined popular leisure and recreational activities – and this has been hotly disputed – the further growth of population and urbanization in the second half of the century was paralleled by a burgeoning in the facilities for mass participation in sport and leisure pursuits.[38] Finally, at least in the British case, population growth and its geographic re-location has been accompanied by a rise, not a fall, in opportunities for individual political representation and in society's concern for the welfare of its individual members.

The social consequences of recent increases in rates of human geographic mobility are equally difficult to assess. It is certainly too facile to assume that high rates of migration necessarily promote social instability and tension. The fact is that the political and social implications of migratory movements vary considerably with the size of the communities losing and receiving them, the economic, social, cultural and topographical circumstances of the populations between which people move, the age, sex, marital and socio-occupational composition of the migrant flows themselves and the distances they cover.[39] Such a complexity of influences makes it impossible to assess the social impact of migratory trends in Britain since the middle of the eighteenth century.

In short, while demographic variables undoubtedly have some influence on political and social structures and behaviour, the relative extent and direction of their influence is neither easily measured nor consistent and easily predicted. The extent of the demographic influence and the way in which it works to fashion political and social institutions and attitudes is very much the prisoner of the cumulative environment within which it operates and by which it is itself shaped. Demography is no more an independent initiator of social change than it is of economic change.

NOTES AND REFERENCES

1. Between 1806 and 1871 36%–40% of the English population was under fifteen years of age, 42%–47% between fifteen and sixty and 6%–7% over sixty (Wrigley and Schofield 1981).

2. The proportion of the Irish population in the age-group 0–14 was only 15% less in 1936/7 than in 1891.

3. Aggregate data on eighteenth-century sex ratios are scant. But the data which are available compare closely with the pattern for the nineteenth and twentieth centuries. In Scotland the number of males per hundred females was 91 in the 1750s and 90 in the 1790s (Flinn 1977). In eighteenth-century England sex ratios varied between 76 and 90 for urban populations and between 95 and 98 for rural communities, though in some rural areas numbers of males actually exceeded numbers of females (Law 1969). The only evidence for eighteenth-century Ireland is that for the city of Armagh in 1770 where, typically for urban populations, the ratio of males to females was as low as 84 (Clarkson 1978).

4. Except for Scotland during the first half of the nineteenth century where, even allowing for the exclusion of men serving in the armed forces and the merchant navy, the official data suggest that the number of males per

hundred females was abnormally low. Large-scale male emigration, to England and overseas, may account for this.

5. The 'household' or 'co-resident domestic group' is defined as 'that unit or block of persons which was recognized ... to be distinct from other units or blocks of persons when the inhabitants of a community were listed' (Laslett 1969, p. 202). A pattern of small, nuclear households was common to much, though not all, of Western and Central Europe and North America. In South and East Europe and in parts of Asia larger and more complex households were generally the norm (Laslett 1972, 1977; Wachter, Hammel and Laslett 1978; Flandrin 1979; Anderson 1980; Mitterauer and Sieder 1982).

6. The proportion of households containing resident kin (other than offspring), for example, ranged from 10% in 61 pre-industrial English communities (Armstrong 1972) to 16% at Bow St. (Cardiganshire) in 1851 (Lewis 1966), 17% in mid-nineteenth century Nottingham (Armstrong 1972), 21% at Ashford (Kent) and York (Armstrong 1972, 1974) and 23% at Preston (Anderson 1971). At Bethnal Green in 1955 the proportion was 10%, at Swansea in 1960 14% and for England and Wales as a whole in 1966 only 9% (Armstrong 1974).

7. In one hundred English communities covering the period 1574–1821 MHS varied from 6.63 among the gentry, to 5.83 for the clergy, 5.91 for yeomen, 5.09 for husbandmen, 4.65 for tradesmen and craftsmen, 4.51 for labourers, 3.96 for paupers and 3.72 for 'others' (Laslett 1969). At Stratford-on-Avon in the 1760s MHS was larger in the wealthier than the poorer wards of the town and also varied directly with the wealth of the household head – 7.0 among the town's principal manufacturers and tradesmen, 5.46 for more modest tradesmen and craftsmen, 4.30 for all households (Martin 1978). At York in 1841 MHS ranged from 5.19 in socio-occupational classes I and II to 4.46 in class III and 4.32 in classes IV and V: in 1851 from 5.31, 4.66 to 4.48 respectively (Armstrong 1974).

8. MHS in late seventeenth-century Scotland was between four and five (Flinn 1977): at Avos-in-Mull in 1779 it was 5.25 (Carney 1978): in the Wigtownshire parish of Portpatrick 4.9 in the early 1830s, 5.1 in 1851, 4.2 in 1871 and 4.4 in 1891 (Tranter 1980): according to the published census returns the average size of 'separate families' in Scotland in 1871 and 1891 was 4.5 and 4.6 respectively. In the early 1830s 15% of all Portpatrick households included resident kin other than offspring, the proportion rising to 28% in 1851, 33% in 1871 and 35% in 1891. Even so, the majority of Portpatrick households comprised only the nuclear family (Tranter 1980). MHS at Portpatrick varied positively with the socio-occupational status of the household head: in the early 1830s, for example, it was 6.3 among farmers, 5.7 for craftsmen, 5.0 for tradesmen, 4.4 among labourers and 3.4 for heads without recorded occupation. The differences were due to variations in the numbers of offspring and servants (Tranter 1974).

9. Except for the market town of Armagh in 1770 no reliable data are available on the size and structure of the Irish household before the early nineteenth century. At Armagh MHS was as low as four and the presence in the household of kin (other than offspring), servants and 'lodgers' was rarer than in eighteenth-century England. It may be that the small size and simple structure of the Armagh household was due to the ease of securing

a house (Clarkson 1978). We cannot yet tell whether Armagh was typical or atypical of late eighteenth-century Irish household structure.

10. MHS = mean family size plus servants: mean family size = all members of the household related by blood or marriage to the household head; 'inmates' = all members who were neither servants nor related to the household head by blood or marriage. MHS in a sample of English communities over the period 1574–1821 was 4.45 and in England as a whole in 1821, 4.62. Mean family size in English communities between 1574 and 1821 was 3.82, the mean number of servants 0.63 and of 'inmates' 0.32 (Carney 1978).

11. Gibbon and Curtin 1978. The simultaneous presence of stem-family household patterns and a mean size of household not much greater in Ireland than in England in 1911 suggests that there was considerably more variance in Irish than English household sizes, with relatively large numbers of very small households in the former. This needs to be investigated.

12. The effects of economic depression on the frequency of kin residence are clearly illustrated by the cases of Portpatrick and the three Cornish mining parishes of St Just, Camborne and Redruth. At Portpatrick, following the abandonment of the harbour project and the demise of the port as a principal focus for trade and communication between Scotland and northern Ireland during the 1830s and 1840s, the proportion of households containing kin rose from 15% in the early 1830s to 28% in 1851, 33% in 1871 and 35% in 1891 (Tranter 1980). The slump in the copper mining industry at St Just, Camborne and Redruth after the mid-1860s was accompanied by a similar increase in kin residence (mainly comprising grandchildren whose parents had left in search of work and partly of unmarried young adult females) and in the frequency of 'multiple' households (households containing two or more separate nuclear families) (Brayshay 1980). In both the Cornish and Portpatrick cases the growing complexity of the household at times of economic and demographic depression was associated with a decrease in MHS. But this was not always so. The decline in MHS in eleven North Cardiganshire parishes during a period of agricultural depression between 1851 and 1871 was accompanied by a 28% drop in the number of resident kin and a 26% decrease in the number of 'lodgers' (Lewis 1979).

13. **Harley, C. K.** (1982), 'British industrialization before 1841: evidence of slower growth during the Industrial Revolution,' *Journal of Economic History,* XLII, 2; **Crafts, N. F. R.** (1983), 'British economic growth, 1700–1831: a review of the evidence', *Economic History Review,* XXXVI, 2.

14. **McCloskey, D. N.** (1981), 'The industrial revolution, 1780–1860: a survey' in **Floud, R. C.** and **McCloskey, D. N.** (1981) (eds), *The economic history of Britain since 1700,* vol. I, Cambridge.

15. **Smelser, N. J.,** *Social change in the Industrial Revolution,* London, 1959.

16. Berkner 1975, for example.

17. On trends in parental deprivation see Laslett 1974.

18. It is significant that at Preston in 1851 the tendency to share households with kin rose among the working classes as incomes fell. In view of the unpopularity of the poor law, until the twentieth century there was no

viable alternative to kinship as a source of help in times of difficulty (Anderson 1971).

19.   Berkner 1972a and b; Hareven 1975, 1978; Wheaton 1975; Bradley and Mendels 1978; Anderson 1980. Family and individual life cycle analysis requires population listings which include data on age, marital status and family relationship. Few private listings contain such detail, a fact which explains the concentration on static methods of analysis. Life cycle methods become feasible with the introduction of civil census enumerators' books and need to be more often used (Berkner 1975).

20.   Anderson 1971, 1980; Berkner 1975; Hareven 1975; Bradley and Mendels 1978; Mills 1973. See also Laslett 1977.

21.   **Cary, J.,** *An essay on the state of England,* London, 1695; **Tucker, J.** (1755), 'The elements of commerce and the theory of taxes' in **Schuyler, R. L.** (ed.), *Josiah Tucker. A selection from his Economic and Political Writings,* New York, 1931; **Grahame, J.,** *An Inquiry into the Principle of Population,* Edinburgh, 1816; **Ensor, G.** *An Inquiry Concerning the Population of Nations,* London, 1818; **Gray, S.,** *The Happiness of States,* London, 1815; **Alison, A.** *The Principles of Population and their Connection with Human Happiness,* Edinburgh, 1840.

22.   *Report of the Departmental Committee appointed to consider Mr Rider Haggard's report on agricultural settlements in British Colonies,* BPP, 1906, LXXVI, pp. 559–60; Royal Commission on the Natural Resources, Trade and Legislation of certain portions of His Majesty's Dominions, *First Interim Report, Part I, Migration,* BPP, 1912–13, XVI, pp. 242, 286–90.

23.   *Haggard,* 1906, pp. 672, 693; *Natural Resources,* 1912–13, p. 173.

24.   Report from the Select Committee on Colonisation, 1889, p. 233, 1890, pp. 290–1, 306, in Reports from the Select Committees on Colonisation, 1889–91, *Emigration,* 9, Irish University Press, Shannon, 1969.

25.   Commission on Emigration, 1955; Connell 1958, 1961–2, 1968; Douglas 1963; Kennedy 1973; O'Grada 1973.

26.   **Petty, W.** (1683), 'Another essay on political arithmetic' in **Hull, C. H.** (ed.), *The economic writings of Sir William Petty,* New York, 1963; **Malthus, T. R.,** *First essay on population,* London, 1798.

27.   It has been suggested, for example, that the greater spatial movement of people in England than America in the seventeenth century helps to explain why the latter was a more *'ordered, stable and traditional society'* (Prest 1976). Such data as exist on seventeenth century mobility, however, do not indicate that the difference between English and American experience was large enough to have had significant social implications. In any case, the fact that short-distance, inter-parochial migration was more common in Britain may simply reflect the smaller size of British than American parishes.

28.   See *Haggard,* 1906, pp. 644, 646, 768–71, 896–7; *Natural Resources,* 1912–13, pp. 124, 148–9, 165–7, 178.

29.   See *Natural Resources,* 1912–13, pp. 142, 245–7, 286–90; *The Times,* 16 April 1910.

30.   *The Times,* 6 March 1886.

31.   *The Times,* 8 February 1870.

32.   Crotty 1966; Connell 1972; Donnelly 1975; O'Grada 1979.

33.   **Dingle, A. E.** (1972), 'Drink and working class living standards in Britain, 1870–1914', *Economic History Review,* XXV, 4.

34. **Hair, P. E.** (1970), 'A note on the incidence of Tudor suicide', *Local Population Studies,* 5; **Hair, P. E.** (1971), 'Deaths from violence: a tentative secular survey', *Population Studies,* 25, 1.

35. **Anderson, O.** (1980), 'Did suicide increase with industrialization in Victorian Britain?', *Past and Present,* 86.

36. **Gatrell, V. A. C.** and **Hadden, T. B.** (1972), 'Criminal statistics and their interpretation' in **Wrigley, E. A.** (ed.), *Nineteenth Century Society,* Cambridge U.P., 1972.

37. **Hair, P. E.** (1972), 'Homicide, infanticide and child assault in late Tudor Middlesex', *Local Population Studies,* 9; Hair, *Population Studies,* 1971.

38. **Malcolmsen, R.** *A History of Popular Recreations in English Society, 1700–1850,* Cambridge U.P., 1973; **Mellor, H.,** *Leisure and the Changing City, 1870–1914,* London, 1976; Bailey, P., *Leisure and Class in Victorian England: Rational Recreation and the Contest for Control, 1830–85,* London, 1978; **Walvin, J.,** *Leisure and Society, 1830–1950,* London, 1978; **Dunning, E.** and **Sheard, K.,** *Barbarians, Gentlemen and Players: a Sociological Study of the Development of Rugby Football,* Oxford, 1979; **Cunningham, H.,** *Leisure in the Industrial Revolution, c.1780–1880,* London, 1980; **Mason, Tony,** *Association Football and English Society, 1863–1915,* Brighton, 1980; **Walton, J. K.** (1981), 'The demand for working class seaside holidays in Victorian England', *Economic History Review,* XXXIV, 2.

39. Walker 1972; Parish 1972–3; Werly 1973; Lees 1976; Prest 1976.

BIBLIOGRAPHY

The following abbreviations are used for periodicals:

Ag.H.R.	Agricultural History Review
A.H.R.	American Historical Review
C.S.S.H.	Comparative Studies in Society and History
Ec.D.C.C.	Economic Development and Cultural Change
Ec.H.R.	Economic History Review
Econ.Jnl.	Economic Journal
E.Econ.H.	Explorations in Economic History
Hist. Jnl.	Historical Journal
Hist. St.	Historical Studies
Hist. Workshop Jnl.	History Workshop Journal
Irish Econ. & Soc. Hist.	Irish Economic and Social History
I.H.S.	Irish Historical Studies
J.Ec.H.	Journal of Economic History
J.Eur.Econ.H.	Journal of European Economic History
J.Fam.Hist.	Journal of Family History
J.Hist.Soc. of Ch. Wales	Journal of the Historical Society of the Church of Wales
J.I.H.	Journal of Interdisciplinary History
J.R.S.S.	Journal of the Royal Statistical Society
J.Soc.Hist.	Journal of Social History
Loc.Hist.	The Local Historian
L.P.S.	Local Population Studies
Med.Hist.	Medical History
P. and P.	Past and Present
Pop.St.	Population Studies
Procs. of R.I.A.	Proceedings of the Royal Irish Academy
S.J.S.	Scottish Journal of Sociology
Soc.Hist.	Social History
T. & P. of Inst. of British Geogs.	Transactions and Papers of the Institute of British Geographers
T.R.H.S.	Transactions of the Royal Historical Society
Vict.St.	Victorian Studies

Aalen, F. H. A. (1963–4), 'A review of recent Irish population trends', *Pop.St.*, 17.

Abel-Smith, B. (1964), *The Hospitals, 1800–1948*, Harvard U.P.

Adams, W. F. (1932), *Ireland and Irish Emigration to the New World From 1815 to the Famine*, New Haven.

Adelstein, A. M. and **Ashley, J. S. A.** (1980), 'Recent trends in mortality and morbidity in England and Wales' in **Hiorns, R. W.** (ed.), *Demographic Patterns in Developed Societies*, London.

Almquist, E. K. (1979), 'Pre-famine Ireland and the theory of European proto-industrialization: evidence from the 1841 census', *J.Ec.H.*, XXXIX, 3.

Ambler, R. W. (1972), 'Non-parochial registers and the local historian', *Loc.Hist.*, 10, 2.

Ambler, R. W. (1974), 'Baptism and christening: custom and practice in nineteenth-century Lincolnshire', *L.P.S.*, 12.

Anderson, M. (1971), *Family Structure in Nineteenth Century Lancashire*, Cambridge U.P.

Anderson, M. (1972), 'Standard tabulation procedures for the census enumerators' books, 1851–91' in **Wrigley, E. A.** (ed.), *Nineteenth Century Society*, Cambridge U.P.

Anderson M. (1976), 'Marriage patterns in Victorian Britain: an analysis based on registration district data for England and Wales, 1861', *J.Fam.Hist.*, 1, 1.

Anderson, M. (1977), 'The national sample from the 1851 census', *Urban History Yearbook*.

Anderson, M. (1980), *Approaches to the History of the Western Family, 1500–1914*, London.

Andorka, R. (1979), 'Birth control in the eighteenth and nineteenth centuries in some Hungarian villages', *L.P.S.*, 22.

Anning, S. T. (1974), 'The Leeds public dispensary', *Thoresby Society Publications*, LIV.

Appleby, A. B. (1975), 'Nutrition and disease: the case of London, 1550–1750', *J.I.H.*, VI, 1.

Appleby, A. B. (1979), 'Grain prices and subsistence crises in England and France, 1590–1740', *J.Ec.H.*, XXXIX, 4.

Appleby, A. B. (1980a), 'Epidemics and famine in the Little Ice Age', *J.I.H.*, X, 4.

Appleby, A. B. (1980b), 'The disappearance of plague: a continuing puzzle', *Ec.H.R.*, XXXIII, 2.

Aries, P. (1972), *Centuries of Childhood*, London.

Armstrong, W. A. (1965), La population de l'Angleterre et du pays de Galles, 1789–1815, *Etudes et chroniques de démographie historique*.

Armstrong, W. A. (1966), 'Social structure from the early census returns' in **Wrigley, E. A.** (ed.), *An introduction to English historical demography*, London.

Armstrong, W. A. (1972), 'A note on the household structure of mid-nineteenth century York in comparative perspective' in **Laslett, P.** (ed.), *Household and Family in Past Time*, Cambridge U.P.

Armstrong, W. A. (1974) *Stability and change in an English county town: a social study of York, 1801–51*, Cambridge U.P.

Armstrong, W. A. (1981a), 'The trend in mortality in Carlisle between the 1780s and 1840s; a demographic contribution to the standard of living debate', *Ec.H.R.*, XXXIV, 1.

Armstrong, W. A. (1981b), 'The influence of demographic factors on the position of the agricultural labourer in England and Wales, 1750–1914', *Ag.H.R.*, 29, II.

Ayers, G. M. (1971), *England's first State Hospitals, 1867–1930*, London.

Baines, D. (1972), 'The use of published census data in migration studies' in Wrigley, E. A. (ed.), *Nineteenth-Century Society*, Cambridge U.P.

Baker, D. (1973), 'The inhabitants of Cardington in 1782', *Publications of the Bedfordshire Historical Record Society*, 52.

Banks, J. A. (1954) *Prosperity and Parenthood*, London.

Banks, J. A. (1967–8), 'Population change and the Victorian city', *Vict.St.*, 11.

Banks, J. A. (1981), *Victorian Values: Secularism and the Size of Families*, London.

Banks, J. A. and O. (1954), 'The Bradlaugh–Besant trial and the English newspapers', *Pop.St.*, 8, 1.

Banks, J. A. and O. (1964), *Feminism and Family Planning in Victorian England*, Liverpool.

Barrett, J. C. (1971), 'Fecundability and coital frequency', *Pop.St.*, 25, 2.

Barrett, J. C. and **Marshall, J.** (1969), 'The risk of conception on different days of the menstrual cycle', *Pop.St.*, 23, 3.

Beaujot, R. P., Krotki, K. J. and **Krishan, P.** (1978), 'Socio-cultural variations in the applicability of the economic model of fertility', *Pop.St.*, 32, 2.

Beaver, M. W. (1973), 'Population, infant mortality and milk', *Pop.St.*, 27, 2.

Becker, G. S. (1960), 'An economic analysis of fertility' in National Bureau of Economic Research, *Demographic and Economic Change in Developed Countries*, Princeton U.P.

Benjamin, B. (1954–5), 'Quality of response in census-taking', *Pop.St.*, 8.

Benjamin, B. (1963–4), 'The urban background to public health changes in England and Wales, 1900–50', *Pop.St.*, 17.

Benson, B. (1976), 'The modern rise of population', *L.P.S.*, 17.

Berent, J. (1952), 'Fertility and social mobility', *Pop.St.*, 5, 3.

Berkner, L. K. (1972a), 'Rural family organization in Europe: a problem in comparative history', *Peasant Studies Newsletter*, 1.

Berkner, L. K. (1972b), 'The stem family and the development cycle of the peasant household: an eighteenth century Austrian example', *A.H.R.*, lxxv.

Berkner, L. K. (1975), 'The use and misuse of census data for the historical analysis of family structure', *J.I.H.*, V, 4.

Bhal, S. de (1973), 'A Dublin voluntary hospital: the Meath', *Dublin Historical Records*, XXVII, 1.

Bhattacharyya, A. K. (1975), 'Income inequality and fertility: a comparative view', *Pop.St.*, 29, 1.

Bienefeld, M. A. (1972), *Working Hours in British Industry: an Economic History*, London.

Biller, P. P. A. (1982), 'Birth control in the west in the thirteenth and early fourteenth centuries', *P. and P.*, 94.

Binford, M. C. (1975), 'Never trust the census-taker even when he's dead', *Urban History Yearbook*.

Bisset-Smith, G. T. (1909), 'A statistical note on birth registration in Scotland previous to 1855', *J.R.S.S.*, 72.

Blacker, J. G. C. (1957–8), 'Social ambitions of the bourgeoisie in 18th century France and their relation to family limitation', *Pop.St.*, 11.

Blake, J. (1968), 'Are babies consumer durables?', *Pop.St.*, 22, 1.

Blaug, M. (1963) 'The myth of the Old Poor Law and the making of the New', *J.Ec.H.*, XXIII, 2.

Boulding, K. E. (1974), 'The shadow of the stationary state', *Daedalus*, 102, 4.

Bourke, P. M. A. (1965), 'The agricultural statistics of the 1841 census of Ireland: a critical review', *Ec.H.R.*, XVIII.

Bovenkirk, F. (1973), 'On the causes of Irish emigration', *Sociologica Ruralis*, XIII, 3–4.

Bowen, I. (1976), *Economics and Demography*, London.

Bradley, B. P. and Mendels, F. F. (1978), 'Can the hypothesis of a nuclear family organization be tested statistically?' *Pop.St.*, 32, 2.

Bradley, L. and Razzell, P. (1973), 'Smallpox: a difference of opinion', *L.P.S.*, 10.

Brass, W. and Kabir, M. (1978), 'Regional variations in fertility and child mortality during the demographic transition in England and Wales' in Hobcraft, J. and Rees, P. (eds), *Regional Demographic Development*, London.

Brayshay, M. (1979), 'Using American records to study nineteenth century emigrants from Britain', *Area*, 11, 2.

Brayshay, M. (1980), 'Depopulation and changing household structure in the mining communities of west Cornwall, 1851–71', *L.P.S.*, 25.

Brown, R. (1976), 'Clandestine marriages in Wales', *J.Hist.Soc. of Ch. Wales*, XXV.

Brown, V. N. (1971), 'Wider reconstitution', *L.P.S.*, 7.

Brownlee, J. (1916), 'History of birth and death rates in England and Wales taken as a whole, from 1570 to the present time', *Public Health*, XXIX.

Buckatsczh, E. J. (1951), 'The constancy of local populations and migration in England before 1800', *Pop.St.*, V, 1.

Buer, M. C. (1926), *Health, Wealth and Population in the Early Days of the Industrial Revolution*, London.

Buissink, J. D. (1971), 'Regional differences in marital fertility in the Netherlands in the second half of the nineteenth century', *Pop.St.*, 25, 3.

Busfield, J. and Paddon, M. (1977), *Thinking About Children*, Cambridge U.P.

Cairncross, A. K. (1949), 'Internal migration in Victorian England', *Manchester School*, 17.

Cairncross, A. K. (1973), *Home and Foreign Investment, 1870–1913*, Cambridge U.P.

Caldwell, J. C. (1979), 'Education as a factor in mortality decline; an examination of Nigerian data', *Pop.St.*, 33, 3.

Caldwell, J. C. (1981), 'The mechanisms of demographic change in historical perspective', *Pop.St.*, 35, 1.

Camp, W. D. (1961), *Marriage and the family in France since the Revolution*, New York.

Campbell, F. (1960–1), 'Birth control and the Christian churches', *Pop.St.*, 14.

Carlsson, G. (1966), 'The decline of fertility: innovation or adjustment process', *Pop.St.*, 20, 2.

Carlsson, G. (1970), 'Nineteenth-century fertility oscillations', *Pop.St.*, 24, 3.

Carney, F. J. (1975), 'Pre-famine Irish population: the evidence from the Trinity College estates', *Irish Econ. & Soc. Hist.*, II.

Carney, F. J. (1978), 'Aspects of pre-famine Irish household size: composition and differentials' in **Cullen, L. M.** and **Smout, T. C.** (eds), *Comparative Aspects of Scottish and Irish Economic and Social History, 1600–1900*, Edinburgh.

Carrier, N. H. and **Jeffery, J. R.** (1953), 'External migration: a study of the available statistics', *General Register Office Studies on Medical and Population Subjects, No. 6*, London.

Carrier, N. H. (1955), 'An examination of generation fertility in England and Wales', *Pop.St.*, 9.

Carrothers, W. A. (1929), *Emigration from the British Isles*, London.

Carter, I. (1977), 'Illegitimate births and illegitimate inferences', *S.J.S.*, 2, 1.

Chambers, J. D. (1953), 'Enclosure and labour supply in the Industrial Revolution', *Ec.H.R.*, V.

Chambers, J. D. (1957), 'The Vale of Trent, 1670–1800', *Economic History Review Supplement No. 3*, London.

Chambers, J. D. (1972), *Population, Economy and Society in Pre-Industrial England*, Oxford U.P.

Chaytor, M. (1980), 'Household and kinship: Ryton in the late sixteenth and early seventeenth centuries', *Hist. Workshop Jnl.*, X.

Cherry, S. (1972), 'The role of a provincial hospital: the Norfolk and Norwich hospital, 1771–1880', *Pop.St.*, 26, 2.

Cherry, S. (1980a), 'The hospitals and population growth: Part I', *Pop.St.*, 34, 1.

Cherry, S. (1980b), 'The hospitals and population growth: Part II, *Pop.St.*, 34, 2.

Chojnacka, H. (1976), 'Nuptiality patterns in an agrarian society', *Pop.St.*, 30, 2.

Clark, C. (1968), *Population Growth and Land Use*, London.

Clark, P. (1979), 'Migration in England during the late seventeenth and early eighteenth centuries', *P. and P.*, 83.

Clarkson, L. A. (1978), 'Household and family structure in Armagh city, 1770', *L.P.S.*, 20.

Clarkson, L. A. (1981), 'Irish population revisited, 1687–1821' in **Goldstrom, J. M.** and **Clarkson, L. A.** (eds), *Irish Population, Economy and Society: Essays in Honour of the late K. H. Connell*, Oxford U.P.

Coale, A. J. and **Hoover, E. M.** (1958), *Population Growth and Economic Development in Low Income Countries*, Princeton U.P.

Coale, A. J. (1963), 'Population and economic development' in **Hauser, P. M.** (ed.), *The Population Dilemma*, Columbia U.P.

Coleman, D. A. (1980), 'Recent trends in marriage and divorce in Britain and Europe', in **Hiorns, R. W.** (ed.), *Demographic Patterns in Developed Societies*, London.

Coleman, T. (1974), *Passage to America*, Harmondsworth.

Collins, B. and **Anderson, M.** (1978), 'The administration of the 1851 census in the county of East Lothian', *L.P.S.*, 20.

Collins, B. (1982), 'Proto-industrialization and pre-famine emigration', *Soc.Hist.*, 7, 2.

Collins, E. J. T. (1975), 'Dietary change and cereal consumption in Britain in the nineteenth century', *Ag.H.R.*, 23, 2.

Collins, E. J. T. (1976), 'Migrant labour in British agriculture in the nineteenth century', *Ec.H.R.*, XXIX, 1.

Commission on Emigration and other population problems (1955), *Reports, 1948-54*, Dublin.

Connell, K. H. (1950a), *The Population of Ireland, 1750-1845*, Oxford U.P.

Connell, K. H. (1950b), 'Land and population in Ireland, 1780-1845', *Ec.H.R.*, II.

Connell, K. H. (1951), 'The colonization of waste land in Ireland, 1750-1845', *Ec.H.R.*, III.

Connell, K. H. (1958), 'The land legislation and Irish social life', *Ec.H.R.*, XI, 1.

Connell, K. H. (1961-2), 'Peasant marriage in Ireland: its structure and development since the Famine', *Ec.H.R.*, XIV.

Connell, K. H. (1968a), 'Catholicism and marriage in the century after the Famine' in **Connell, K. H.** (ed.), *Irish Peasant Society*, Oxford U.P.

Connell, K. H. (1968b), 'Illegitimacy before the Famine' in *ibid.*

Connolly, S. J. (1979), 'Illegitimacy and pre-nuptial pregnancy in Ireland before 1864: the evidence of some Catholic parish registers', *Irish Econ. & Soc. Hist.*, VI.

Cook, M. (1980), 'Birth-baptism intervals in some Flintshire parishes', *L.P.S.*, 24.

Cook, M. S. L. and **Repetto, R.** (1982), 'The relevance of the developing countries to demographic transition theory: further lessons from the Hungarian experience', *Pop.St.*, 36, 1.

Coombs, L. C. and **Freedman, R.** (1970), 'Pre-marital pregnancy, child spacing and later economic achievement', *Pop.St.*, 24, 3.

Cope, Z. (1964), 'The history of the dispensary movement' in Poynter, F. N. L. (ed.), *The Evolution of Hospitals in Britain*, London.

Corcoran, M. (1971), 'A Drogheda census list of 1798', *County Louth Archaelogical and Historical Journal*, XVII, 2.

Cousens, S. H. (1960), 'The regional pattern of emigration during the Great Irish Famine, 1846-51', *T. & P. of Inst. of British Geogs.*, 28.

Cousens, S. H. (1960-1), 'Regional death rates in Ireland during the Great Famine from 1846 to 1851', *Pop.St.*, 14.

Cousens, S. H. (1961-2), 'Emigration and demographic change in Ireland, 1851-61', *Ec.H.R.*, XIV.

Cousens, S. H. (1963), 'Regional variations in population change in Ireland, 1881-91', *T. & P. of Inst. of British Geogs.*, 33.

Cousens, S. H. (1963-4), 'The regional variations in population changes in Ireland, 1861-81', *Ec.H.R.*, XVI.

Cousens, S. H. (1964), 'Population trends in Ireland at the beginning of the twentieth century', *Irish Geography*, V.

Cousens, S. H. (1965), 'The regional variation in emigration from Ireland between 1821 and 1841', *T. & P. of Inst. of British Geogs.*, 37.

Cousens, S. H. (1966), 'The restriction of population growth in pre-famine Ireland', *Procs. of R.I.A.*, 64, 4.

Cowan, P. (1970), 'Some observations concerning the increase of hospital provision in London between 1850 and 1960', *Med.Hist.*, 14, 1-2.

Cox, J. C. (1910), *The Parish Registers of England*, London.

Cox, P. R. (1970), *Demography*, 4th ed., Cambridge U.P.

Crafts, N. F. R. (1974), 'Eighteenth century local population studies in the context of aggregate estimates for England and Wales', *L.P.S.*, 13.

Crafts, N. F. R. and **Ireland, N. J.** (1976a), 'Family limitation and the English demographic revolution: a simulation', *J.Ec.H.*, XXXVI, 3.

Crafts, N. F. R. and **Ireland, N. J.** (1976b), 'A simulation of the impact of changes in age at marriage before and during the advent of industrialization in England', *Pop.St.*, 30, 3.

Crafts, N. F. R. (1978), 'Average age at first marriage in mid-nineteenth century England and Wales: a cross-section study', *Pop.St.*, 32, 1.

Crotty, R. D. (1966), *Irish Agricultural Production: its Volume and Structure*, Cork U.P.

Crouzet, F. (1967), 'England and France in the eighteenth century: a comparative analysis of two economic growths' in **Hartwell, R. M.** (ed.), *The Causes of the Industrial Revolution in England*, London.

Cullen, L. M. (1968), 'Irish history without the potato', *P. and P.*, 40.

Cullen, L. M. (1972), *An Economic History of Ireland Since 1660*, London.

Cullen, L. M. (1981), 'Population growth and diet, 1600–1850' in **Goldstrom, J. M.** and **Clarkson, L. A.** (eds), *Irish Population, Economy and Society: Essays in Honour of the late K. H. Connell*, Oxford U.P.

Cullen, M. J. (1974), 'The making of the civil registration act of 1833', *Journal of Ecclesiastical History*, XXV, 1.

Damme, C. (1978), 'Infanticide: the worth of an infant under law', *Med.Hist.*, 22.

D'Arcy, F. (1977), 'The Malthusian League and the resistance to birth control propaganda in late Victorian Britain', *Pop.St.*, 31, 3.

Daultrey, S., Dickson, D., O'Grada, C. (1981), 'Eighteenth century Irish population: new perspectives from old sources', *J.Ec.H.*, XLI, 3.

Deane, P. and **Cole, W. A.** (1967), *British Economic Growth, 1688–1959*, Cambridge U.P.

Dennis, R. J. (1977), 'Inter censal mobility in a Victorian city', *T. & P. of Inst. of British Geogs.*, II, 3.

Deprez, P. (ed.) (1970), *Population and Economics*, Manitoba U.P.

Devine, T. M. (1979), 'Temporary migration and the Scottish Highlands in the nineteenth century', *Ec.H.R.*, XXXII, 3.

Dickson, D. (1972), 'A census of the parish of Tullow in 1795', *Carlovinia*, II, 21.

Dixon, R. B. (1978), 'Late marriage and non-marriage as demographic responses: are they similar?', *Pop.St.*, 32, 3.

Donaldson, G. (1966), *The Scots Overseas*, London.

Donnelly, J. S. (1975), *The Land and People of Nineteenth Century Cork*, London.

Doolittle, I. G. (1980), 'Age at baptism: further evidence', *L.P.S.*, 24.

Douglas, J. H. N. (1963), 'Emigration and Irish peasant life', *Ulster Folklife*, IX.

Drake, M. (1962), 'An elementary exercise in parish register demography', *Ec.H.R.*, XIV.

Drake, M. (1963–4), 'Marriage and population growth in Ireland, 1750–1845', *Ec.H.R.*, XVI.

Drake, M. (1969), 'Population growth and the Irish economy' in **Cullen, L. M.** (ed.), *The Formation of the Irish Economy*, Dublin.

Drake, M. (1972a), 'Marital age patterns in peasant societies: Ireland and Norway, 1800–1900 in **Eversley, D. E. C.** (ed.), *Third International Conference of Economic History, Munich, 1965*.

Drake, M. (1972b), 'The census, 1801–91' in **Wrigley, E. A.** (ed.), *Nineteenth Century Society*, Cambridge U.P.

Duncan, R. (1963–4), 'Case studies in emigration: Cornwall, Gloucestershire and New South Wales, 1877–86', *Ec.H.R.*, XVI.

Dunkley, P. (1980), 'Emigration and the state, 1803–42: the nineteenth century revolution in government reconsidered', *Hist.Jnl.*, 23, 2.

Dyer, A. D. (1978), 'The influence of bubonic plague in England, 1500–1667', *Med.Hist.*, 22.

Dyhouse, C. (1978), 'Working class mothers and infant mortality in England, 1895–1914', *J.Soc.Hist.*, 12, 2.

Easterlin, R. A. (1968), *Population, Labour Force and Long Swings in Economic Growth*, Columbia U.P.

Easterlin, R. A. (1978), 'The economics and sociology of fertility: a synthesis' in Tilly, C. (ed.), *Historical Studies of Changing Fertility*, Princeton U.P.

Editorial (1970), 'Pre-1841 census enumerators' schedules', *L.P.S.*, 5.

Edwards, K. J. (1969), 'Norwich Bills of Mortality, 1707–1830', *Yorkshire Bulletin of Economic and Social Research*, 21, 2.

Edwards, W. J. (1976a), National marriage data: a reaggregation of John Rickman's marriage returns', *L.P.S.*, 17.

Edwards, W. J. (1976b), 'National parish register data: an evaluation of the comprehensiveness of the areal cover', *L.P.S.*, 17.

Elliott, V. (1973), 'Marriage licences and the local historian', *Loc.Hist.*, 10, 6.

Eltis, D. (1983), 'Free and coerced transatlantic migrations: some comparisons', *A.H.R.*, 88, 2.

Engelman, H. O. and Wanner, R. A. (1969), 'Population size and industrial technology', *American Journal of Economics and Sociology*, 28, 3.

Enke, S. (1971), 'Economic consequences of rapid population growth', *Econ.Jnl.*, 81.

Erickson, C. J. (1972), 'Who were the English and the Scots emigrants to the United States in the late nineteenth century?' in Glass, D. V. and Revelle, R. (eds), *Population and Social Structure*, London.

Erickson, C. J. (1981), 'Emigration from the British Isles to the USA in 1831', *Pop.St.*, 35, 2.

Ermisch, J. (1979), 'The relevance of the "Easterlin" hypothesis and the "New Home Economics" to fertility movements in Great Britain', *Pop.St.*, 33, 1.

Espenshade, T. J. (1972), 'The price of children and socio-economic theories of fertility', *Pop.St.*, 26, 2.

Espenshade, T. J. (1975), 'The impact of children on household savings: age effect versus family size', *Pop.St.*, 29, 1.

Eversley, D. E. C. (1957), 'A survey of population in an area of Worcestershire from 1660 to 1850', *Pop.St.*, 10.

Eversley, D. E. C. (1966), 'Exploitation of Anglican parish registers by aggregative analysis' in Wrigley, E. A. (ed.), *An Introduction to English Historical Demography*, London.

Eversley, D. E. C. (1967), 'The home market and economic growth' in Jones, E. L. and Mingay, G. E. (eds), *Land, Labour and Population in the Industrial Revolution*, London.

Eversley, D. E. C. (1981), 'The demography of the Irish Quakers, 1650–1850' in Goldstrom, P. A. and Clarkson, L. A. (eds), *Irish Population, Economy and Society: Essays in Honour of the late K. H. Connell*, Oxford U.P.

Ferenczi, I. and Willcox, W. (1929), *International Migrations*, vol. I, New York.

Field, A. J. (1981), 'What is wrong with neoclassical institutional economics: a critique with special reference to the North-Thomas model of pre-1500 Europe', *E.Econ.H.*, 18, 2.

Fieldhouse, R. (1971), 'The 1811 census of Thirsk', *L.P.S.*, 7.

Finlay, R. (1980), 'Distance to church and registration experience', *L.P.S.*, 24.

Fischer, W. (1973), 'Rural industrialization and population change', *C.S.S.H.*, 15, 2.

Fitzpatrick, D. (1980), 'Irish emigration in the later nineteenth century', *I.H.S.*, XXII, 86.

Fitzpatrick, D., Gibbon, P. and **Curtin, C., Varley, A.** (1983), 'The stem family in Ireland: a debate', *C.S.S.H.*, 25, 2.

Flandrin, J-L. (1979), *Families in Former Times: Kinship, Household and Sexuality*, Southern, R., trans., Cambridge U.P.

Flegg, A. T. (1979), 'The role of inequality of income in the determination of birth rates', *Pop.St.*, 33, 3.

Flinn, M. W. (ed.) (1965), *E. Chadwick, Report on the Sanitary Condition of the Labouring Population of Great Britain, 1842*, Edinburgh.

Flinn, M. W. (1974), 'The stabilization of mortality in pre-industrial Western Europe', *J.Eur.Econ.H.*, 3, 2.

Flinn, M. W. (ed.) (1977), *Scottish Population History*, Cambridge U.P.

Flinn, M. W. (1979), 'Plague in Europe and the Mediterranean countries', *J.Eur.Econ.H.*, 8, 1.

Flinn, M. W. (1981), *The European Demographic System, 1500–1820*, Brighton.

Flinn, M. W. (1982), 'The population history of England, 1541–1871', *Ec.H.R.*, XXXV, 3.

Forbes, T. R. (1971), 'The regulation of English midwives in the eighteenth and nineteenth centuries', *Med.Hist.*, 15, 3–4.

Foster, D. (1975), 'Mobility and economy in new towns: the case of Fleetwood', *L.P.S.*, 14.

Freedman, R. (1961–2), 'The sociology of human fertility: a trend report and bibliography', *Current Sociology*, 10–11.

Freudenberger, H. and **Cummins, G.** (1976), 'Health, wealth and leisure before the Industrial Revolution', *E.Econ.H.*, 13, 1.

Friedlander, D. and **Roshier, R. J.** (1966), 'A study of internal migration in England and Wales, Part I', *Pop.St.*, 19, 3.

Friedlander, D. (1969), 'Demographic responses and population change', *Demography*, 6.

Friedlander, D. (1970), 'The spread of urbanization in England and Wales, 1851–1951', *Pop.St.*, 24, 3.

Friedlander, D. (1973), 'Demographic patterns and socio-economic characteristics of the coalmining population in England and Wales in the nineteenth century', *Ec.D.C.C.*, 22, 1.

Froggatt, P. (1965), 'The census in Ireland of 1813–15', *I.H.S.*, XIV.

Fryer, P. (1965), *The Birth Controllers*, London.

Galloway, L. E. and **Veddar, R. K.** (1971), 'Emigration from the United Kingdom to the USA: 1860–1913', *J.Ec.H.*, XXXI, 4.

Gant, R. (1977), 'Employment and migration: a study from civil registration records', *L.P.S.*, 18.

Gaskin, K. (1978), 'Age at first marriage in Europe before 1850: a summary of family reconstitution data', *J.Fam.Hist.*, 3, 1.

Gaunt, D., Levine, D., Moodie, E. (1983), 'The population history of England 1541–1871: a review symposium', *Soc.Hist.*, 8, 2.

Gibbon, P. and **Curtin, C.** (1978), 'The stem family in Ireland', *C.S.S.H.*, 20, 3.

Gittins, D. (1982), *Fair Sex: Family Size and Structure, 1900–39*, London.

Glass, D. V. (1951), 'A note on the underregistration of births in Britain in the nineteenth century', *Pop.St.*, V, 1.

Glass, D. V. (1963–4), 'Some indications of differences between urban and rural mortality in England and Wales and Scotland', *Pop.St.*, 17.

Glass, D. V. and **Eversley, D. E. C.** (eds) (1965), *Population in History,* London.

Glass, D. V. (1968), 'Fertility trends since the Second World War', *Pop.St.*, 22, 1.

Glass, D. V. (1973a), *Numbering the People*, Farnborough.

Glass, D. V. (1973b), *The Development of Population Statistics*, Farnborough.

Glass, D. V. (1973c), 'The population problem and the future', *The Eugenics Review*, XXIX, 1.

Glass, D. V. and **Taylor, P. A. M.** (1976), *Population and Emigration in Nineteenth Century Britain*, Dublin.

Glasser, J. H. and **Lachenbruch, P. A.** (1968), 'Observations on the relationship between frequency and timing of intercourse and the probability of conception', *Pop.St.*, XXII, 3.

Goldstrom, J. M. and **Clarkson, L. A.** (eds) (1981), *Irish Population, Economy and Society: Essays in Honour of the late K. H. Connell*, Oxford U.P.

Goubert, P. (1968), 'Legitimate fecundity and infant mortality in France during the 18th century: a comparison', *Daedalus*.

Gould, J. D. (1979), 'European intercontinental emigration, 1815–1914: patterns and causes', *J.Eur.Econ.H.*, 8, 3.

Gould, J. D. (1980a), 'European intercontinental emigration the road home: return migration from the USA', *J.Eur.Econ.H.*, 9, 1.

Gould, J. D. (1980b), 'European intercontinental emigration: the role of "diffusion" and feedback', *J.Eur.Econ.H.*, 9, 2.

Griffiths, G. T. (1926), *Population Problems in the Age of Malthus,* Cambridge U.P.

Grigg, D. B. (1980), *Population Growth and Agrarian Change*, Cambridge U.P.

Guillet, E. C. (1963), *The Great Migration: the Atlantic crossing by Sailing Ships Since 1700*, Toronto U.P., 2nd ed.

Gwynne, T. and **Sill, M.** (1977), 'Census enumerators' books: a study of mid-nineteenth century immigration', *Loc.Hist.*, XII, 2.

Habakkuk, H. J. (1953), 'English population in the 18th century', *Ec.H.R.*, VI, 2.

Habakkuk, H. J. (1958), 'The economic history of modern Britain', *J.Ec.H.*, XVIII.

Habakkuk, H. J. (1962), *American and British Technology in the Nineteenth Century*, Cambridge U.P.

Habakkuk, H. J. (1963a), 'Second thoughts on British and American technology in the nineteenth century', *Business Archives and History*, III.

Habakkuk, H. J. (1963b), 'Population growth and economic development in the late eighteenth and nineteenth centuries', *American Economic Review, Papers and Proceedings*, LIII.

Habakkuk, H. J. (1971), *Population Growth and Economic Development Since 1750*, Leicester U.P.

Haines, M. R. (1977), 'Fertility, nuptiality and occupation: a study of British mid-nineteenth century coalmining populations', *J.I.H.*, VIII, 2.

Hair, P. E. (1966), 'Bridal pregnancy in rural England in earlier centuries', *Pop.St.*, XX, 2.

Hair, P. E. (1970), 'Bridal pregnancy in earlier rural England further examined', *Pop.St.*, XXIV, 1.

Hajnal, J. (1947), 'Aspects of recent trends in marriage in England and Wales', *Pop.St.*, 1, 1.

Hajnal, J. (1953), 'Age at marriage and proportions marrying', *Pop.St.*, 7, 2.

Hammerton, A. J. (1975), 'Without natural protectors: female immigration to Australia, 1832–6', *Hist.St.*, 16, 65.

Hammerton, A. J. (1979), *Emigrant Gentlewomen: Genteel Poverty and Female Emigration, 1830–1914*, London.

Hansen, A. H. (1939), 'Economic progress and declining population growth', *American Economic Review*, XXIX, 1, 1.

Hareven, T. K. (1975), 'Household and family in past time', *History and Theory*, XIV, 2.

Hareven, T. K. (ed.) (1978), *Transitions: the Family and the Life Course in Historical Perspective*, New York.

Harris, P. M. G. (1974), 'Family and household across time and culture', *J.Eur.Econ.H.*, 3, 3.

Hastings, R. P. (1973), 'A nineteenth-century dispensary at work', *Loc.Hist.*, 10, 5.

Heaseman, K. (1964), 'The medical mission and the care of the sick poor in nineteenth-century England', *Hist.Jnl.*, 7.

Heer, D. M. (1966), 'Economic development and fertility', *Demography*, 3.

Heer, D. M. (1968), 'Economic development and the fertility transition', *Daedalus*.

Henderson, L. O. (1959–60), 'Parish registers', *Amateur Historian*, 4, 6.

Henry, L. (1956), *Anciennes familles genevoises, étude démographique: XVIe– XXe siècle*, I.N.E.D., 26, Presses universitaires de France.

Henry, L. and **Lévy, C.** (1960), 'Ducs et pairs sous l'Ancien Régime', *Population*.

Henry, L. (1965), 'The population of France in the 18th century in **Glass, D. V.** and **Eversley, D. E. C.** (eds), *Population in History*, London.

Henry, L. (1968), 'The verification of data in historical demography', *Pop.St.*, 22, 1.

Henry, L. (1976), *Population: Analysis and Models*, London.

Henstock, A. (1973), 'House repopulation from the census returns of 1841 and 1851', *L.P.S.*, 10.

Himes, N. E. (1963), *Medical History of Contraception*, New York.

Hitchins, F. H. (1931), *The Colonial Land and Emigration Commission*, Pennsylvania U.P., Philadelphia.

Hobcraft, J. and **Rees, P.** (eds) (1978), *Regional demographic development*, London.

Hollingsworth, T. H. (1964), 'The demography of the British peerage', *Population Studies Supplement*, XVIII, 2.

Hollingsworth, T. H. (1968), 'The importance of the quality of the data in historical demography', *Daedalus*, 97.

Hollingsworth, T. H. (1969), *Historical Demography*, London.

Hollingsworth, T. H. (1972), 'Migration and temporary migration in nominative demographic research', *Annales de démographie historique.*

Holmes, R. S. (1973), 'Ownership and migration from a study of rate-books', *Area*, V. Part 4.

Hopkin, W. A. B. and **Hajnal, J.** (1947), 'Analysis of births in England and Wales, 1939, by father's occupation', *Pop.St.*, 1, 2.

Hopkins, E. (1982), 'Working hours and conditions during the Industrial Revolution: a reappraisal', *Ec.H.R.*, XXXV, 1.

Horner, A. A. (1969), 'The pre-famine population of some Kildare towns', *Journal of the County Kildare Archaeological Society*, XIV, 4.

Howard-Jones, N. (1972), 'Cholera therapy in the nineteenth century, *Journal of History of Medicine and Applied Science*, XXVII, 4.

Howells, B. (1973), 'The historical demography of Wales: notes on some sources', *Loc.Hist.*, 10, 6.

Hunt, E. H. (1973), *Regional Wage Variations in Britain, 1850–1914*, Oxford.

Hunter, J. A. (1971), 'Population changes in the Lower Roe Valley, 1831–61', *Ulster Folklife*, XVII.

Hutchinson, B. (1970), On the study of non-economic factors in Irish economic development', *Economic and Social Review, Dublin*, 1, 4.

Huzel, J. P. (1969), 'Malthus, the Poor Law and population in early nineteenth century England', *Ec.H.R.*, XXII, 3.

Huzel, J. P. (1980), 'The demographic impact of the old poor law: more reflexions on Malthus', *Ec.H.R.*, XXXIII, 3.

Innes, J. W. (1938), *Class fertility trends in England and Wales, 1876–1934*, Princeton U.P.

Irvine, H. S. (1960), 'Some aspects of passenger traffic between Britain and Ireland, 1820–50', *Journal of Transport History*, V.

Jackson, G. and **Laxton, P.** (1977), 'Of such as are of riper years? A note on age at baptism', *L.P.S.*, 18.

John, A. H. (1961), 'Aspects of English economic growth in the first half of the eighteenth century'. *Economica*, N.S., 28.

John, A. H. (1965), 'Agricultural productivity and economic growth in England, 1700–60', *J.Ec.H.*, XXV.

Johnson, J. A. (1970), 'Family reconstitution and the local historian', *Loc.Hist.*, 9, 1.

Johnson, J. H. (1957–8), 'Marriage and fertility in nineteenth century Londonderry', *Journal of Statistical Society of Ireland*, XX, Part I, Section III.

Johnson, J. H. (1959), 'Population movements in County Derry during a pre-famine year', *Procs. of R.I.A.*, Section C, No. 3.

Johnson, J. H. (1967), 'Harvest migration from nineteenth century Ireland', *T. & P. of Inst. of British Geogs.*, 41.

Johnson, J. H. (1970), 'Rural population changes in nineteenth century Londonderry, *Ulster Folklife*, XV–XVI.

Johnson, S. C. (1913), *A History of Emigration from the United Kingdom to North America, 1763–1912*, London.

Johnston, H. J. M. (1972), *British Emigration Policy, 1815–30: 'shovelling out paupers'*, Oxford.

Jones, E. L. (1965), 'Agriculture and economic growth in England, 1660–1750: agricultural change', *J.Ec.H.*, XXV.

Jones, R. E. (1968), 'Population and agrarian change in an eighteenth century Shropshire parish', *L.P.S.*, 1.

Jones, R. E. (1976), 'Infant mortality in rural North Shropshire, 1561–1810', *Pop.St.*, 30, 2.

Jones, R. E. (1980), 'Further evidence on the decline in infant mortality in pre-industrial England: North Shropshire, 1561–1810', *Pop.St.*, 34, 2.

Kelley, A. C. (1965), 'International migration and economic growth: Australia, 1865–1935', *J.Ec.H.*, XXV.

Kelley, A. C. (1972), 'Scale economies, inventive activity and the economics of American population growth', *E.Econ.H.*, 10, 1.

Kennedy, R. E. (1973), *The Irish: Emigration, Marriage and Fertility*, California U.P.

Kenwood, A. G. and **Lougheed, A. L.** (1982), *Technological Diffusion and Industrialization Before 1914*, London.

Kett, J. F. (1964), 'Provincial medical practice in England, 1730–1815', *Journal of the History of Medicine and Science*, 19, 1–2.

Keyfitz, N. (1973), 'Individual mobility in a stationary population', *Pop.St.*, 27, 2.

Keynes, J. M. (1937), 'Some economic consequences of a declining population', *The Eugenics Review*, XXIX, Part I.

Kington, J. A. (1977), 'Fluctuations climatiques: une étude synoptique du climat, fin XVIIIe–début XIXe siècle', *Annales, Economies, Sociétés, Civilisations*, 32, 2.

Knight, P. (1977), 'Women and abortion in Victorian and Edwardian England', *Hist. Workshop Jnl.*, 4.

Knodel, J. (1977), 'Family limitation and the fertility transition: evidence from the age patterns of fertility in Europe and Asia', *Pop.St.*, 31, 2.

Knodel, J. and **Wilson, C.** (1981), 'The secular increase in fecundity in German village populations: an analysis of reproductive histories of couples married 1750–1899', *Pop.St.*, 35, 1.

Krause, J. T. (1958), 'Changes in English fertility and mortality, 1781–1850', *Ec.H.R.*, XI.

Krause, J. T. (1958–9), 'Some implications of recent work in historical demography', *C.S.S.H.*, 1.

Krause, J. T. (1965), 'The changing adequacy of English registration, 1690–1837' in **Glass, D. V.** and **Eversley, D. E. C.** (eds), *Population in History*, London.

Krotki, K. J. and **Krishnan, P.** (1978), 'Socio-cultural variations in the applicability of the economic model of fertility', *Pop.St.*, 32, 2.

Kuchemann, C. F. (1973), 'A demographic and genetic study of a group of Oxfordshire villages' in **Drake, M.** (ed.), *Applied Historical Studies*, London.

Kyd, J. G. (ed.) (1952), *Scottish Population Statistics*, Edinburgh.

Langer, W. L. (1963), 'Europe's initial population explosion', *A.H.R.*, LXIX, 1.

Langer, W. L. (1975), 'American foods and Europe's population growth, 1750–1850', *J.Soc.Hist.*, Winter.

Laslett, B. (1973a), 'Family structure and social history: a methodological review essay', *Historical Methods Newsletter*, 24, 3.

Laslett, B. (1973b), 'The family as a public and private institution: a historical perspective', *Journal of Marriage and the Family*, XXXV.

Laslett, P. (1969), 'Size and structure of the household in England over three centuries', *Pop.St.*, 23, 2.

Laslett, P. (1970–1), 'The comparative history of household and family', *J.Soc.Hist.*, 4.

Laslett, P. (1970), ' "The decline of the size of the domestic group in England": a comment on J. W. Nixon's note', *Pop.St.*, 24, 3.

Laslett, P. (ed.) (1972), *Household and family in past time*, Cambridge U.P.

Laslett, P. and **Oosterveen, K.** (1973), 'Long term trends in bastardy in England: a study of the illegitimacy figures in the parish registers and in the reports of the Registrar-General, 1561–1960', *Pop.St.*, 27, 2.

Laslett, P. (1974), 'Parental deprivation in the past: a note on the history of orphans in England', *L.P.S.*, 13.

Laslett, P. (1977), *Family Life and Illicit Love in Earlier Generations*, Cambridge U.P.

Law, C. M. (1967), 'The growth of urban population in England and Wales, 1801–1911', *T. & P. of Inst. of British Geogs.*, XLI.

Law, C. M. (1969), 'Local censuses in the eighteenth century', *Pop.St.*, 23, 1.

Law, C. M. (1972), 'Some notes on the urban population of England and Wales in the eighteenth century', *Loc.Hist.*, XLI.

Lawton, R. (1968), 'Population changes in England and Wales in the later nineteenth century: an analysis of trends by registration districts', *T. & P. of Inst. of British Geogs.*, XLIV.

Lawton, R. (1978), 'Regional population trends in England and Wales, 1750–1971' in **Hobcraft, J.** and **Rees, P.** (eds.), *Regional demographic development*, London.

Lawton, R. (1979), 'Mobility in nineteenth century cities', *The Geographical Journal*, 145, 2.

Lebergott, S. (1964), *Manpower in Economic Growth: the American Record Since 1800*, New York.

Ledbetter, R. (1976), *A History of the Malthusian League, 1877–1927*, Ohio State U.P.

Lee, J. (1968), 'Marriage and population in pre-famine Ireland', *Ec.H.R.*, XXI, 2.

Lee, J. (1981), 'On the accuracy of the pre-famine Irish censuses' in **Goldstrom, J. M.** and **Clarkson, L. A.** (eds.), *Irish Population, Economy and Society: Essays in Honour of the late K. H. Connell*, Oxford U.P.

Lee, R. (1963), 'Population in pre-industrial England: an econometric analysis', *Quarterly Journal of Economics*, 87.

Lee, R. (1974), 'Estimating series of vital rates and age structures from baptisms and burials: a new technique with application to pre-industrial England', *Pop.St.*, 28, 3.

Lee, R. (1978), 'Models of pre-industrial population dynamics with application to England' in **Tilly, C.** (ed.), *Historical Studies in Fertility*, Princeton U.P.

Lee, W. R. (1979), 'Introduction: population growth, economic development and social change in Europe, 1750–1970' in **Lee, W. R.** (ed.), *European Demography and Economic Growth*, London.

Lee, R. and **Schofield, R.** (1981), 'British population in the eighteenth century' in **Floud, R.** and **McCloskey, D.** (eds.), *The Economic History of Britain Since 1700*, vol. 1, Cambridge U.P.

Lees, L. (1976), 'Mid Victorian migration and the Irish family economy', *Vict.St.*, XX, 1.

Lesthaege, R. (1971), 'Nuptiality and population growth', *Pop.St.*, XXV, 3.

Levine, D. (1976a), 'The reliability of parochial registration and the representativeness of family reconstitution', *Pop.St.*, 30, 1.

Levine, D. (1976b), 'The demographic implications of rural industrialization: a family reconstitution study of Shepshed, Leicestershire, 1600–1851', *Soc.Hist.*, 2.

Levine, D. (1977), *Family Formation in an Age of Nascent Capitalism*, London.

Levine, D. (1978), 'Some competing models of population growth during the First Industrial Revolution', *J.Eur.Econ.H.*, 7, 2.

Lewis, G. J. (1966), 'The demographic structure of a Welsh rural village during the mid-nineteenth century', *Ceredigion*, 5, 3.

Lewis, G. J. (1979), 'Mobility, locality and demographic change: the case of North Cardiganshire, 1851–71', *Welsh History Review*, 9, 3.

Lewis, J. (1979), 'The ideology and politics of birth control in inter-war England', *Women's Studies International Quarterly*, 2.

Liebenstein, H. (1968), 'Population theories, non-traditional inputs and the interpretation of economic history' in **Deprez, P.** (ed.), *Population and Economics*, Manitoba U.P.

Liebenstein, H. (1974), 'An interpretation of the economic theory of fertility: promising path or blind alley', *Journal of Economic Literature*, XII, 2.

Lindert, P. H. (1983), 'English living standards, population growth, and Wrigley-Schofield', *E.Econ.H.*, 20.

Litchfield, R. B. (1969), 'Demographic characteristics of Florentine patrician families, sixteenth to nineteenth centuries', *J.Ec.H.*, XXIX, 2.

Lithell, U-B. (1981), 'Breastfeeding habits and their relation to infant mortality and marital fertility', *J.Fam.Hist.*, 6, 2.

Lockhart, D. G. (1978), 'Chartulary books: a source for migration in Scotland, 1740–1850', *L.P.S.*, 21.

Logan, W. P. D. (1950), 'Mortality in England and Wales from 1848 to 1947', *Pop.St.*, 4.

Long, M. and **Maltby, B.** (1980), 'Personal mobility in three West Riding parishes, 1777–1812', *L.P.S.*, 24.

Loschky, D. J. (1967), 'The usefulness of England's parish registers', *Review of Economics and Statistics*, 49.

Loschky, D. J. and **Krier, D. F.** (1969), 'Income and family size in three eighteenth century Lancashire parishes: a reconstitution study', *J.Ec.H.*, XXIX, 3.

Loschky, D. J. (1972), 'Urbanization and England's eighteenth century crude birth and death rate', *J.Eur.Econ.H.*, 1, 3.

Loschky, D. J. (1976), 'Economic change, mortality and Malthusian theory', *Pop.St.*, 30, 3.

Luckin, B. (1977), 'The decline of smallpox and the demographic revolution of the eighteenth century', *Soc.Hist.*, 6.

Maillat, D. (1978), 'Economic growth' in Council of Europe, *Population Decline in Europe*, London.

Malchow, H. L. (1979), *Population Pressures: Emigration and Government in late Nineteenth Century Britain*, Palo Alto.

Malcolmson, W. (1977), 'Infanticide in the eighteenth century' in **Cockburn, J. S.** (ed.), *Crime in England, 1550–1800*, London.

Maltby, B. (1971), 'Parish registers and the problem of mobility', *L.P.S.*, 6.

Marshall, J. S. (1972), 'Irregular marriages in Scotland as reflected in Kirk sessions records', *Records of the Scottish Church History Society*, XVIII, 1.

Marshall, T. H. (1929), 'The population problem during the Industrial Revolution: a note on the present state of the controversy', *Economic History*, I, 4.

Martin, J. M. (1977a), 'Marriage and economic stress in the Felden of Warwickshire during the eighteenth century', *Pop.St.*, 31, 3.

Martin, J. M. (1977b), 'An investigation into the small size of the household as exemplified by Stratford-upon-Avon', *L.P.S.*, 10.

Martin, J. M. (1978), 'The rich, the poor and the migrant in eighteenth century Stratford-upon-Avon', *L.P.S.*, 20.

Massey, D. S. and **Tedrow, L. M.** (1976), 'Economic development and fertility: a methodological re-evaluation', *Pop.St.*, 30, 3.

Mathias, P. (1975), 'Swords and ploughshares: the armed forces, medicine and public health in the late eighteenth century' in **Winter, J. M.** (ed.), *War and Economic Development*, Cambridge U.P.

Matossian, M. K. and **Schafer, W. D.** (1977), 'Family, fertility and political violence, 1700–1900', *J.Soc.Hist.*, 11, 2.

Matras, J. (1965), 'Social strategies of family formation: data for British female cohorts born 1831–1906', *Pop.St.*, 19, 2.

McCallum, D. (1980), 'Age at baptism: further evidence', *L.P.S.*, 24.

MacDonald, D. F. (1937), *Scotland's shifting population, 1770–1850*, Glasgow.

McDonald, R. W. (1976), 'The parish registers of Wales', *Journal of the National Library of Wales*, XIX, 4.

MacFarlane, A. (1978), *The Origins of English Individualism: the Family, Property and Social Transition*, Oxford U.P.

MacFarlane, A. (1979), 'Review of L. Stone', *History & Theory*, XVIII.

McKenna, E. (1974), 'Marriage and fertility in post-Famine Ireland', *American Journal of Sociology*, 80, 3.

McKenna, E. (1978), 'Age, region and marriage in post-Famine Ireland', *Ec.H.R.*, XXXI, 2.

McKeown, T. and **Brown, R. G.** (1955), 'Medical evidence related to English population changes in the eighteenth century', *Pop.St.*, 9.

McKeown, T. and **Record, R. G.** (1962–3), 'Reasons for the decline in mortality in England and Wales during the nineteenth century', *Pop.St.*, 16.

McKeown, T., Record, R. G. and **Turner, R. D.** (1975), 'An interpretation of the decline in mortality in England and Wales during the twentieth century', *Pop.St.*, 29, 3.

McKeown, T. (1976), *The Modern Rise of Population*, London.

McKeown, T. (1978), 'Fertility, mortality and causes of death: an examination of issues related to the modern rise of population', *Pop.St.*, 32, 3.

McLaren, A. (1976), 'Contraception and the working classes: the social ideology of the English birth control movement in its early years', *C.S.S.H.*, 18, 2.

McLaren, A. (1977), 'Women's work and regulation of family size: the question of abortion in the nineteenth century', *Hist. Workshop Jnl.*, 4.

McLaren, A. (1978), *Birth Control in Nineteenth Century England*, London.

McLaren, D. (1978), 'Fertility, infant mortality and breastfeeding in the seventeenth century', *Med.Hist.*, 22.

McLaren, D. (1979), 'Nature's contraceptive: wet nursing and prolonged lactation: the case of Chesham, Buckinghamshire, 1578–1601', *Med.Hist.*, 23, 4.

MacMillan, D. S. (1963), 'Sir Charles Trevelyan and the Highlands and Islands Emigration Society, 1849–59', *Journal and Proceedings of the Royal Australian Historical Society*, 49, Part 3.

Meade, J. E. et. al (1970), 'Demography and economics', *Population Studies Supplement.*

Meenan, J. F. (1958), 'Eire' in Thomas, B. (ed.), *The Economics of International Migration*, London.

Mendels, F. F. (1972), 'Proto-industrialization: the first phase of the industrialization process', *J.Ec.H.*, XXXII, 1.

Meteyard, B. (1980), 'Illegitimacy and marriage in eighteenth-century England', *J.I.H.*, X, 3.

Meteyard, B. (1981), 'Comment and controversy: a reply', *J.I.H.*, XI, 3.

Mills, D. R. (1973), 'The christening custom at Melbourn, Cambridgeshire', *L.P.S.*, 11.

Minge-Kalman, W. (1978), 'The Industrial Revolution and the European family: the institutionalization of "childhood" as a market for family labour', *C.S.S.H.*, 20, 3.

Mitchell, B. R. and **Deane, P.** (1962), *Abstract of British Historical Statistics*, Cambridge U.P.

Mitchison, R. (1977), *British Population Change Since 1860*, London.

Mitterauer, M. and **Sieder, R.** (1982), *The European Family*, translated by **Oosterveen, K.** and **Hörzinger, M.**, Oxford U.P.

Mokyr, J. (1977), 'Demand vs supply in the Industrial Revolution', *J.Ec.H.*, XXXVII, 4.

Mokyr, J. (1980), 'Malthusian models and Irish history', *J.Ec.H.*, XL, 1.

Mokyr, J. (1981), 'Irish history without the potato', *Irish Econ. & Soc. Hist.*, VIII.

Mokyr, J., O'Grada, C. (1982), 'Emigration and poverty in pre-Famine Ireland' *E.Econ.H.*, 19.

Morgan, V. (1973), 'The Church of Ireland registers of St Patrick's, Coleraine, as a source for the study of a local pre-Famine population', *Ulster Folklife*, XIX.

Morgan, V. (1974), 'Mortality in Magherafelt, County Derry, in the early eighteenth century', *I.H.S.*, XIX.

Morgan, V. (1976), 'A case study of population change over two centuries; Blaris, Lisburn, 1661–1848', *Irish Econ. & Soc. Hist.*, III.

Namboodiri, N. K. (1970), 'On the relation between economic status and family size preference when status differentials in contraceptive instrumentalities are eliminated', *Pop.St.*, XXIV, 2.

National Birth Rate Commission (1917), *The Declining Birth Rate: its Causes and Effects*, 2nd ed., London.

National Birth Rate Commission (1920), *Problems of Population and Parenthood*, London.

Nixon, J. W. (1970), 'Comments on Peter Laslett's paper', *Pop.St.*, 24, 3.

Noonan, J. T., junior (1968), 'Intellectual and demographic history', *Daedalus*, 97.

North, D. C. and **Thomas, R. P.** (1970), 'An economic theory of the growth of the western world', *Ec.H.R.*, XXIII, 1.

North, D. C. and **Thomas, R. P.** (1973a), *The Rise of the Western World: a New Economic History*, Cambridge U.P.

North, D. C. and **Thomas, R. P.** (1973b), 'Reply to Professor Ringrose', *Ec.H.R.*, XXVI, 2.

Oddy, D. J. (1970), 'Working-class diets in late nineteenth-century Britain', *Ec.H.R.*, XXIII, 2.

O'Grada, C. (1973), 'Seasonal migration and post-Famine adjustments in the west of Ireland', *Studia Hibernica*, 13.

O'Grada, C. (1975), 'A note on nineteenth-century Irish emigration statistics', *Pop.St.*, 29, 1.

O'Grada, C. (1978), 'Some aspects of nineteenth-century Irish emigration' in **Cullen, L. M.** and **Smout, T. C.** (eds), *Comparative Aspects of Scottish and Irish Economic and Social History, 1600–1900*, Edinburgh.

O'Grada, C. (1979), 'The population of Ireland, 1700–1900: a survey', *Annales de démographie historique*, 199.

O'Grada, C. (1980), ' Irish emigration to the United States in the nineteenth century' in **Doyle, D. N.** and **Edwards, O. D.** (eds), *America and Ireland, 1776–1976: the American Identity and the Irish Connection*, London.

Ohlin, G. (1960–1), 'Mortality, marriage and growth in pre-industrial populations', *Pop.St.*, 14.

O'Rourke, D. (1972), 'A stocks and flows approach to a theory of human migration with examples from past Irish migration', *Demography*, 9.

Outhwaite, R. B. (1973), 'Age at marriage in England from the late seventeenth to the late nineteenth centuries', *T.R.H.S.*, 5th series, 23.

Parish, W. L. junior (1972–3), 'Internal migration and modernisation: the European case', *Ec.D.C.C.*, 21.

Pearce, C. G. (1973), 'Expanding families: some aspects of fertility in a mid-Victorian community', *L.P.S.*, 10.

Peel, J. (1963–4), 'The manufacture and retailing of contraceptives in England', *Pop.St.*, 17.

Peel, J. (1964–5), 'Contraception and the medical profession', *Pop.St.*, 18.

Pennington, C. I. (1977), 'Mortality, public health and medical improvements in Glasgow, 1855–1911', unpublished Ph.D. thesis, University of Stirling.

Pentland, H. C. (1972), 'Population and labour growth in Britain in the eighteenth century' in **Eversley, D. E. C.** (ed.), *Third International Conference of Economic History, Munich, 1965*, Paris.

Perry, P. J. (1969), 'Working class isolation and mobility in rural Dorset, 1837–1936: a study of marriage distances', *T. & P. of Inst. of British Geogs.*, 46.

Philpot, G. (1975), 'Enclosure and population growth in eighteenth century England', *E.Econ.H.*, 12, 1.

Pollard, S. (1978), 'Labour in Great Britain' in **Mathias, P.** and **Postan, M.** (eds), *Cambridge Economic History of Europe*, VII, Part I, Cambridge U.P.

Pollard, S. (1981), *Peaceful Conquest: the Industrialization of Europe, 1760–1970*, Oxford U.P.

Post, J. D. (1976), 'Famine, mortality and epidemic disease in the process of modernization', *Ec.H.R.*, XXIX, 1.

Post, J. D. (1977), *The Last Great Subsistence Crisis in the Western World*, Baltimore.

Poynter, F. N. L. (ed.) (1964), *The Evolution of Hospitals in Britain*, London.

Prest, W. R. (1976), 'Stability and change in Old and New England: Clayworth and Dedham, *J.I.H.*, VI, 3.

Preston, S. and Nelson, V. E. (1974), 'Structure and change in causes of death: an international summary', *Pop.St.*, 28, 1.

Preston, S. (1975), 'The changing relation between mortality and the level of economic development', *Pop.St.*, 29, 2.

Pryce, W. T. R. (1971), 'Parish registers and visitation returns as primary sources for the population geography of the eighteenth century', *Transactions of the Cymmrodorian Society*, 11.

Ravenstein, E. G. (1885), 'The laws of migration', *J.R.S.S.*, XLVIII.

Razzell, P. (1965), 'Population change in eighteenth century England: a reappraisal', *Ec.H.R.*, XVIII.

Razzell, P. (1967), 'Population growth and economic change in eighteenth and early nineteenth century England and Ireland' in **Jones, E. L.** and **Mingay, G. E.** (eds), *Land, Labour and Population in the Industrial Revolution*, London.

Razzell, P. (1969), 'Population change in Moreton Say', *L.P.S.*, 2.

Razzell, P. (1972), 'The evaluation of baptism as a form of birth registration through cross-matching census and parish register data', *Pop.St.*, 26, 1.

Razzell, P. (1974a), 'An interpretation of the modern rise of population in Europe – a critique', *Pop.St.*, 28, 1.

Razzell, P. (1974b), 'The smallpox controversy', *L.P.S.*, 12.

Ringrose, D. (1973), 'European economic growth: comments on the North-Thomas theory', *Ec.H.R.*, XXVI, 2.

Rogers, G. (1976), 'Mobility and economy in mid-nineteenth century Lancashire coastal towns: the case of Fleetwood and Lytham', *University of Lancaster Regional Bulletin*, XV.

Royal Commission on Population (1949), *Report*, London.

Royal Commission on Population (1950), *Report of the Economics Committee*, London.

Royle, S. (1982), 'Irish manuscript ecclesiastical census returns: a survey with an example from Clogherny parish, Co. Tyrone, 1851–2', *L.P.S.*, 29, 1982.

Rubin, E. (1958), 'United States' in **Thomas, B.** (ed.), *The Economics of International Migration*, London.

Ryan, W. J. L. (1955), 'Some Irish population problems', *Pop.St.*, 9.

Ryder, N. B. (1975), 'Notes on stationary populations', *Population Index*, 41, 1.

Santini, A. (1972), 'Techniques and methods in historical demography (17th-18th centuries)', *J.Eur.Econ.H.*, 1.

Sauer, R. (1978), 'Infanticide and abortion in nineteenth-century Britain', *Pop.St.*, 32, 1.

Sauvy, A. (1969), *General Theory of Population*, London.

Schnaiberg, A. (1973), 'The concept and measurement of child dependency: an approach to family formation analysis', *Pop.St.*, 27, 1.

Schnuker, R. V. (1975), 'Elizabethan birth control and puritan attitudes', *J.I.H.*, V, 4.

Schofield, E. M. (1979), *Medical Care of the Working Class about 1900*, Federation of Local History Societies in the County Palatine of Lancaster.

Schofield, R. S. (1970a), 'Age specific mobility in an English rural parish', *Annales de démographie historique*.

Schofield, R. S. (1970b), 'Some notes on aggregative analysis in a single parish', *L.P.S.*, 5.

Schofield, R. S. (1971), 'Historical demography: some possibilities and some limitations', *T.R.H.S.*, 5th series, 21.

Schofield, R. S. and **Berry, B.** (1971), 'Age at baptism in pre-industrial England', *Pop.St.*, 25, 3.

Schofield, R. S. (1972a), 'The representativeness of family reconstitution', *L.P.S.*, 8.

Schofield, R. S. (1972b), 'Crisis mortality', *L.P.S.*, 9.

Scott, J. W. and **Tilly, L. A.** (1975), 'Women's work and the family in nineteenth-century Europe', *C.S.S.H.*, 17, 1.

Select Committee on Parochial Registration, BPP, 1833, 669, XIV.

Serow, W. J. and **Espenshade, T. J.** (1978), 'The economics of declining population growth: an assessment of the current literature' in **Espenshade, T. J.** and **Serow, W. J.** (eds), *The Economic Consequences of Slowing Population Growth*, London.

Sharlin, A. (1978), 'Methods for estimating population total, age distribution and vital rates in family reconstitution studies', *Pop.St.*, 32, 3.

Shepperson, W. S. (1957), *British Emigration to North America: Projects and Opinions in the Early Victorian Period*, Oxford U.P.

Shiels, W. J. (1979), 'Mobility and registration in the north in the late eighteenth century', *L.P.S.*, 23.

Shorter, E., Knodel, J. and **van de Walle, E.** (1971), 'The decline of non-marital fertility in Europe, 1880–1940', *Pop.St.*, 25, 3.

Shorter, E. (1973), 'Female emancipation, birth control and fertility in European history', *A.H.R.*, 78.

Shorter, E. (1977), *The Making of the Modern Family*, Glasgow.

Sigsworth, E. (1966), 'A provincial hospital in the eighteenth and early nineteenth centuries', *College of General Practitioners, Yorkshire Faculty Journal*.

Simon, J. L. (1969), 'The effect of income on fertility', *Pop.St.*, 23, 3.

Simons, J. (1978), 'Developments in the interpretation of recent fertility trends in England and Wales in **Hobcraft, J.** and **Rees, P.** (eds), *Regional Demographic Development*, London.

Singer, C. and **Underwood, E. A.** (1962), *A Short History of Medicine*, London.

Slack, P. (1981), 'The disappearance of plague: an alternative view', *Ec.H.R.*, 34, 3.

Smith, V. (1969), 'The analysis of census-type documents', *L.P.S.*, 2.

Smout, T. C. (1976), 'Aspects of sexual behaviour in nineteenth century Scotland' in **Maclaren, A. A.** (ed.), *Social class in Scotland*, Edinburgh.

Smout, T. C. (1977) Illegitimacy – a reply, *S.J.S.*, 2, 1.

Snow, E. C. (1935), 'The limits of employment II. The influence of the growth of population on the development of industry', *J.A.S.S.*, XCVIII, Part II.

Soloway, R. A. (1978), 'Neomalthusians, eugenists and the declining birth rate in England, 1900–18', *Albion*, 10, 3.

Speake, R. (1975), 'Under-registration in the Warton (Lancs.) registers', *L.P.S.*, 15.

Spencer, B., Hunn, D. and Deprez, P. (1976), 'Spectral analysis and the study of seasonal fluctuations in historical demography', *J.Eur.Econ.H.*, 5, 1.

Spengler, J. (1968), 'Demographic factors and early modern economic development', *Daedalus*.

Spufford, P. (1970), 'Population movement in seventeenth century England', *L.P.S.*, 4.

Stark, J. (1851), 'Contribution to the vital statistics of Scotland', *Journal of the Statistical Society of London*, 14, March.

Steele, D. J. (ed.) (1970), 'Sources for Scottish genealogy and family history', *National Index of Parish Registers*, 12, London & Chichester.

Stone, L. (1977), *The Family, Sex and Marriage in England, 1500–1800*, London.

Stone, L. (1981), 'Illegitimacy in the 18th century England: again', *J.I.H.*, XI, 3.

Sweezy, A. (1971), 'The economic explanation of fertility changes in the United States', *Pop.St.*, 25, 2.

Szymanski, A. (1974), 'Economic development and population', *Comparative Studies in International Development*, 9, 2.

Taylor, A. J. (1951), 'The taking of the census, 1801–1951', *The British Medical Journal*, 7 April.

Teitelbaum, M. S. (1974), 'Birth underregistration in the constituent counties of England and Wales, 1841–1910', *Pop.St.*, 28, 2.

Terry, G. B. (1975), 'Rival explanations in the work-fertility relationship', *Pop.St.*, 29, 2.

Thomas, B. (1954), *Migration and Economic Growth: a Study of Great Britain and the Atlantic Economy*, Cambridge U.P.

Thomas, B. (ed.) (1958), *The Economics of International Migration*, London.

Thomas, E. G. (1980), 'The old poor law and medicine', *Med.Hist.*, 24.

Thompson, E. P. (1967), 'Time, work discipline and industrial capitalism', *P. and P.*, 38.

Thomson, D. (1980), 'Age reporting by the elderly and the nineteenth century census', *L.P.S.*, 25.

Tillott, P. (1968), 'The analysis of census returns', *Loc.Hist.*, 8, 1.

Tillott, P. (1969), 'An approach to census returns', *L.P.S.*, 2.

Tillott, P. (1972), 'Sources of inaccuracy in the 1851 and 1861 censuses' in Wrigley, E. A. (ed.), *Nineteenth Century Society*, Cambridge U.P.

Tilly, C. (ed.) (1978), *Historical Studies in Fertility*, Princeton U.P.

Tilly, L. A., Scott, J. W. and Cohen, M. (1976), 'Women's work and European fertility patterns', *J.I.H.*, VI, 3.

Titmuss, R. and K. (1942), *Parents' Revolt*, London.

Tomaske, J. A. (1970–1), 'Enclosures and population movements in England, 1700–1830: a methodological comment', *E.Econ.H.*, 8, 2.

Tomaske, J. A. (1971), 'The determinants of inter-country differences in European emigration, 1881–1900', *J.Ec.H.*, XXXI, 4.

Tranter, N. L. (1966), *Demographic Change in Bedfordshire, 1670–1800*, unpublished Ph.D. thesis, University of Nottingham.

Tranter, N. L. (1967), 'Population and social structure in a Bedfordshire parish: the Cardington listing of inhabitants, 1780', *Pop.St.*, 21, 3.

Tranter, N. L. (1973a), *Population since the Industrial revolution: the case of England and Wales*, London.

Tranter, N. L. (1973b), 'The social structure of a Bedfordshire parish in the mid-nineteenth century', *International Review of Social History*, XVIII, 1.

Tranter, N. L. (1974), 'The Reverend Andrew Urquhart and the social structure of Portpatrick in 1832', *Scottish Studies*, 18.

Tranter, N. L. (1978), 'The demographic impact of economic growth and decline: Portpatrick, 1820–91', *Scottish Historical Review*, LVII, 163.

Tranter, N. L. (1980), 'Nineteenth century Portpatrick: an empirical study of the relationship between economic change, population growth and social structure', *S.J.S.*, 4, 3.

Tranter, N. L. (1981), 'The labour supply, 1780–1860' in **Floud, R.** and **McCloskey, D.** (eds), *The Economic History of Britain Since 1700*, vol. I, Cambridge U.P.

Trumbach, R. (1978), *The Rise of the Egalitarian Family: Aristocratic Kinship and Domestic Relations in Eighteenth Century England*, New York.

Tucker, G. S. L. (1970), Irish fertility ratios before the Famine', *Ec.H.R.*, XXIII, 2.

Tucker, G. S. L. (1975), 'The old poor law revisited', *E.Econ.H.*, XII.

Turner, M. (1976), 'Parliamentary enclosure and population change in England 1750–1830', *E.Econ.H.*, 13.

United Nations (1953), *The Determinants and Consequences of Population Trends*, New York.

United Nations (1956), 'The ageing of populations and its economic and social implications', *Population Studies*, 26, New York.

Van de Walle, E. (1974), *The Female Population of France in the Nineteenth Century*, Princeton U.P.

Van de Walle, E. (1978), 'Alone in Europe: the French fertility decline until 1850' in **Tilly, C.** (ed.), *Historical Studies in Fertility*, Princeton U.P.

Vaughan, W. E. and **Fitzpatrick, A. J.** (eds) (1978), *Irish Historical Statistics: Population, 1821–1971*, Dublin.

Verrière, J. (1979), *La Population d'Irlande*, Paris.

Wachter, K. W., Hammel, E. and **Laslett, P.** (1978), *Statistical Studies of Historical Social Structure*, New York.

Walker, W. M. (1972), 'Irish immigrants in Scotland: their priests, politics and parochial life', *Hist.Jnl.*, XV, 4.

Wall, R. (1974), 'Mean household size in England from printed sources' in **Laslett, P.** (ed.), *Household and Family in Past Time*, Cambridge U.P.

Wall, R. (1978), Regional and temporal variations in English household structure from 1650' in **Hobcraft, J.** and **Rees, P.** (eds), *Regional Demographic Development*, London.

Walsh, B. (1970a), 'An empirical study of the age structure of the Irish population', *Economic and Social Review (Dublin)*, 1, 2.

Walsh, B. (1970b), 'Marriage rates and population pressure: Ireland 1871 and 1911', *Ec.H.R.*, XXIII, 1.

Walshaw, R. S. (1941), *Migration to and from the British Isles*, London.

Weaver, F. S. (1974), 'Relative backwardness and cumulative change: a comparative approach to European industrialization', *Studies in Comparative International Development*, IX, 2.

Webb, J. N. (1963), 'Natural and migrational components of population change in England and Wales, 1921–31', *Economic Geography*, 39.

Weeks, J. (1981), *Sex, Politics and Society*, Longman.

Wells, R. V. (1975), 'Family history and the demographic transition, *J.Soc.Hist.*, 9, 1.

Welton, T. A. (1911), *England's Recent Progress*, London.

Werly, J. (1973), 'The Irish in Manchester, 1832–49', *I.H.S.*, XVIII, 71.

West, F. (1974), 'Infant mortality in the East Fen parishes of Leake and Wrangle', *L.P.S.*, 13.

Wheaton, R. (1975), 'Family and kinship in western Europe: the problem of the joint family household', *J.I.H.*, V, 4.

Williams, J. A. (1973), 'A local population study at a college of education', *L.P.S.*, 11.

Williamson, J. G. (1974), 'Migration to the New World: long-term influences and impact', *E.Econ.H.*, 11.

Willis, R. J. (1973), 'A new approach to the economic theory of fertility behaviour', *Journal of Political Economy*, 81, 2, Part II.

Winter, J. M. (1976), 'Some aspects of the demographic consequences of the First World War on Britain', *Pop.St.*, 30, 3.

Winter, J. M. (1977a), 'The impact of the First World War on civilian health in Britain', *Ec.H.R.*, XXX, 3.

Winter, J. M. (1977b), 'Britain's "lost" generation of the First World War', *Pop.St.*, 31, 3.

Winter, J. M. (1979), 'Infant mortality, maternal mortality and public health in Britain in the 1930s', *J.Eur.Econ.H.*, 8, 2.

Winter, J. M. (1980), 'The fear of population decline in western Europe, 1870–1940' in **Hiorns, R. W.** (ed.), *Demographic Patterns in Developed Societies*, London.

Wood, J. D. (1964–5), 'Scottish migration overseas', *Scottish Geographical Magazine*, 80–1.

Woods, R. (1978), 'Mortality and sanitary conditions in the "Best governed city in the world" – Birmingham, 1870–1910', *Journal of Historical Geography*, 4, 1.

Woods, R. and **Smith, C. W.** (1983), 'The decline of marital fertility in the late nineteenth century: the case of England and Wales', *Pop.St.*, 37, 2.

Woodward, J. (1974), *To Do the Sick No Harm*, London.

Wrightson, K. (1975), 'Infanticide in earlier seventeenth century England', *L.P.S.*, 15.

Wrigley, E. A. (ed.) (1966a), *An Introduction to English Historical Demography*, London.

Wrigley, E. A. (1966b), 'Family limitation in pre-industrial England', *Ec.H.R.*, XIX, 1.

Wrigley, E. A. (1968), 'Mortality in pre-industrial England: the example of Colyton, Devon, over three centuries', *Daedalus*, Spring.

Wrigley, E. A. (1969a), 'Baptism/marriage ratios in the late seventeenth century', *L.P.S.*, 3.

Wrigley, E. A. (1969b), *Population and History*, London.

Wrigley, E. A. (ed.) (1972a), *Nineteenth Century Society: Essays in the Use of Quantitative Methods for the Study of Social Data*, Cambridge U.P.

Wrigley, E. A. (1972b), 'Some problems of family reconstitution using English parish register material: the example of Colyton' in **Eversley, D. E. C.** (ed.), *Third International Conference of Economic History, Munich, 1965*, Paris.

Wrigley, E. A. (1973), 'Clandestine marriage in Tetbury in the late seventeenth century', *L.P.S.*, 10.

Wrigley, E. A. (1975), 'Baptism coverage in early nineteenth century England: the Colyton area', *Pop.St.*, 29, 2.

Wrigley, E. A. (1976), 'Checking Rickman', *L.P.S.*, 17.

Wrigley, E. A. (1977a), 'Births and baptisms: the use of Anglican baptism registers as a source of information about the number of births in England before the beginning of civil registration', *Pop.St.*, 31, 2.

Wrigley, E. A. (1977b), 'A note on the lifetime mobility of married women in a parish population in the later eighteenth century', *L.P.S.*, 18.

Wrigley, E. A. (1978), 'Fertility strategy for the individual and the group' in **Tilly, C.** (ed.), *Historical Studies in Fertility*, Princeton U.P.

Wrigley, E. A. (1983), 'The growth of population in eighteenth-century England: a conundrum resolved, *P. and P.*, 98.

Wrigley, E. A. and **Schofield, R. S.** (1981), *The Population History of England, 1541–1871, a Reconstruction*, London.

Wrigley, E. A. and **Schofield, R. S.** (1983), 'English population history from family reconstitution: summary results, 1600–1799', *Pop.St.*, 37, 2.

Yasumoto, M. (1981), 'Industrialization and demographic change in a Yorkshire parish', *L.P.S.*, 27.

Youngson, A. J. (1961–2), 'Alexander Webster and his "Account of the Number of people in Scotland in the year 1755"', *Pop.St.*, 15.

Ziegler, P. (1969), *The Black Death*, London.

Zimmer, B. G. (1981), 'The impact of social mobility on fertility', *Pop.St.*, 35, 1.

Zwanenberg, D. W. (1978), 'The Suttons and the business of inoculation', *Med.Hist.*, XXII.

INDEX

Aalen, 49
Abel-Smith, 70–1
Aberdeen Union of Women Workers, 135
Abortion, 92, 97, 110–11
Adulteration of Food, Drink and Drugs Act, 80
Age structure: and age at marriage, 50; and fertility, 60; and household size, 184; economic and social effects of, 153, 156, 159, 162, 168, 170, 173, 178, 181; trends in, 178–9
Aggregative techniques, 22–3: problems of, 23–4
Agriculture: and the Industrial Revolution, 163; productivity of, and diet, 83
Aliens, records of, 28
Almquist, 103
Ambler, 14, 16
Anaesthetics, 75
Anderson, 13–14, 41, 104, 188
Andorka, 111
Animal diseases, 79
Anning, 69, 71, 73
Antiseptics, 75–6
Appleby, 67, 84
Armstrong, 14, 45, 80, 188
Aseptics, 75–6

Baines, 26
Banks, 109, 113–16, 119, 121–2
Barnardos, 135
Batchelor, 56
Beaver, 80–1, 83
Benson, 87
Berkner, 188
Besant, 109
Bhal, 69

Biller, 111
Bills of mortality, 14
Birth control: and education, 121–2; and marital fertility, 109–12; attitudes towards, 110–12, 119; frequency and availability of, 109–12; methods of, 109–12; social evils of, 190
Birth rates see Fertility
Blacker, 111
Blake, 118
Blaug, 102
Bovenkirk, 138
Bradlaugh, 109
Bradlaugh-Besant trial, 109
Bradley, 76, 188
Brass, 60, 113
Brayshay, 28, 185
Breast-feeding, 111
Bridal pregnancy: birth control and, 95; problems of measuring, 55; rates of, 55–7
Bristol Emigration Society, 135
Bronchitis, 75
Brown, 16, 26
Buckatsczh, 27
Buer, 68
Buissinck, 111
Busfield, 108

Caldwell, 88, 121–2
Camp, 112
Carlsson, 111–12
Carney, 183
Carrothers, 130–1
Carter, 99
Celibacy: and fertility, 109; and household size, 183; rates of, 53–4, 58; sex ratios and, 181
Census: civil, 3–5, 8–14, 26–8; reliability

census (cont.)
of, 9–14; private, 3–4, 6–8, 26–7;
deficiencies in, 6–8; motives for, 7
Census enumerators, competence of, 13
Chambers, 84, 155–6, 159, 161, 163
Chartulary books, 27
Chaytor, 189
Cherry, 73–7
Children's Friend Society, 129
Chojnacka, 100
Cholera, 75
Church Army, 135
Church of England: Emigration Society,
135, 140; Waifs and Strays Society,
133
Clark, 41, 142, 145
Clarkson, 8
Cohen, 98
Coitus interruptus, 97, 111
Cole, 42, 104, 142, 155–6
Coleman, 53
Collins, 13, 43, 103, 139, 167
Colonial Intelligence League, 140
Colonial Land and Emigration
Commisioners, 129, 132
Commission on Emigration, 173, 181
Connell, 7, 47, 49–50, 55, 57, 69, 97,
99, 107, 183
Connolly, 14, 55, 96–7
Consumption, and bread prices, 84
Contraception *see* Birth control
Cook, 118
Cope, 71
Cowan, 70
Cox, 191
Crafts, 21, 49, 111
Crime, 194
Crotty, 105
Crouzet, 159–60
Cullen, 19, 172–3
Curtin, 185

Daultrey, 7
Deane, 42, 104, 142, 155–6
Deaths *see* Mortality
Demography *see* Population
Dennis, 27
Deprez, 22
Devine, 43
Diarrhoea, infantile, 67
Dickson, 7–8
Diet: and mortality, 82–7; trends in, 85–7
Dispensaries, 68: ailments treated in,
74–5; 'cured and relieved' rates in, 73;
friendly society, 71; mortality in, 73;
poor law, 70–1; voluntary, 69–71

Dixon, 53
Domestic service, decline in, 186–7
Donaldson, 130
Donnelly, 138
Douglas, 192
Drake, 12, 47, 49–50
Drugs, effectiveness of, 75, 78
Drunkenness, 194
Drysdale, 192
Duncan, 135, 166
Dunkley, 131
Dyer, 155, 192
Dyhouse, 72, 81

East End Emigration Fund, 135
Easterlin, 117
Ecclesiastical records, 3–4, 6–7
Edinburgh Committee for the Relief of
Highland Destitution, 129
Edwards, 14, 21
Elliott, 22, 27
Emigrants' Information Office, 132,
140–1
Employment, and diet, 83
Enclosure: and mortality, 79; maps, 25
Engelmann, 157
Erickson, 28, 128, 166
Estate maps, 6
Estate records, 25
Eversley, 14, 23, 45, 58, 100–1, 163

Family reconstitution, 15, 22–6:
problems of, 24–6
Family size, 60–1: and the Industrial
Revolution, 185; causes of variations
in, 185–6; economic effects of, 153,
156
Farr, 20
Fecundity, 92
Female Colonization Loan Society, 130
Female Emigration Fund, 130
Fenwick Emigration Society, 129
Ferenczi, 29
Fertility: deficiencies in models of,
108–9; economic consequences of, 153,
159, 162, 164, 168, 170–1; effect on age
structure, 178–9; family and household
size, 183–6; political and social
progress, 189–90; marital, and
nuptiality, 100; and population
growth, 60; causes of decline in,
107–23; causes of increase in, 100–7;
relation with illegitimacy and bridal
pregnancy, 57; rates of, 4, 56–60, 92;
by socio-occupational class, 61;
non-marital *see* Illegitimacy

Fertility ratios, 58: and poor relief, 102
Fertility transition, causes of, 112–23
Fever, 47, 75: rheumatic, 66; hospitals for, 69, 75
Field, 158
Fieldhouse, 9
Fischer, 104
Fitzpatrick, 9, 30, 39, 183
Flandrin, 188
Flinn, 8, 14, 16, 18, 20, 22, 29, 37, 39, 41, 46, 56, 58, 69, 76–7, 79–80, 82–3, 93–4, 97, 99, 102, 110–11, 142, 178
Food adulteration, 79–80
Food supply, administration of, 82–3
Freedman, 112
Friedlander, 26, 40, 42, 117
Froggatt, 9

Galloway, 136
Gant, 27
Gibbon, 185
Gild and corporation rolls, 27
Gittins, 114
Glasgow Committee for the Relief of Highland Destitution, 129
Glass, 14, 19–20, 49
Gould, 126, 128, 135–6, 139–41
Griffiths, 68
Grigg, 164, 173
Gross Reproduction Rate, 58–9
Gwynne, 27

Habakkuk, 103, 156–7, 160–1, 169
Haines, 61, 110, 115
Hair, 57
Hajnal, 53, 61
Hammel, 186
Hammerton, 130, 133, 136
Hanley, 43
Hardwicke's Act, 15–16, 94
Harris, 186, 188
Hastings, 69, 71, 73, 75
Heaseman, 71–2, 74
Heer, 107
Henry, 24, 111
Himes, 111
Hitchens, 129
Hollingsworth, 14, 24–5, 45, 61, 111
Holmes, 27
Homicide, 194
Hopkin, 61
Hopkins, 101
Hospitals, 68; ailments treated in, 74–5; 'cured and relieved' rates in, 74; mortality in, 73–4; poor law, 70; voluntary, 69–71

Household: and the family, 187–8; definition of, 12–3; economic consequences of, 153, 156; size and structure, 181–4, 189; techniques of analyzing, criticisms of, 188–9; variations in size, causes of, 184–8
Hubback, 189
Hunn, 22
Hunt, 168
Hunter, 138
Hutchinson, 173
Huzel, 102
Hygiene, 77–81

Illegitimacy: causes of, 92–100; problems in measuring, 55; rates of, 55–7, 93–100; ratios, 56–7
Infanticide, 97, 111
Influenza, 75
Innes, 61
Inoculation, 47: effectiveness of, 76–8
Ireland, 49, 111, 168
Irvine, 30

John, 163
Johnson, 30, 50, 129, 139
Johnston, 131
Jones, 46, 111, 163
Junior Imperial Migration Committee, 135

Kabir, 60, 113
Kelley, 137
Kennedy, 49, 105, 119–20, 137–8, 183, 193
Kenwood, 158, 170
Kett, 69
Kinship, 4
Knight, 110
Knodel, 95, 110
Knowlton, 109
Krause, 16–17, 58, 102–3
Krier, 61, 111
Kuchemann, 42

Langer, 111
Laslett, 57, 93, 96–7, 182, 186
Law, 8, 142
Lawton, 36, 40, 43
Lee, 8–9, 50, 86, 156–9
Leisure, 194
Lesthaege, 100
Levine, 17, 45, 60, 80, 104, 111
Levy, 111
Lewis, 41, 145, 185
Liebenstein, 108

Life expectancy, 45, 49, 80: and
  household size, 187; and nutrition,
  83–5; motives for improving, 88; rise
  in, summary of reasons for, 87–8
Listings of inhabitants *see* Census,
  private
Litchfield, 111
Lithell, 111
Liverpool Self Help Emigration Society,
  133, 135
Lockhart, 27, 41
Loschky, 45, 61, 80, 86, 111
Lougheed, 158, 170

McDonald, 15
McKeown, 48, 64, 66–7, 75–6, 78–9, 81,
  83, 87
McLaren, 110–11, 114–15
Maillat, 153
Maize, 85
Malaria, 67
Maltby, 27
Malthusian League, 192
Marital structure, economic effects of,
  153
Marketing, and diet, 82
Marriage: age at, 49–53, 60, 103;
  relationship with economic growth,
  159; fertility, 58; illegitimacy and
  bridal pregnancy, 57; and poor relief,
  102; causes of variations in, 103–7,
  119–20; clandestine, 16, 94; rates of,
  51, 60; effect on economic growth, 173;
  fertility, 49–50, 53, 110, 119;
  household size, 183, 187; Irish
  community life, 181; statistics on, 4, 49
Martin, 51
Maternity and Child Welfare Act, 72
Maternity and child welfare clinics, 72
Mathias, 78
Matossian, 191
Matras, 61
Measles, 66, 75
Medical missions, 70, 74: reasons for
  popularity of, 71
Medical Relief Charities Act, 71
Medical services: coverage and location,
  72–3; effectiveness, 73–8; nature of,
  68–77
Meenan, 173
Menarche, age at, 92
Mendels, 157, 188
Meteyard, 94
Metropolitan Asylums Act, 71
Metropolitan Asylums Board, 70
Migration: and age structure, 178–9; and

household size, 183–5; economic
  effects of, 153, 156, 164–8, 170, 173;
  general influences on, 127–8; political
  and social effects of, 190–5; internal,
  and regional population growth, 40,
  126–7; causes of, 141–6; direction, 40,
  142–3, 145; frequency and distance, 24,
  41–3, 126–7, 142–5; sources and
  statistics on, 4–5, 26–7; overseas, and
  population growth, 39–40; assistance
  for, 129, 131–3; attitudes towards,
  128–35, 138, 140–1, 190–2; causes of,
  128–41; direction of, 137; extent of,
  37–8, 126–7, 129; legislation
  concerning, 134, 136; sources for, 5,
  27–30; seasonal, causes of, 145–6;
  definition of, 141; extent of, 25, 43;
  sources for, 30
Militia rolls, 25
Milk, and infant mortality, 80–1, 83–5
Minge-Kalman, 121
Mitchison, 48, 56, 58
Mitterauer, 186, 188
Mokyr, 85, 105, 158
Morgan, 14, 43, 48, 55
Mortality: and household and family
  size, 185, 187; causes of decline in,
  64–88; economic consequences of, 153,
  155; rates of, 45–9; statistics on, 4,
  44–5, 47

National Health Service Act, 73
Natural increase, 21–2, 43–4, 126; and
  regional demand for labour, 168; and
  regional rates of population growth,
  40
Nephritis, 66
Net Reproduction Rate, and household
  size, 186
Nixon, 182
North, 155–6, 158
Nuptiality *see* Marriage

O'Grada, 7, 30, 128, 139, 192
Ohlin, 100
Oosterveen, 57, 93, 96–7
Ordnance survey maps, 14
O'Rourke, 127
Outhwaite, 22
Overseers' assessment and accounts, 25

Paddon, 108
Parish, 42, 145
Passenger Act, motives for, 130–1
Passenger agents, 140

Passengers, sources of statistics on, 4–5, 28–30
Pearce, 61
Peel, 109
Pennington, 69
Pentland, 159–60
Perry, 145
Phelps Brown, 101
Phelps Brown and Hopkins, price and real wage index, criticisms of, 101–2
Philpot, 79
Plague: and bread prices, 84; causes of disappearance of, 65–7, 77; economic effects of, 155; social effects of, 192
Pneumonia, 75
Police charge books, 14, 27
Political representation, 194
Pollard, 157, 168
Population: economic consequences of, 153–74; growth of, 34–7; methods of estimating, 20–3; reliability of statistics on, 3–5; social and political effects of, 177, 189–95
Population (Statistics) Act, 19
Post, 77, 79
Potato: and diet, 82, 85; and marriage and fertility, 103
Preston, 87
Pryce, 7
Public health, 47, 78–81, 83

Quarantine, significance of, 77

Rate books, 14, 27
Razzell, 17–18, 45–6, 76, 78, 172
Record, 48
Registers: civil, 4–5, 10–11, content and reliability of, 19–20; opposition to, 18; origins of, 18–19; nonconformist, 14; parochial, 4, 14–8, 21, 27; underregistration in, 15–18, 21; uses of, 20–6
Repetto, 118
Rickman, 9–10, 21
Ringrose, 158
Robertson, 193
Rose's Act, 14, 18
Roshier, 26, 40, 42
Royal Commission on Population, 115, 165–6
Royle, 14
Rubin, 134
Ryan, 173

Sale of Food and Drugs Act, 80–1

Salvation Army, 133, 135, 140–1
Sanitation *see* Public health
Santini, 24
Sauer, 110
Scarlatina, 75
Scarlet fever, 66
Schafer, 191
Schnuker, 111
Schofield, 21–3, 25, 27, 40–1, 44–5, 49–50, 53, 58–60, 67, 73, 75, 84, 86, 101–2, 107, 158–62, 181
Schumpeter, 154
Scott, 98, 185
Select Committee on Emigration, 129, 131
Settlers' Emigration League, 140
Sex structure: and celibacy, 53; economic consequences of, 153; life expectancy and, 180; migration and, 180; population growth and, 179–80; social consequences of, 181; trends in, 179–80
Sexual morality, 95, 98; female employment and, 95–6; industrialization and, 95
Sharlin, 23
Shepperson, 129
Ship lists, 28
Shorter, 95–9, 109
Sieder, 186, 188
Sigsworth, 74
Sill, 27
Simons, 60
Singer, 70
Smallpox, 8, 47, 64, 67, 75–8: and bread prices, 84
Smith, 122
Smout, 93–4, 97, 99
Snow, 165
Social welfare, 194
Society for the Promotion of Colonization, 132
Society for the Suppression of Juvenile Vagrancy, 129
South African Colonization Society, 135–6, 141
Spencer, 22
Spengler, 159
Spufford, 41
Steele, 14
Stem family, 183–4
Sterility, 92
Stone, 95, 98
Strachan, 56
Suicide, 194
Surgery, techniques of, 75–6

Tax returns, 3, 6–7, 27
Teitelbaum, 20
'The Church's Care for Emigrants', 140
'The Emigrant', 140
Thomas, 29–30, 69, 134, 155–6, 158, 166
Thomson, 12
Tillott, 12–13
Tilly, 98, 185
Tithe award plans, 14
Tomaske, 136, 141
Transport, and diet, 82
Tranter, 1, 17, 56, 158, 185
Travellers' Aid Society, 140
Tuberculosis, 64, 75: and bread prices,
    84
Tucker, 47–8, 58, 102
Turner, 48, 79
Typhus, 66, 75: and bread prices, 84

Underwood, 70

Vaccination, 47: effectiveness of, 76–8
Vaughan, 9, 30
Veddar, 136
Verrière, 38–9, 47

Wachter, 186
Wages: and mortality, 86–7; and
    nutrition, 82–3, 86–7
Wall, 182
Walle, 95, 109, 112
Wanner, 157
Weaver, 157
Weeks, 98
Wells, 122
West, 46
Willcox, 29
Williams, 27
Wills, 25, 189
Winter, 81, 83, 190
Wood, 130
Woods, 81, 122
Woodward, 69, 74
Wrigley, 2, 16–17, 21–3, 40–2, 44–5,
    49–50, 53, 58–60, 67, 84, 86, 101–2,
    105–7, 111–12, 159–62, 181

Yasumoto, 46, 104
Young, 106

Ziegler, 192
Zwanenberg, 76–7